BIOGRAPHICAL

* AND *

HISTORICAL

* MEMOIRS *

× × OF × ×

Natchitoches Parish
Louisiana

EXTRACTED FROM
Biographical and Historical Memoirs
of Northwest Louisiana

WITH A NEW INDEX BY
Donna Rachal Mills

HERITAGE BOOKS
2008

HERITAGE BOOKS

AN IMPRINT OF HERITAGE BOOKS, INC.

Books, CDs, and more—Worldwide

For our listing of thousands of titles see our website
at
www.HeritageBooks.com

A Facsimile Reprint
Published 2008 by
HERITAGE BOOKS, INC.
Publishing Division
100 Railroad Ave. #104
Westminster, Maryland 21157

Originally published 1890, Nashville and Chicago
The Southern Publishing Company

Index Copyright © 1985 Donna Rachal Mills

Other Heritage Books by Donna Rachal Mills:
The First Families of Louisiana: An Index
Florida's First Families: Translated Abstracts of Pre-1821 Spanish Censuses, Volume 1
Florida's Unfortunates: The 1880 Federal Census: Defective, Dependent, and Delinquent Classes
Some Southern Balls: From Valentine to Ferdinand and Beyond

Library of Congress Catalog Card No. 85-060815

— Publisher's Notice —
In reprints such as this, it is often not possible to remove blemishes from the
original. We feel the contents of this book warrant its reissue despite these
blemishes and hope you will agree and read it with pleasure.

International Standard Book Numbers
Paperbound: 978-0-7884-4896-6
Clothbound: 978-0-7884-7499-6

✦ PREFACE.

n the late nineteenth century, America underwent an historical reawakening, a birth and growth of a heightened interest in our nation's past and its builders. Lineage and patriotic societies mushroomed. County and state histories rolled off the presses of local newspaper shops and major publishing companies. Included in their number was an 1890 production of The Southern Publishing Company of Nashville and Chicago, which promised its readers "a large fund of biography of actual residents, and an interesting historical sketch of thirteen counties [parishes]" of the Pelican State.

Biographical and Historical Memoirs of Northwest Louisiana lived up to its promise: 703 pages -- **unindexed**, in keeping with the custom of the times. For researchers fortunate enough to obtain one of the now-rare copies, the publication presents a delightful treat -- one missed by many other researchers who lack the time to pore through all pages of such a voluminous work in search of an ancestor who may or may not be included. A limited reprint edition offered in 1976 by the North Louisiana Historical Association offered a small improvement -- an index to the 648 biographies. However, an everyname index to the estimated 15,000 individuals included in the volume does not yet exist.

The present publication begins to fill this void with the reproduction of one major chapter -- the major chapter, in a sense, since Natchitoches was the mother parish from which all but two of the other parishes were carved -- together with a **new, everyname index** to people, places, and firms discussed in both the historical narrative and the biographical sketches.

The class of book to which the original volume belongs is also one which offers mixed blessings. An almost rigid formula was followed, offering an overview of the region's past and, **most importantly,** biographies of "prominent" citizens. The emphasis upon the latter had a dual purpose, a fact that genealogists and historians would do well to keep in mind. The "tribute" given to most of the featured individuals were well-deserved, and a published account of their lives has served as an important reference for subsequent writers. At the same time, the featuring of **living** individuals was an effective guarantee that a viable number of copies would be sold. The men (and, occasionally, the women) "chosen" for inclusion were commonly those willing to subscribe to the volume.

The finished product was a "parlor table book," one to be found in all the "right" homes of the county. Those who submitted accounts of their lives, their parentage and, in many cases, their ancestry, were well aware of this fact. Given the peculiarities of human nature, it is not surprising that many individuals of ordinary origins acquired a more noteworthy past, nor is it surprising that potentially embarrassing family skeletons were glossed over. It is consequently no wonder this type of publication is now often referred to as "mug books."

In the preparation of both the historical narratives and the biographical accounts, orthography proved to be a major cause of errors. Particularly was this the case in volumes produced on Louisiana, where the bulk of the population carried names "foreign" to the Anglo-oriented Americans who usually were responsible for the overall compilation of the manuscripts. Present readers who are experienced in Louisiana research, particularly in the Natchitoches area, will recognize many mutilated names of both places and people within the pages that follow. The less experienced will have more difficulties. In an effort to forestall as many such problems as possible, the publishers of this particular work forwarded typewritten copies of personal sketches to each biographee, requesting that the text be approved and returned. Not all individuals did so, however. No such proofing of the historical narrative appears to have been made by any party familiar with the people and the places of the parish of Natchitoches.

Serious researchers will use this volume with discretion. The quantity, nature and content of its data does offer a marvelous research tool -- as long as the reader is cognizant of the potential for error and the necessity of using the material as clues to find other **original source material** that will solidly document the statements made herein.

drm

Biographical and Historical Memoirs
of Natchitoches Parish, Louisiana

NATCHITOCHES PARISH, LOUISIANA

NATCHITOCHES PARISH—THE ORIGINAL PARISH—SOIL, PRODUCTIONS, ETC.—THE SPANISH AND THE FRENCH
—GRANTS OF LAND—SLAVEHOLDERS—THE COURTS AND ATTORNEYS—RECORDS OF THE POLICE
JURY—DUELING—MILITARY RECORD—NEWSPAPERS—NATCHITOCHES—ITS BUSINESS AND
INSTITUTIONS—ITS CHURCHES, SCHOOLS, ETC.—PRUDHOMME—ROBELINE—CLOUTIER-
VILLE — MARTHAVILLE — GRANT'S POINT — PROVENCAL — GRAND ECORE—
CAMPTI — TRADITIONS, REMINISCENCES, ETC. — STATE OFFICIALS—
MEMORIAL AFFAIRS.

"I love everything that's old—old friends,
Old times, old manners, old books, old wine."—Anon.

THE act of April 10, 1805, divided Louisiana Territory into twelve parishes, Orleans, German Coast, Acadia, La Fourche, Iberville, Pointe Coupee, Attakapas, Opelousas, Natchitoches, Rapides, Ouachita and Concordia. Avoyelles was established in 1808. The Constitution of 1812 established three parishes out of original Orleans. In the fall of this year Dr. Sibley reported to Congress on the topography and people of the Red River Valley.

The original parish comprised all the territory in the ecclesiastical parish of St. Francis, or an area 120 miles long by seventy broad, Caddo, Claiborne, Webster, Bossier, part of Lincoln, Sabine, De Soto, Bienville, part of Winn, Red River, and part of Grant, all were organized out of Natchitoches. Natchitoches, in 1880, ranked third in number of inhabitants and fifth in cotton production of all the upper parishes. South of the old town and outside the bottom the uplands partake of a pine-hill character, except on Bayou Kasatchie. Of its total area, 1,290 miles, long-leaf pine hills cover 600, oak uplands 300, and Red River bottom-lands 300 square miles. Of 58,969 acres cultivated in 1879–80, there were 26,784 acres in cotton, which yielded 15,320 bales, or .57 bales per acre; 813 pounds of seed cotton, or 271 of cotton lint; 17,871 acres of corn; 197 of sweet potatoes, and 28 of sugar cane. Joseph Henry, of Willow, stated that the cotton plant reaches eight feet in height, and that fresh land produces 2,000 pounds of seed cotton, and after fifteen years of cultivation yields 1,800 pounds.

The alluvial land produces one bale and the hill land a half bale of cotton per acre. The statistics for 1889 are as follows: Cotton, acres, 32,783; cotton, bales, 20,115; corn, acres, 84,200; corn, bushels, 202,150; potatoes, acres, 1,605; potatoes, bushels, 56,000; hay, acres, 4,000; hay, bales, 110,100; alluvial land, acres, 230,018; pine and oak land, acres, 548,702; cultivated land, acres, 79,633; uncultivated land, acres, 523,060; government land, acres, 196,037; yellow pine, long and short leaf, feet, 1,300,000,000; cypress, feet,

500,000,000, and hardwood, feet, 2,000,000,000. Assessor Safford in his very careful review of the assessment of 1890, fixes the total taxable property at $2,787,260,* which is less than that of 1889. The poll tax is $4,400, $1,000 more than last year, and the taxes accruing from all sources at 16 mills, State and parish, are $49,030. The decrease in the taxable property is due to the fact that the assessment of the railroads was reduced from $7,500 to $6,000 a mile.

In 1785 the population of Natchitoches was 756, the figures being obtained for Capt. Gen. Galvez. The total population of Natchitoches in 1810 was 2,870, including 1,213 Caucasians, 181 free colored, and 1,476 slaves; in 1820, 7,486 or 4,725 whites, 415 free colored, and 2,326 slaves; in 1830, 7,095 or 3,802 whites, 532 free colored, and 3,571 slaves; in 1840, 14,350 or 7,042 whites, 657 free colored, and 6,651 slaves; in 1850, 14,228 or 5,466 whites, 881 free colored, and 7,881 slaves; in 1860, 16,699 or 6,306 whites, 958 free colored, and 9,434 slaves; in 1870, 18,265 or 7,312 whites and 10,928 colored; in 1880, 19,722 or 7,642 whites and 12,080 colored.

For 1890 the State statistics show 5,569 white male and 7,942 colored male, 3 Indian male, 4 Chinese male, and 5,295 white female and 7,513 colored female inhabitants, or a total of 26,326. There are 2,068 white and 2,791 colored voters; 5,612 colored and 3,782 white children of school age; 2,110 farm owners and 3,090 farm laborers. The United States census for 1890 places the population of the parish at 25,836.

The village of the Boluxa Indians (near Colfax) stood where the river divides into two branches, forming an island about fifty miles in length and three to four in width. On the right hand ascending was the stream called Rigolet de Bon Dieu (now Red River), on which there were no settlements in 1812. On the left hand (now Cane River) was the boat channel to Natchitoches, and on this branch, for twenty-four miles, were several rich plantations. Above the old River Cane settlement the river divided again, forming an island thirty miles in length, called Isle Brevel. This island was subdivided by a bayou, which crossed it from one river to the other. The middle or Cane River was called Little River, and was the boat channel. The westward channel, old river or false river, was navigable; but, owing to the lowness of its banks there were no settlements visible in 1812. The river passed through Lac Occasee (where Prudhomme now is), and above, at Natchitoches, the two channels met, while the Rigolet du Bon Dieu (now the main channel) left the present Cane River at Perot's plantation, one mile below Grand Ecore Bluffs, six miles up the stream from Natchitoches.

When De Soto came here in 1540 the Chickasaws were the most ferocious of all the tribes, and Red River deserved its name then as it does now. The gallant discoverer died at the mouth of this river, conferring the command on Muscoso de Alvarado. After the death of the chief, the Spaniards essayed to reach Mexico, but had not yet arrived at the mountains when Quiqualtanqui, chief of the Indian confederacy, opposed their advance and drove them back to the Gulf, reduced in number to 300 men. July 7, 1673, the venerable Marquette and the daring Joliet entered the Mississippi and floated down to the mouth of the Arkansas. In 1682 La Salle sailed down the Mississippi to its mouth. His second voyage, on which he discovered the Indian village where Natchitoches stands, resulted in his unfortunate death in 1687. A few years later the French and English hastened to claim part of the Spaniard's discovery, and the "Pelican," under Iberville and Bienville, silenced forever the British ships which attacked her. In March, 1699, the two captains with Pere Anastase (who was on La Salle's expedition of 1682) entered the Mississippi and explored the country to the Red River.

---

*The assessment of the parish in 1858 fixed the value of real estate at $1,640,800; of 7,095 slaves, $4,010,950; horses, $301,100; carriages and vehicles, $15,550; moneys at interest, $265,800, and capital in trade, $187,250. On this total of $6,429,750 a State tax of $16.66⅔ per $100 was levied, amounting to $10,741.83; the trade and profession tax yielded $2,100; the one-mill school tax $6,430.35; the poll tax, $1,068, and the internal improvement tax, $1,607.59, or a total of $21,967.77. Of 212,386 acres cultivated there were 36,765 under cotton, and 16,803 under corn, which produced 22,663 bales of cotton and 381,700 bushels of corn.

In 1870 the total assessed value was $2,601,330.50. On this a 4-mill State tax amounting to $10,405.31, and school and State bond taxes amounting to $15,737.65 were levied or $26,142.96. Of 362,182 acres in cultivation there were 20,999 acres of cotton and 18,603 acres of corn. The former yielded 9,189 bales and the latter 172,214 bushels.

Prior to 1694 the Spaniards established a colony of Canary Islanders at and around Adayes.

In 1713 the Marquis de la Jonquiere, and the officers appointed under Crozat's charter arrived in Louisiana. Lamotte Cadillac, one of the principal officers disappointed in trading with the Gulf Spaniards, determined to push French commercial enterprise into the interior of Mexico and to hold back the Spaniards. He established the post at Natchitoches, sending thither St. Denys with thirty Canadians and a number of Indians. This was in 1714, but St. Denys left only a few Canadians there, and pushed westward to the Presidio del Norte on Rio Bravo. In 1715 Du Pisne was sent to build a fort on Natchitoches Island. In 1716 St. Denys returned to Natchitoches, received supplies there from the Canadians and set out for the village of Adayes, where thirty warriors resided. Fording the river they very soon arrived at the Adeyches village, where there were ten cabins. The Catholic mission was at this point, and near by was the house of the two friars, the barrack of three soldiers and the cabin of the devout housekeeper of the convent. Thirty miles farther up was the first village of the Assinais, where a church was attended by two friars, and some distance away was the first Spanish Presidio, a captain, lieutenant and twenty-five troops. Immense herds of buffalo were seen.

When La Harpe arrived at Natchitoches with his fifty men he found Commandant Blondel in charge, with Father Manuel, of the Adayes Mission, as his guest. On an island near the fort were 200 members of the Natchitoches, Dulcinoes and Yattassee tribes. La Harpe went as far as latitude 33° 35', and erected a post there, 250 miles from Natchitoches. In 1718 St. Denys was commandant. After a short investigation, he learned that the Marquis de Gallo, governor of Texas, was in the vicinity with 400 cavalry and $50,000 worth of goods, and had begun to burn brick for a fort. Again he brought diplomacy to aid him, and received a promise from De Gallo that the French territory would not be occupied.

Biloxi was settled by the French under Iberville in 1699; Natchez, settled by the French under Iberville and De Touti in 1700; Fort St. Louis, settled by the French under Bienville in 1701; Mobile, settled by the French under Bienville in 1710; Fort Rosalie, settled by the French under Bienville in 1716; Natchitoches Fort, erected by the French under Bienville in 1717; New Orleans, settled by the French under Bienville in 1718.

At this time (1699) the Natchez numbered 600 warriors. In 1700 Bienville arrived at Natchitoches and Yattassee, forty miles above, where St. Denys subsequently had a post. They attacked Natchez Post, and in January, 1730, attacked the settlers at the Yazoos. St. Denys, who was commander at Natchitoches in 1730, won the respect of the Texan Indians. Against this post the Natchez directed their strength, but their approach was discovered. After diplomacy failed them to gain possession of the post, they burned a Frenchwoman in sight of the fort. At this time St. Denys had forty French soldiers and twenty settlers inside the stockade, and forty Natchitoches warriors close by. Driven to vengeance by the sight of the burning woman, he made a sortie, killed sixty savages, wounded a greater number and drove all to flight. Later the Avoyelles, Tunicas and other small tribes became allies of the French. In December, 1730, the Red River expedition set out under Salverte, brother of Gov. Perier. The third and last stand of the Natchez was made at Battle Ground plantation, on Sicily Island, Catahoula Parish, La., forty miles across the swamp from Natchez, Miss. Here they were found by Gov. Perier, January 20, 1732, and many of them torn to pieces by the artillery. That night a heavy rain storm came up to end the butchery, as it were, and in the darkness the remnant of the tribe escaped, leaving the wounded warriors, an aged woman and some non-combatants in the stockade. The refugees reorganized under Chief of the Flour, and attacked Natchitoches early in 1831. The old post, called by the Yankees Fort Claiborne, was surrounded by a deep ditch. In the northeastern section was the cemetery, and there in 1827, the last interment was made. An iron cross marks the grave and date. In January, 1717, M. de La Motte's expedition arrived at Natchitoches, but six years before this the church of San Miguel at Adayes, near Robeline, was established. During the century ending in 1816, Adayes disappeared, and the newer town on Cane River could only boast of 150 houses. On March 29, 1823, the church, presbytery and Rost's house were burned. On March 17, 1838, fire destroyed the new church here, being the second fire in the history of the town. The fort at Bayou Pierre Bluffs, near Grand Ecore, was a substantial set of structures covering one acre and surrounded by a stone wall. Parts of the wall and house foundations are still to be seen. On the Natchitoches and San Antonia trace evidences of a fort exist, and throughout the country bordering the old western trails the crosses of the missionaries or the swords of the soldiers of ancient days are unearthed at intervals.

The Sanchez' grant at Los Tres Llanos, where Louis Latham resided in the twenties, was one of the oldest Spanish grants by Gov. Lavois, who resided at Adizes. Sanchez' son was eighty-six years old in 1820, when District Judge William Murray took testimony in the case. In June, 1772, the inhabitants were driven out of Adizes, by Gov. Rippardo, leaving their crops and three sick families behind.

In 1770 Pierre and Julien Besson settled on the Ecore Rouge, six leagues above Natchitoches, granted by Athanase Mazieres, commandant at this post. The Michael Crow claim on the Sabine, was presented in 1797. His father, Isaac, married the widow Chabineau, and purchased lands on the east bank of the river from Vincente Michele, on the Natchitoches road. In September, 1769, Chevalier de St. Denys, commandant, granted to Marie de St. Denys, wife of De Soto, a tract in this vicinity.

Athanase Poisot claimed lands at Three Cabins, and also Prairie Nabutscahe, under a deed given by chief Antoine and other Indians of the Hyatasses, approved by Vaugine in 1784. This land is near the large bayou flowing into Natchitoches. In 1790 Andrew Rambin purchased from the Indians, Cayacaille and wife, some lands in this parish, and in 1778 a lot in the town from Chevalier Poiret.

In 1813 Richard K. McLaughlin, representing twenty-six claimants each for a square league in Natchitoches, signed the claims in presence of justice Marcel De Soto. The fraudulent methods were exposed by De Soto soon after, and the claims set aside.

In 1787 Francois Grappe purchased from Cahada or Cajahdet, an Indian of the Caddo tribe, a tract at Lake Bastiano, on the road from Campti to Little Caddo. Pierre Gagnier bought lands on Lake auk Meures from John Sohano and other Chesteaur Indians at Natchitoches. In 1790 Hypolite Bourdelin bought lands from the Indian chief, Dehuste, of Natchitoches, under whom the tribe was removed from the post to the lake named, ten leagues above the post, after the death of Chief Tomac.

In 1787 Estwan Mird, governor, granted lands to Francois Bossier, at the old Yatassé village. Lands were also granted to Nanet Larnodier and Alexis Grappe. In 1812 Pierre Elie, Berthelemi Shamberg and Hypolite Bordelon, testified that John B. Roujot and Madame F. Lemaitre owned, successively, the lots in Natchitoches village, claimed by Maria Louise Villfranche, wife of Gaspard Badin at that time. The names of Marie J. Crette, widow of Louis Anty, Gaspard Lacour, Alexis Cloutier, Pierre Labombarde, Louis Dearbonne, Baptiste Trichel, Armaud Lauve, Jean J. Poillet, Louis Vascoeu, of Black Lake; P. Villedaigle, J. F. Lavasseur, F. Mercier Madam Rouquiere, Marie B. Chamard, John M. Pierro, of Rigolet du Bon Dieu; Antoine Rachal, Michel Du Roy, Geago Rami, Manuel De Soto (died in 1799, after freeing his old slave, Papillon, then aged fifty-two years), Pierre Kairey, Jacques Vercheve, Alexis Cloutier, on river Aux Cannes, opposite the Old Village, bought from Miguel Rosalie Craz, in 1808; Joseph Taurus, Paul Coutant, B. L. Estage, Old River; Eben Leech, Spanish Lake; J. B. Morin, Marie A. Dupré, Joseph Rabalais, J. B. Boisnette, Joseph and Dominic Mettoyer, Little River; Nicholas, a free negro (Bunch of Canes), Marie Palige and Marie Perine (free mulatto woman) Drunkard's Bayou; P. T. Mettoyer, Bayou Blue; Marie R. Frederique, Florentine Conan, Marcellet Martin, Pierre Charrio, F. Laurent and S. B. Wiley (Campti), Augustin (a free negro) above Grand

Ecore; Jose de la Vega, John Quinnity, John Young, Young's Bayou; Joseph Hill, Little River; Pierre Schilletree, Old River; Valery Anty, Baltazar Brevel, John Litton and Joseph Santes, Bayou Tortoise; Louis Courtesse, Paul Prudhomme, Neuville Gallien, Leandre Lasso, Widow Antoine, Bayou Tete du Cheval; Pierre Sans Quartier, Bayou Pierre; Gregoire Gizernac, Lachoniere Island; Joseph Procelle, Bayou Dearbonne; Jean Legur, Bayou Deyet; the Martins, Bermudas; J. B. Piedfirme, Lac Poule de Eau; B. Ratbois, Antoine Lenoir, Remy Lamber, Saline Lake, eight leagues above Post; Antoine Dubois, P. Bonvellon, near Grand Marsh; U. Ortise, A. Le Blanc, Baptiste Plaisance and M. Levasseur, near Post; Ambrose Le Campti and James Teal, Prairie Yanecoocoo; Etienne La Caze, John A. Agnes and A. Langlois, River Tahon; J. B. T. Grillet, near Campti; Pierre Gagne, Rene Perrault, Jean Narces, Louis Sydic, Felicite Guillory and E. Derouen, four on Rigolet du Bon Dieu; Paul Poisseau, Attahoo River; Asa Beckham, Bayou Tortoise; J. M. Leando, sold to James F. Porter; Pierre Captain, a Christian Indian, resided on du Aux Cannes, near Antys settlement, in 1780; James Bludsworth claimed the Rouquiere lands, opposite Petite Ecore; Pierre Mailleux, Gilbert Closseau, Jean Francois Hartzog, Little River, 1794; he kept a store on Cane River, distant one and one-half leagues; William B. Quirk, Rio Pedro; Roger McPike, Bayou Nantache; Edmond Quirk, Bayou Dieu Domini; John Walker built a hunting cabin on Bayou Castor, in 1801, sold to John and Sarah Thompson; L. Robinson, Bayou Boine, seven miles west of post, and one mile above the old town of Adayes; Therese Lamalthie, Elizabeth David, Maria F. Hemell, Old River; Placide Bossier, Clear Lake; John Smith, Bayou Jeat; B. Savoy, Brosse Island.

In July, 1764, Director General Dabadie granted to J. B. Dubois, near the La Cour de la Prelle Islands at Ecore, 480 superficial arpens on the right bank of a branch of Red River, called River Cane.

In 1795 there were granted to Francis Rouquiere 1,600 arpens on Grand Batture Island in

Lac Terre Noire, one and one-half leagues from Natchitoches Post.

In August, 1787, 280 superficial arpens at the extremity of the Grand Ecore, near the lands of Joseph Martin, were granted to Francois Varcocu.

The Bernarda Pantaloon claim for four square leagues, twenty or twenty-five miles northwest of Natchitoches village, was founded on the grant by Commandant Ugarte, of Nacogdoches, in 1798; Dr. Sibley was witness for claimants. The village of Tapalcote, on the Arroyo del Durasno, and the stream called Tierra Blanca and Spanish Lake are mentioned among the boundaries. John Sibley's claim for the old Francois Morvant lands, seven leagues from Natchitoches, on the Bayou Pierre road, was sustained by a deed from Patrick Murphy, sheriff of Natchitoches in 1814.

In 1820 Felix Trudeau testified before Parish Judge Charles Slocum, of Natchitoches, that the claim of Emanuel Prudhomme for fifty-one acres on Red River, opposite the post of Natchitoches (lodged in the name of Widow Chaiqneau), was cultivated in 1796, when he came and was one of the first settled plantations in the parish. In 1782 the widow petitioned for title, and this petition was endorsed by M. de Vaugine, then commandant. At this time also the petition for title by Madame Widow St. Denys was recommended.

The slaveholders of Natchitoches in 1862, who paid taxes on ten or more slaves, are named in the following list. Such names as Gen. Bossier, Gen. Gagnie, Dr. Normand, and other large owners of slaves in pioneer days, do not occur in this list, as they had passed away long years before, while others took their slaves to Texas in 1862: C. C. Anthony, 29; Giles Berry, 24; James Beasley, 17; W. O. Breazeale, 56; J. W. Butler, 36; Breazeale, Payne & Harrison, 114; Mrs. M. N. Breazeale, 12; F. G. Bartlett, 44; Michael Boyce, 84; J. P. Breda, 21; J. D. Blair, 51; J. J. Blair, 45; Mrs. S. Bossier, 10; M. C. Buckstone, 15; Inil Brown, 11; Mrs. L. A. Buard, 57; J. L. Bullard, 11; C. B. Baird, 16; B. H. Baird, 14; O. P. Blanchard, 100; J. C. Brooks, 25; T. D. Brown, 24; A. W. Baird, 36; J. R. Bosley, 28; Hardy Bryant, 170; E. S. Blackstone, 13; Mary Brown,

30; D. & W. W. Brown, 80; J. R. Bosley, 24; J. W. Brown, 26; M. Bundanis, 12; L. F. Bordelon, 21; Hilaire Bordelon, 11; J. G. Campbell, 17; G. L. and M. F. Clanton, 36; Joseph Clark, 29; S. M. Cade, 49; Etienne Chelletre, 10; W. R. Cowser, 10; N. D. Calhoun, 107; W. S. Campbell & Co., 22; Emile Chevalier, F. M. C., 10; Noel Coudet, F. M. C., 25; A. Chaler, 14; Terence Chaler, 66; P. O. Chaler, 15; Jean Conant, F. M. C., 10; Chopin & Benoit, 42; Cockfield & Benoit, 49; A. Carnahan, 18; J. M. Compere, 15; J. B. Cloutier estate, 29; M. Carroll, 28; J. M. Dixon, 12; Widow Mary Dixon, 11; A. Deblieux, 11; L. Duplex, 20; J. A. Ducournau, 20; E. V. Deblieux, 36; J. N. Deblieux, 36; F. M. Dickerson, 10; Widow E. B. Daniel, 20; Mrs. L. F. Davis, 27; Widow Adolphe Dupre, 21; F. Derlouches, 10; L. G. Derbonne, 10; R. L. Duncan, 16; E. Davion, 10; J. H. Ellzey, 10; William Ellzey, 42; Joe Ezenack, 9; T. J. Foster, 18; E. B. Fleming, 46; G. Fontenot, 16; widow of Edward Frederic, 22; Honori Frederic, 13; Ben. Frederic, 11; Azenor Farson, Sr., 10; W. D. Gooch, 21; widow of Louis Gentry, 27; widow of F. Gonin, 18; George Gurney, 26; Mrs. E. J. Gallien, 10; L. A. & C. E. Greneaux, 22; Dezzelin Gallion, 16; Marco Givanovitch, 128; Richard Grant, 17; J. P. Grappe, 25; T. T. Hollis, 18; M. Henderson, 16; J. F. Hendricks, 11; Hypolite Hertzog, 56; widow of Richard Hertzog, 37; Joe Henry & Co., 56; R. E. Hammett, 20; Matthew Hertzog, 39; S. M. Hyams, 62; E. L. Hyams estate, 87; T. C. Hunt, 29; W. F. Howell estate, 23; Mrs. L. Hailey, 10; Thomas Hunter, 69; S. M. Hart, 13; Widow J. B. T. Happi, 15; Emile Hertzog's heirs, 18; Widow J. F. Hertzog, 78; Henry Hertzog, 51; Widow M. L. Hanrut, 59; S. D. Harper, 73; B. M. Hines, 33; widow of H. Harville, 18; A. G. Jordan, 79; F. Johnson, 16; Joseph Janin, 40; B. F. Jones, 12; W. S. Ketcheart, 12; Jacob Kile, 14; R. R. King, 40; J. C. Leopold, 10; Mrs. F. Lynch, 14; J. S. Levy, 8; John La Place, 8; Ambroise Lecomte, 233 (valued at $119,800, taxed, $199.67); Mrs. Eugenie Lemee, 68; Ursin Lambie, 26; Mrs. Valsin Lambie, 26; F. Lecomte, 37; Gasparite Lacour, 18; Benoist Lavispierre, 15; Theodore de Lattin,

18; Marcel Laplante, 10; Finnin Lattier, 22; F. B. Lee, 14; H. M. N. McKnight, 52; L. Marcy, 14; L. Moreau, 12; J. B. Moreau, 16; William Matthews, 16; Joseph and J. H. Martin, 17; W. P. Morrow, 17; J. L. McLaurin, 52; Reine McFier, 15; J. B. Marontini, 11; Widow Louis Morin, F. W. C., 10; Widow Alex Moreau, 23; Jerome Messie, 25; N. P. Metoyer, F. M. C., 12; P. G. Metoyer, 26; Widow J. B. Metoyer, F. W. C., 18; Franqullen Metoyer, F. M. C., 10; T. F. Metoyer, F. M. C., 15; widow of August Metoyer, F. W. C., 16; Widow J. B. A. Metoyer, F. W. C., 23; A. P. Metoyer, F. M. C., 18; widow of Ben Metoyer, 120; Benj. Metoyer, 35 (twenty-three years before this Dr. Norman was a slave owner); Amelia Owings, 29; Widow Lucy Oliver, 14; D. A. W. Patterson, 11: James E. Prothro, 32; Joshua Prothro, 28; Joseph E. Prothro, 28; Achille Prudhomme, 78; W. A. Ponder, 25; A. W. Pearre, 17; A. H. Pierson, 31; S. C. Prothro, 26; Charles Perot, 14; Phanor Prudhomme, 146; Adolphe Prudhomme, 26; Theophite Prudhomme, 22; J. B. Prudhomme, 91; Narcisse Prudhomme, 110; St. Ann Prudhomme, 72; John Prudhomme, 80; G. & E. Prudhomme, 49; Neuville Prudhomme, 51; Leetan Prudhomme, 50; Isaac Plaisance, 19; F. Plaisance, 18; Omer Perot, 11; John L. Perot, 28; Cyriac Perot, 23; L. Q. C. Puckett, 13; C. J. C. Puckett, 20; J. P. Packer, 20; James B. Porter, 19; Luke Poche, 10; Watson Read, 25; Francois Ronbieu, 40; widow of Francois Ronbieu. 46; L. B. Rachal, 26; Victor Rachal, 42; L. J. Rachal estate, 20 (there were five free colored males and one free colored female of this name who owned two to five slaves each, and there were thirty-three tax-payers of this name in the parish); J. B. O. Rouquier, 13; W. B. Robinson, 13; Widow C. N. Roques, F. W. C., 10; Emile Rost, 69; J. W. Roper, 17; J. W. Reynolds, 12; J. F. Scarborough, 11; T. M. Smith, 44; William Smith, 23; Jerry Smith, 19; C. E. Sompayrac, 63; J. S. Stephens, 12; Strong & Morse, 30; A. H. Stathart, 15; William Sprowl, 15; W. B. Stewart, 23; Jonathan Sprowl, 11; A. B. Sompayrac, 33; Damas St. Germain, 10; A. Samptte, 16; C. A. Sarpy (colored), 17; John B. Smith, 43; J. F. St. Amans,

15; C. E. St. Amans, 13; B. St. Amans, 66; Jerome Sarpy, Jr. (colored), 13; S. O. Scruggs, 27; Edward Severin, 12; Joseph Soldini, 15; S. S. Simmons, 12; John Simms, 77; Richard H. Turner, 10; Marcellin Tauzin, 35; T. E. Tauzin, 10; Strong, Walcott & Morse, 30; John N. Smith, 162; Ambroise Sompayrac, 100; Jules Sompayrac, 33; J. E. Tauzin, 11; J. M. B. Tucker, 10; T. B. Turner, 23; W. A. Tharp, 22; Mrs. T. E. Tauzin, 10; Severin Trichel, 20; Leo Trichel, 14; Lucien Trichel, 16; J. B. Trezziur, 14; H. V. Tessier, 12; Gabriel Vienne, 10; Adolphe Vienne, 17; widow of Emile Vienne, 10; G. W. Whitfield, 10; Philip Wagley, 10; G. S. Walmsley, 46; H. P. Walsh, 12; Warren Williams, 18; widow of F. E. Williams, 31; William Williams, 10; Rawle Williams, 19; E. Whitted, 10, and William Whitted, 12. There were 1,579 resident tax-payers and 82 non-resident tax-payers in 1862. The non-resident slave owners were: A. L. Abbott, 17; Berry & Thompson, 43; D. A. Blacksher; 58; G. M. Braimer, 19; W. M. Burns, 34; John Carnahan, 16; J. W. Foster, 13; John Frazier, 63; W. D. Gooche, 23; T. B. Hale & J. R. Williams, 14; John Jordan, 67; John R. Jones, 28; King & Blacksher, 17; J. L. Lewis & J. D. Harper, 73; Morse & Butler, 29; E. L. Patterson, 19; J. B. Planche, 81; G. W. Stone & C. R. Johnson, 21; J. T. Thorn, 52; G. W. Thompson, 36, and William Wyche, 35.

The first session of the district court was held at Natchitoches Post, July 19, 1813, with Josiah S. Johnson, of the (then) Sixth District, presiding. A judgment for $878.18¼ was returned in favor of M. Murphy against Augustus Langlois. In November, of that year, Isaac McNutt, William Murray, J. Winship, Isaac Baldwin and Robert K. McLaughlin were admitted to the bar, and James Wallace was given special permission to practice. Isaac McNutt was appointed district attorney. Nine persons were sentenced to one year's imprisonment for taking a prisoner from the jail. On March 13, 1814, Mr. George Strickland, a United States soldier at Fort Claiborne, was sentenced to death for the murder of Ross McCabe. Judge Johnson ordered him to be taken to the place of execution between 11 o'clock in the morning and 4 o'clock in the afternoon, closing in the old form, "and that you be hung by the neck, between the heaven and the earth, until you be dead, dead, dead, and may the Lord have mercy on your soul." Edward Love was indicted for the murder of James Crawford in 1817, but acquitted; while in 1819, Samuel Sims was sentenced to a ten years' term for perjury. In July, 1817, James Dunlap was judge, vice Johnson, recused; P. Bludworth was coroner, and L. S. Hazelton, sheriff. Henry A. Bullard was judge in 1819, but Judge S. Lewis tried the suit of the Civil Parish vs. the Ecclesiastical Parish, and decreed that all the territory claimed by the Civil Parish, with the exception of a comparatively small area, belonged to the claimant. In June, 1820, William Murray succeeded Judge Bullard. In November, 1823, the suit of Post vs. Catholic Congregation was tried. This grew out of the fire of March 29, 1823, the plaintiff claiming $2,000 for loss of his house near by and other property. It appears that in August, 1822, Padre Magney left Natchitoches, and no other priest took his place until after the fire. Meantime a negro named Joe, who had been beadle for twenty years before, looked after the buildings.

The second oldest record of the district court in possession of Clerk Hyams is dated May, 1824, William Murray as judge and George Smith, deputy clerk being present. The estate of Gary and Shadrack Thomas was assigned to Mr. J. G. Hotham for the use of their creditors, the pay of the assignee being $100, subsequently the debtors were discharged from all liabilities under the insolvent law. On May 4 the cases known as the Town of Natchitoches vs. Tauzin, Lennon and Jackson, Obe & Loupart and Landreaux were tried, and a jury of whom A. Bludworth was foreman, returned a verdict that the buildings of defendants were on public property and should be removed. Parish Judge J. C. Carr took Judge Murray's place in special cases during this term. In November, 1824, Charles Provots was indicted for murder and found guilty. Benjamin Bullett, the sheriff with others, was ordered to pay $800 for a slave. In November, 1826, S. Lewis succeeded Murray as judge, and C. E. Greneaux, clerk, succeeding M.

Bronaugh. In January, 1833, C. E. Greneaux succeeded John C. Carr as parish judge, and served until 1846. Judge Carr was parish judge as early as 1807, *ex-officio* recorder, clerk, and president of police jury, and a man of all work under the American regime.

E. K. Wilson, judge of the Seventh District, was present in 1836 and Henry Boyce of the Sixth in December. In April, 1840, George R. King of the Fifth District presided here. In April the trial of Francois M. Normand was begun—the Judge refused a jury *de meditate lingue*. The charge of murder against him was without the shadow of a foundation; but the jury found him guilty of manslaughter, recommending him to mercy. This jury moved round the town at will during the dinner hour and by other methods brought the court into contempt.

The November term of 1840 was opened by Judge J. G. Campbell of the Tenth District, who with George R. King of the Fifth District transacted court affairs here until April, 1843, when Henry Boyce of the Sixth District presided, Judge Campbell, however, held court here that year and in 1844-45 and 1846. In August of 1846 James Taylor, judge of the Sixteenth District, was present, and served here until 1851, when Charles A. Bullard was commissioned. Judges Olcutt and Jones tried many special cases here during Taylor's term. In 1853 Chichester Chaplin was commissioned judge of the Sixteenth District and served uninterruptedly up to December, 1864. In April, 1865, no court was held, but the fall term was presided over by Judge Michael Ryan of the Ninth District. William B. Lewis, of the same district, opened court in March, 1866, and John Osborn in December, 1868. He was succeeded in 1874 by H. C. Myers, but in 1875 C. Chaplin was commissioned and served until June, 1877, when Judge David Pierson was commissioned to preside over the Seventeenth District.

Edward D. Turner was judge of the parish court of Natchitoches in 1806, when Isaac Baldwin, Josiah S. Johnson and William Murray were admitted to the bar. George McTier was interpreter; Patrick Clark, crier. In 1810 John C. Carr

signed the records as probate judge. In May, 1813, P. D. Cailleau Lafontaine was parish judge, followed by John C. Carr, who served until January, 1833, when C. E. Greneaux succeeded him. The latter served until the office was abolished in 1845-46. On October 5, 1868, W. H. Hiestand presided as parish judge; in 1870, H. C. Myers, D. H. Boult, Jr., in 1874; J. E. Breda in 1875; P. A. Simmons in 1877 and in January, 1879, J. M. B. Tucker presided. He held the office until March, 1880, when the constitutional term ended.

A. W. Hamilton was clerk in 1867, and John A. Barlow, deputy clerk. Mayor James Cromie, a Federalist, was clerk in 1868, with A. E. Lemee, deputy. J. Jules Bossier then followed as clerk in 1871, with L. A. Bossier as deputy. In 1873 H. P. Meziere was clerk, and John A. Barlow, deputy, who has been in the clerk's office as deputy since that year. Edward Ezernack was clerk in 1875, W. H. Tunnard, 1877; in 1880, George W. Kearney was elected clerk and served until his death in June, 1885, when Henry M. Hyams, the present clerk, was appointed to fill vacancy, and subsequently elected.

The members of the bar of 1890 are T. C. Armstrong, Phanor Breazeale, J. Ernest Breda, H. Bernstein, E. E. Buckner, C. Chaplin, Thomas P. Chaplin, M. H. Carver, W. A. Carter, J. F. Carter, M. J. Cunningham, J. H. Cunningham, M. L. Dismukes, C. F. Dranguet, William H. Jack, W. G. MacDonald, M. F. Machen, James C. Morse, M. C. Moseley, Amos Ponder (Many), Silas D. Ponder, Charles V. Porter, D. C. Scarborough (district attorney), J. M. B. Tucker, James B. Tucker, John M. Tucker and L. B. Watkins. (J. F. Smith, of Many, died in 1890.) The students who expect to be admitted to the bar are S. J. Henry, B. H. Litchenstein, R. L. Caspari and Briant Tauzin.

In 1813 Patrick Murphy was sheriff; 1814, Bartholmie Fleming; 1815, James Loccard; 1818, L. S. Hazelton; 1823, Benjamin Bullitt; 1830, W. R. Johnson; 1832, Henry Jones; 1835, Benjamin F. Chapman; 1838, David S. Burnett; 1839, John A. De Russy; 1841, Benjamin V. Cortes; 1846, Theophele E. Tauzin; 1847, Samuel M. Hyams;

1854, Francois Vienne; 1860, William S. Campbell; 1861, Joseph W. Norris; 1864; P. C. Rogers; 1865, Theophile Bossier; 1866, James C. Hughes; 1868, Samuel Parson; 1872, R. E. Burke; 1875, Virgel A. Barron; 1877, D. H. Boult; 1878, Louis A. Deblieux; 1880, Samuel P. Raines; 1884, G. L. Trichel, with Charles E. Trichel, deputy. J. H. Cosgrove qualified as public printer in 1880.

In 1815 S. H. Sibley qualified as clerk of the district court, and appears to have held this office up to 1832. In January, 1833, F. Williams filed his bond as clerk, and in 1837 S. M. Hyams qualified as clerk of the district and probate courts; in 1846, C. E. Greneaux; 1847, William P. Morrow; 1851, C. E. Greneaux; 1853, William P. Morrow; 1858, L. A. Greneaux; November, 1860, Benjamin Joseph Bouis, and A. W. Hamilton in 1865. The clerks from 1867 to the present time are named above.

Thomas P. Jones qualified as recorder, October 1, 1846; William Payne in 1858; George W. Kearney, 1866; Charles F. Christy, 1868; L. H. Burdick, 1870; George W. Kearney, 1872; L. D. C. Lafontaine was recorded in 1813, succeeding J. C. Carr; Charles Slocum in March, 1819; J. C. Carr, 1821, and C. E. Greneaux, 1833.

Louis F. Martin was surveyor in 1834, and John H. Mahle, coroner; D. F. Tabor was auctioneer in 1837, and J. L. Gillispie, surveyor; Isaac Holmes, coroner in 1839; James D. Cannon in 1843; George W. Morse, surveyor in 1844; F. Williams, coroner, 1845; D. H. Boult, 1846; J. F. Payne, auctioneer, 1846, and D. F. Tabor, 1847–52; Simon Cockrell, coroner, 1852; J. A. Wolfson, auctioneer, 1855; T. Bossier, coroner, 1858; T. M. Hart, auctioneer, 1858; J. W. Walker, surveyor, 1859; P. C. Rogers, coroner, 1860, and T. Bossier in 1864.

Edward O. Blanchard filed his bond as major of the Eighteenth Louisiana Militia in 1837; G. W. Reese, quartermaster, and S. M. Hyams, adjutant. In 1842 P. E. Bossier, major-general of Second Division Louisiana Militia, took the oath; Dr. Charles Hamlin, coroner, 1866; Harry Percy, surveyor, 1866; William H. Boult, 1869; Philip Breda, coroner, 1873; Denis V. Murphy, auction-

eer, J. S. Stephens, coroner, 1890; H. Percy succeeded W. H. Boult, and served until 1886.

The oldest record of the police jury was found in the office of Ambroise H. Lecomte, justice of the peace, September 25, 1890. It is a venerable volume without cover or pretensions, written in French, and dating back to October 29, 1846. B. St. Amans was then president and F. Williams, clerk; T. M. Brown, S. H. Benoist, S. S. Bossier, N. Furlong, R. E. Hammett, S. M. Hyams, G. W. Morse (inventor of Morse rifle), and H. W. Powell were members of the jury, and later the names of Lestan Prudhomme, T. Thompson, Landry Delouches, and W. T. Walmsley appear. A. H. Pierson was parish attorney. Two slaves, Victor and Hypolite, were emancipated on petition of Michael Boyce and Ambrose Sompayrac, who gave bonds for their departure from the State. The Chronicle was then the official paper. Michael Boyce, James Taylor, P. A. Morse, C. E. Greneaux and T. H. Airey were appointed school directors. The last named parish treasurers, Jules Sompayrac and Jesse Wamack were elected jurors in 1847, and in October the expenses for the current year were estimated at $11,100. In June, 1848, H. Y. Waddell, William Williams, S. S. Bossier, William Townsend, James McKnight, L. Delouches and L. Prudhomme were jurors. T. H. Areaux was chosen constable, and the other jury officers were re-elected. In June, 1849, M. L. Squiers, W. A. Strong, Sylvan Delouches, B. St. Amans, W. Smith and Tally D. Brown were elected or re-elected, while in 1850 James Lester and J. W. McDonald were new members. The unusual benevolence of a legislator is recorded in June of this year. John A. Ragan, representative, donated his mileage to the parish to be used in the purchase of books and papers for the use of orphan scholars. The estimate of expenses was $5,500. In June, 1851, H. Y. Waddell succeeded St. Amans as president. H. T. Jones, D. H. Boult, J. W. Wray and A. Carnahan qualified as jurors, while in 1852 D. H. Boult succeeded Waddell. A. P. Scisson and Leonard Trichel qualified with other old members re-elected. In July the parish was redistricted into seven wards, and in September the question of voting aid to the New Orleans, Opelousas & Great Western Railroad Company was ordered to be submitted to the people. In June, 1853, President Boult with S. S. Bossier and L. Prudhomme old members, and J. Knight, A. P. Scisson and Syl. Trichel, Leonard Trickel, Thomas C. White, T. M. Spurgeon and J. R. Bosley formed the jury. J. Lester, J. J. Rains and G. Fontenot are named in 1854, with H. P. Gallion and F. B. Metoyer. In 1855 A. M. Baird, H. H. Haithorn and Peter Airhart qualified as new jurors, and in 1856 W. P. Owings, and J. B. Fleming qualified. J. B. Smith was elected attorney *vice* A. H. Pierson. At this time a road from Campti to Sparta was authorized, and also a road from Springville to Coushatta Point was declared a public road. The estimate of expenses for the fiscal year was placed at $10,000, and with this entry the old record book closes. In September, 1855, the record ceased to be kept in the French language, and the old clerk, F. Williams, continues the minutes in the English language until 1856. In 1858 John Colton, presided, followed in 1860 by W. O. Breazeale; in June, 1861, by P. M. Backen; in June, 1860, by W. O. Breazeale; in 1864, P. M. Backen. In 1838 J. F. Cortes, V. Lambre, John Freeman, Chme Vascoco and Edmund Smith were jurors.

The first *post bellum* record of the police jury in possession of H. P. Breazeale, clerk of the jury, is dated December 20, 1865. P. M. Backen was president, with F. Jennings, Hyp. Hertzog, G. Fontenot, J. M. Bishop, L. Trichel and L. Marcy, members. C. L. Walmsley was treasurer, and A. E. Lemee, clerk. The liabilities of the parish were estimated at $22,158, exclusive of interest; but the exact amount of bonds and promissory notes issued for war purposes could not be ascertained. An issue of 8 per cent bonds, payable in ten years from April, 1866, was authorized. In June, 1866, a new jury, with William Payne, treasurer, qualified. The members were B. H. Baird, W. C. Ross, R. E. Hammett, E. S. Blackstone, William A. Ponder, J. D. Addison, Jacob Kile, G. Fontenot, B. W. Bullitt and Hosea Pickett. C. Chaplin, Sr., was appointed attorney, and R. E. Burke, treasurer. In 1867 A. E. Lemee was at-

torney, and the estimate of expenses for the year 1867–68 was placed at $16,000, the same as for 1866–67. William Trichel, Henry Dallas, Emile Silvie, Joseph Martin, P. H. Hamilton, J. R. Hornsby, J. B. Vienne and R. L. Faulkner (public school teacher) were the new members in 1868. The estimate of expenditures was placed at $20,-000. V. A. Barron presided in 1869, *vice* Martin and Theo. Monette was a member. In 1870 A. E. Lemee was elected treasurer; J. J. Bossier succeeded him as clerk the year before, and C. A. Bullard succeeded him as attorney. M. P. Blackstone was president and Charles Le Roy (colored) was treasurer in 1871. In August, the estimate of expenditures was placed at $35,600. In October of this year, the "Immigration Bureau," was established, with H. C. Myers agent, and J. J. Bossier secretary, Justine Condet (colored) was a juror at this time with J. B. Vienne (colored) and President Blackstone. The reform association suits against the jury were commenced. John Dumas qualified as juror in 1872. In June, 1873, P. A. Simmons was chosen president, and he with F. Jennings, W. W. Breazeale, J. Addison, V. A. Barron, Ed Mitchell and N. P. Metoyer formed the board. John La Place succeeded Bossier as secretary, but soon after gave place to J. A. Barlow. The re-districting of the parish into five wards was effected in August, 1873, and in September, the ordinance prohibiting all Red River steamboats (except the Grand Ecore packets) from landing at any place in the parish, was adopted. In 1874, Samuel Black and John Holmes are named as jurors, and Charles Le Roy treasurer, but later Willis Holmes held that position, and V. A. Barron, president. Joseph Ezernack was treasurer in 1873, and W. H. Boult, assistant. Joseph P. Johnson was clerk in August, 1874. V. A. Barron, W. A. Ponder, R. E. Hammett and J. C. Metoyer were jurors, and in November the names of W. C. Ross, F. Jennings and H. R. McClendon appear and William Payne qualified as juror. In April, 1875, Joseph Ezernack was chosen president, A. E. Lemee appointed treasurer, *vice* Holmes, but declining Dr. A. P. Breda was elected, W. H. Tunnard was clerk; Carroll Jones, J. A. Clamons,

F. A. Mezierre and L. G. Barron were jurors. The clerks and treasurers' records were then held by Johnson and Holmes, and a request for their prompt transfer to the new officials was made and a notice of the "Payne Police Jury" placed on record. The petition of Col. Burke, M. H. Carver, Leo Caspari and James E. Keegan, to order an election on the question of granting $100,000 aid to the New Orleans & Pacific Railroad was not entertained. In February, 1876, lots for white and colored school buildings were donated, and in July a memorial to Gov. Kellogg asking him to take immediate action in the case of Amos Wright, H. Redmond and William Henry (sentenced to death in 1875 and then in the parish jail) was adopted. In January, 1877, M. B. Florens and J. B. Fleming appear as jurors, with President Ezernack, Secretary Tunnard and Carroll Jones. In June William Payne, president; R. E. Jackson, A. V. Carter, W. B. Butler, L. Chopin, W. C. Ross, H. J. Weaver, with Ezernack, Jones and Fleming were members. A. E. Lemee was treasurer, J. H. Cosgrove, secretary, and C. P. Blanchard, constable. In 1878 F. Jennings was a juror, and in January, 1879, William Payne, W. O. Braezeale, R. W. Freeman, P. E. Prudhomme, J. O. Williams, H. R. McClendon, S. G. Dowden, H. H. Haithorn, A. Maronovich were jurors, and M. L. Dismukes, clerk.

In April, 1880, Jules E. Messi was chosen clerk. R. E. Hammett, Thomas Smith, J. N. Burkett and Charles Wheeler, with Messrs. Payne, Haithorn, Braezeale, Dowden, Maronovich and Jennings, formed the jury. W. O. Braezeale presided in 1881. P. E. Prudhomme was a member in 1882, and F. P. Chaplin and F. Jennings in 1883. In March, 1884, Joseph Henry was appointed World's Fair commissioner from this parish. In July J. C. Trichel, J. H. Normand, Jr., J. T. Smith, W. O. Braezeale and T. L. Grappe appear as new members of the board. S. D. Ponder was chosen clerk in April, and served until January, 1886, when H. P. Braezeale was elected. H. B. Walmsley was chosen treasurer, to succeed A. E. Lemee at this time, and in December a number of delegates to the agricultural convention was appointed.

W. S. Greneaux was elected treasurer in August, 1887, and in April, 1888, J. J. Rains took the place of F. Jennings, deceased. In August of this year W. B. Butler represented Ward 4, and Adolph Lemee, Ward 10.

The assessors from 1847 to 1889 are named as follows: F. Vienne, 1847–54; L. G. De Russy, 1854; M. C. Brosset, 1856; J. J. Rains, 1860; G. P. Rains, 1860; W. J. Robins, 1865; C. J. Smith, 1868; D. H. Boult, 1869; W. H. Redmond, 1874; J. P. Johnson, 1880; Henry Safford, 1889.

The treasurers, from 1849 to 1889, are named as follows: T. H. Airey, 1849–55; L. R. Walmsley, 1853; C. L. Walmsley, 1860; R. E. Burke, 1865; Joseph Ezernack, 1869; A. E. Lemee, 1870; Charles LeRoy, 1871; Joseph Ezernack, 1874; Willis Holmes, 1874; A. P. Breda, 1875; A. E. Lemee, 1877; W. S. Greneaux, 1887.

The collectors from 1861 to 1875 were: H. F. Trichel, collector of war tax, 1861; John E. Murphy, 1863; Morris Lisso, by Confederate appointment, 1864; D. H. Boult, 1867; W. P. Morrow, 1874; C. J. C. Pucketts, 1875.

In 1871 the Tax Reform Association was organized, with M. Boyce president. M. H. Carver and Leopold Caspari were appointed a committee to appeal from the findings of the district court to the Supreme Court. Other steps were taken to check the unlimited issue of warrants. In some matters this association was successful, checkmating the judgment creditors through Arbitrators Joseph Henry, William Payne and R. E. Burke.

In the report of Parish Treasurer Lemee, in September, 1877, he showed that judgments, or parish paper, amounted to $164,663.28; parish paper floating debt $24,561.04, and paper absorbed by taxes, from 1871 to 1875 inclusive, $77,317.13; or a total of $286,541.45.

The duel between W. L. McMillen and George Williams was fought in January, 1836, and resulted in McMillen's death. David Burnett was present as the friend of McMillen, and Adolphe Sompayrac as the friend of Williams, with Dr. F. Johnson, surgeon.

On September 14, 1839, Gen. Pierre E. Bossier, through his friends, Sylvester Bossier, Victor Sompayrac and P. A. Morse (Democrats), challenged Gen. Francois Gaiennie, of Cloutierville, to fight a duel. The latter's friends, L. G. De Russy, F. B. Sherburne and J. G. Campbell (Whigs), accepted the challenge and designated rifles as the weapons. On September 18, 1839, the persons named, with Dr. F. Johnson, Dr. Dingles, T. E. Tauzin, Phanor Prudhomme and John F. Cortez, were present at "The Savannah," in rear of Emile Sompayrac's plantation. The first fire was delivered ineffectually by Gaiennie, and the second effectually by Bossier, who killed his opponent.

In connection with the Bossier-Gaiennie troubles it may be added that eleven citizens lost their lives: Sylvester Rachal, killed by M. Busy (a clerk for Dr. Normand); Brevile Perot, killed by Gaiennie's overseer, who was also killed on Lecompte's race-track at Cloutierville, being among the number.

Col. Prickett, who was killed in a duel early in the forties, is buried on the spot, one and one-half miles from Natchitoches, on Sibley Lake.

Tauzin challenged one of the officers at Fort Jesup to a duel, and the meeting did actually take place. John E. Cortez was Tauzin's second. Capt. May, the wild officer of Fort Jesup, was accustomed to ride over to Natchitoches daily. His duels were many.

In September, 1865, the grand jury of Natchitoches presented the Freedman's Bureau as a nuisance. Lieut. Pope, of the Nineteenth Pennsylvania Cavalry, on duty there, committed suicide in January, 1866.

In September, 1878, a convention of the Democratic party was held at Natchitoches, and the negroes, under A. Rayford Blunt, determined to hold a counter convention. The white citizens were prepared for hostilities, and before Blunt could carry out his designs, himself and men were captured. Next morning a rescuing party, 300 armed negroes, was met at the dirt bridge by the white guards, and driven back.

In November, 1878, a number of citizens were arrested on information sworn by J. R. Hornsby, charging them with interfering with him as a voter for J. M. Wells, candidate for Congress. The men

arrested were Ernest Masson, Dr. S. O. Scruggs, J. Buard, J. C. Johnson, William Airhart, Sr., J. B. Rachal and W. Cockfield. A. Deblieux, then sheriff-elect, and John Hertzog, could not be found by the deputy marshals.

In January, 1879, eleven United States marshals arrived at Natchitoches, with warrants for the arrest of sixty-six citizens; thirty-three of the indicted citizens went at once to New Orleans, where, on March 7, eight were acquitted. The State hailed the verdict with enthusiasm.

In November, 1879, the Union-Greenback-Labor party of Natchitoches nominated Mortimer Perot and Jacob Kile for representatives; John A. Raggio, for sheriff; E. Masson, for clerk of the district court; Dr. Jules Janin, for coroner; J. H. Cunningham, for District attorney, and C. Chaplin, for district judge.

James S. Flournoy represented Natchitoches, Sabine, De Soto and Caddo in 1859 in the Senate. William M. Levy and F. Robieu represented Natchitoches in the House; D. Robson and O. White, Caddo; Henry Phillips and L. L. Tompkins, De Soto, and E. C. Davidson, Sabine. Dr. J. W. Butler was a representative of Natchitoches before the war. Natchitoches recorded 754 votes for Breckinridge; 534 for Bell and 106 for Douglas. A. H. Pierson, of Natchitoches, signed the secession ordinance of 1861. W. H. Jack was representative from Natchitoches during the secession. Jacob Kile and Jules Sompayrac were representatives in 1865, with J. B. Elam and Dr. S. O. Scruggs, senators. In 1868 W. C. Melvin (white) and Charles Le Roy (col.) were chosen representatives, and J. R. Williams (white) and J. B. Lewis (col.), senators. Henry Raby (col.) and M. Blackstone (white) were chosen in 1870. Blackstone was killed during a secret meeting of the Republican executive committee in 1871 and L. R. Barron was chosen to fill vacancy. Rayford Blunt (col.) and J. B. Elam were senators. In 1878 the Democrats elected M. J. Cunningham and W. C. Ross, representatives, and W. D. Sandiford and Boling Williams, senators. They were succeeded by M. J. Cunningham and B. W. Marsden, senators, and J. H. Cosgrove and R. L. Jackson, representatives. In 1884 Joseph Henry and J. Fisher Smith were chosen senators, the latter served until his death in 1890, and the former holds office until 1892. Leo. Caspari and Dr. A. E. Cassidy (died in 1887) were elected representatives in 1884, and in 1888 Leo. Caspari and W. A. Ponder were elected. The latter died in 1890. The vote cast for Francis T. Nicholls (D.) in 1876 was 1,776, and for S. B. Packard (R.), 2,004. In 1879 Louis A. Wiltz (D.), received 1,356 votes and Taylor Beattie (R.), 516. In 1884 there were 2,203 votes cast for Samuel D. McEnery (D.), and 535 for John A. Stevenson (D.). The vote for governor in 1888 shows 3,373 for Francis T. Nicholls (D.), and 285 for Henry C. Warmoth (R.). The number of registered voters in April, 1888, was 5,294—2,314 being white. Of the whites 875 and of the Africans 2,523 were then unable to write their names.

In 1803 a company of United States troops, under Capt. Turner, garrisoned Natchitoches, while one Freeman, in charge of an exploring party, ascended Red River, above the post, until he encountered the Spanish troops, when he quietly returned. Shortly after a post was established within fourteen miles of Natchitoches, on the Nacogdoches road. At this time Spanish troops held the territory to Red River, so that Col. Cushing, with three companies and four guns was ordered to occupy Natchitoches.

In January, 1815, Capt. R. H. Sibley's company of militia joined Col. James Bludworth's Eighteenth Louisiana Regiment, and was present at Camp Villero, below New Orleans. The men failed to arrive prior to January 8, and thus missed participation in the crowning defeat of the British.

John J. La Place, aged seventy-eight, of Natchitoches, and John S. Umphrey, aged forty-six of Rapides, were pensioners of the War of 1812, in 1840.

Gen. U. S. Grant, who, as lieutenant of the Fourth United States Regiment, was stationed at Camp Salubrity, two miles from Natchitoches, in 1844, was well known here, among his friends being A. Deblieux. It is related that he proposed marriage (through Col. Voce) to a lady of this city (now Mrs. Sullivan), but met with a prompt refusal. Col. Voce, then commanding, told her that his young lieutenant would one day be the first man in the United States.

In 1846 Gov. Johnson called for six months' men to serve in the war against Mexico, and among the first to respond were the citizens of Natchitoches. S. M. Hyams raised a company for the Fifth Louisiana Volunteers, and was commissioned captain. The same year this company was mustered out. At the meeting of the Mexican War veterans, held in April, 1879, the commission of E. Valery Deblieux, as lieutenant of the second company of Col. B. Peyson's National Guards, was read. Among the residents entitled to claims were Theodore Hertzog, Samuel Parson, W. P. Morrow, E. J. Cockfield, J. J. A. Martin, James Allen, M. C. Brosset, E. Lavasseur, Emile Vienne, Capt. Samuel M. Hyams and William Airhart and Dr. R. C. Richardson, all of Natchitoches; Josiah S. Scarborough and John Rockwood, near Many, and Ben Prevots, of Mansfield. L. Duplex was constituted a member.

The Veterans' Association, of Central Louisiana, was organized in August, 1887, with H. V. McCain, of Grant, president; R. C. Jones, of Winn, David Pierson, of Natchitoches, J. F. Smith, of Sabine, and C. C. Nash, of Grant, vice-presidents; J. M. McCain, of Winn, secretary; W. E. Russell, of Natchitoches, treasurer; G. L. Trichel and T. Haller, of Natchitoches; J. F. Kelly and W. A. Strong, of Winn; W. W. McNeely and D. W. Self, of Sabine; J. F. Pierson and J. W. Sandiford, of Red River, members of the executive committee.

Company D, Pelican Rangers No. 2, organized in Natchitoches Parish, was mustered in with the Third Louisiana Infantry May 17, 1861. J. D. Blair, who resigned the captaincy in 1861; S. D. Russell, first lieutenant, promoted to colonel; W. E. Russell, second lieutenant, promoted to captain; S. M. Hyams, Jr., second lieutenant, elected lieutenant-colonel of a cavalry regiment; B. P. Morse, first sergeant, chosen second lieutenant in May, 1862; H. B. Walmsley, second sergeant; F. W. Airey, third sergeant, afterward captain in another regiment, and J. H. Peters, fourth sergeant, were the first officers. This company suffered severely at Vicksburg; T. Cobb, H. V. C. Edmondson, W. W. Gandy, and R. C. Hammett being killed, or died of wounds there; O. La Plante died at Iuka from wounds, and J. Williamson at Oak Hills.

Company G, Pelican Rangers No. 1, was mustered in with No. 2; W. W. Breazeale was captian until September 24, 1861; W. O. Breazeale, first and G. W. Halloway, second lieutenant, both of whom resigned before the close of October, 1861. L. Caspari, the second junior lieutenant at muster in, was promoted first lieutenant in October, 1861, and captain in February, 1862. W. B. Butler, the first sergeant was elected captain May 8, 1862, and P. L. Prudhomme, second lieutenant; J. C. Trichel was third, J. A. Derbonne, fourth, and F. F. Chaler, fifth sergeant; the latter died at Maysville, Ark., September 14, 1861. P. Bossier was chosen third lieutenant in May, 1862; B. B. Breazeale, fifth sergeant; F. Gaiennie, first lieutenant; James Kile, third lieutenant; James W. Moss, second lieutenant, and K. Espy, assistant surgeon. The list of deaths, as given in Tunnard's report, is as follows: Placide Bossier, at Oak Hills, V. Bordinave at Castillian Springs, October 3, 1862; C. F. H. Schroeder at Elk Horn; John M. Tauzin, at Iuka, and B. F. Warner at Elk Horn.

The Lecompte Guards were organized in April, 1861, with William M. Levy, captain; R. E. Burke, first lieutenant; J. F. Scarborough, second lieutenant; S. B. Robertson, third lieutenant. This command was mustered into the Second Louisiana Infantry, and served until the close of the war; only seventeen men remained to be mustered out; of this number, very few are now living. The sergeants were T. P. Chaplin, G. P. Rains, L. D. Johnson and G. W. Kearney; the corporals, W. A. Hollon, E. J. Miles, J. S. Kearney, and A. W. Hamilton; Smith Noel was standard bearer, and Dr. C. Hamlin, surgeon. This command left on the steamer "Rapides," April 27, 1861, 107 strong. Capt. W. M. Levy, editor of the Natchitoches Chronicle, and captain of the Lecompte Guards, was promoted colonel of the Second Louisiana Infantry, vice De Russy, resigned, in

August, 1861; at this time J. H. Reid commenced to recruit his select cavalry company.

The Natchitoches Rebels were organized September 9, 1861, with John D. Wood, captain; W. P. Owings, Theodul Latier and Emile Cloutier, lieutenants; S. B. Shackleford, T. J. Foster, Felix Sers, J. C. H. Nemitts, and E. B. Roper, sergeants; Joseph Gallion, A. B. Cunningham, J. A. Clark and L. T. Fontenot, corporals, and W. A. Jenkins, musician. Among the privates were L. L. Lynch, P. Rabelais, M. Vickers, and C. Vircher, who died in October, 1861. Two members of the Hertzog and six of the Rachal families served in this command. On January 24, 1865, a resident of Natchitoches wrote a poem, entitled "Unmarked Graves," dedicating the verses to the women of the South. From this poem the second verse is given thus:

Let Beauty's soft tears, like the dews of the night,
Or the diamond's bright rays, reflecting the light,
Fall on these lonely graves, love's token so pure,
Which memory keeps green, while time shall endure.
While Fame shall proclaim, with his deep, brazen voice,
Names of heroes who, in the land of their choice,
Fell in the strife, on the field of their glory—
Their lives an offering to song and to story.

Company A, Special Militia Force, Fifth Military District, was organized in April, 1890, and mustered in May 7, with C. E. Greneaux, captain; C. Pierson and R. L. Caspari, lieutenants; C. Chaplin, Jr., and E. L. Hyams, sergeants; Aaron Morris, B. F. Dranguet, J. Johnson and P. S. Walmsley, corporals. There were fifty-five private soldiers mustered in.

During the pioneer days of the parish readers were supplied by newspapers and periodicals, both French and Spanish. When the first paper was printed in the English language here can not be ascertained. In 1848, when Mr. Duplex settled here, the Chronicle was published by Thomas C. Hunt.

In 1860 the Natchitoches Union, printed in French and English, was issued by Ernest Le Gendre for the Union Publishing Company. On the editor's death in 1862 L. Duplex took charge as editor; but in 1864 the Federals issued it for one week, and removed two presses and the material. On Banks being driven away, Mr. Duplex refurnished the office and carried on L. 'Union until 1872, under the title Natchitoches Times, when the publication ceased. In 1876 the office was sold to J. H. Cosgrove. The press was sold in 1877 to the Winnsborough Sun.

On April 5, 1864, the Natchitoches Daily Union was issued from the Government printing office. Lieut. Thomas Hughes was editor and Sergt. H. R. Crenshaw & Co., publishers. A beautiful word painting of the happy condition of the people before the war was drawn, the leaders who led them into Rebellion denounced and a promise made that only one flag should wave in the North and South. Among the poems of the war period were the "Marseillaise du Sud," dedicated to the chasseurs a pied des Natchitoches, by E. L. Caporal; "Aux Volontaires," was written in May, 1861, by Malle; "The Soldier's Dirge" in 1864, and "Farewell to the Lafourche Guards" in 1861. During or after the visit of Ex-President Davis, "The Saddest Run of the Storm," was written by Mary E. Bryan for the Spectator.

Natchitoches Spectator was issued December 5, 1867, by J. M. Scanland. On September 22, 1868, Mr. Scanland issued his valedictory and Mr. Cromie purchased the office and filled all contracts from the Red River News—Republican, 1874.

The Red River News was established by James Cromie in 1868. L. H. Burdick became owner in 1870 and continued publication until June, 1874.

The Record was issued here later, and in 1875 D. W. Hubley published the Republican.

The Peoples' Vindicator was issued June 17, 1874, by J. H. Cosgrove, as a Democratic journal, this was the first Democratic paper since the Times suspended. In 1881 the office was sold to to Phanor Breazeale and publication suspended.*

The Daily Vindicator was published in 1876 by J. H. Cosgrove; but owing to the heavy expense of associated press dispatches, this great enterprise was surrendered after six weeks.

The Natchitoches Register was issued in June, 1880, by John E. Hewitt.

The Democratic Review was established May

*On March 29, 1884, the office of the Vindicator was sold to C.V. Porter.

13, 1883, by C. V. Porter. In 1887 Thomas J. Flanner was editor and in May, 1888, J. H. Cosgrove became proprietor. In 1883 the "Race Problem" was written by Mr. Cosgrove and subsequently he contributed to the press of this State many of the ablest, matter-of-fact papers on political and social affairs. He brought the Review into the front rank of Louisiana journals.

The Enterprise was issued here in 1888 by H. P. Breazeale.

The Robeline Reporter was established in February, 1883, by S. M. Potts & Son, who published it until 1884, when J. M. Porter and W. A. Laurent became owners. Later that year the latter sold to W. A. Carter, who a short time after purchased Porter's interest. In 1886 the Reporter became the property of the Robeline Publishing Company, W. A. Ponder, superintendent, and A.V. Carter, editor. After a few months Dr. J. H. Cunningham became editor, and during his illness Mrs. M. E. Cunningham became editress. On the latter's death in 1886, C. R. Lee controlled the office, but publication ceased for a short time, when I. F. Carter revived it. In 1887 Hickson Capers purchased the office, and in February, 1889, when the Publishing Company resumed ownership, another suspension followed until R. M. McIntosh purchased the office, but in 1889 A. V. Carter became owner and changed the name to the News. In January, 1888, R. W. Ferguson was editor and D. W. Hubley, publisher. The valedictory of A.V. Carter as editor, of the Robeline News and of Carter & Son as proprietors, appeared May 30, 1890, and in the same issue, a stirring salutatory was issued by S. C. Presley. J. E. Howe, now connected with the News, entered the office in February, 1883. Martha's Bulletin was issued at Marthaville in 1888, with W. A. Gilbreath publisher. On September 12, 1890, the name was changed to the People's Republic, and Lee & Gilbreath were editors. The size of the paper was doubled at this time.

The enrollment of white pupils in the schools of Natchitoches from 1877 to 1886, inclusive, is as follows: 655, 954, 771, 371, 546, 1,371, 1,422, 1,123, 4,108 and 915. The number of colored pupils enrolled for the years 1878 to 1886 inclusive, is shown as follows: 438, 601, 422, 381, 455, 1,404, 614, 2,613 and 662. In 1888 there were 5,172 children reported attending school and in 1889, 4,738. This parish is one of the most liberal patrons of education in the State. In early years private schools of a first-class character were carried on here, and in 1884 the State recognized the claims of this parish to the normal school. [*Vide* history of town.] Peter Duke was superintendent of free school in 1849; J. H. Stephens in 1850, and later H. P. Breazeale.

In January, 1838, Dr. D. M. Heard presented his diploma as physician of 1831, I. W. Butler his of 1832, Philip Breda his of 1836, and John F. Williams his of 1838. Dr. Normand, of Cloutierville, and other old physicians did not register. Under the law of 1882 the following named registered their diplomas: Penn Crain, Josephus F. Griffin, Charles Hamlin, Joseph S. Stephens, Jules V. Janin, John W. Thomas, Sherman B. Crocheron, Zachary T. Gallion, Joseph A. Leveque, James A. Root, William B. Powell, James E. Thomas, Alexander P. Breda, James Duerson, John A. Lovett, Joseph S. Stephens, Jr., Theophile Goudaux, James N. Lee, John D. Addison, Christopher C. Nash and Samuel H. Scruggs. The old physicians who registered were Lamarque A. Lambert, Andre V. Couty, Thomas B. Sellers, Daniel L. Gillen, Elias I. Persigner, Albert E. Cassady, William W. Pitts, Randolph H. Anderson, Eli Hongo and John F. Carroll.

The town of Natchitoches in latitude 31° 44' and longitude 14° west is the oldest permanent settlement in Louisiana, and with the exception of the ancient Spanish town of Adayes, the oldest without qualification. It is thought by many that Natchitoches is the oldest town in the United States, but this is not the case. St. Augustine, Fla., was founded by the Spaniards in 1565; Port Royal, N. S., by the French, 1605; Jamestown, Va., by the London Company, 1607; Quebec, by the French, 1608; New York, by the Dutch, 1614; Plymouth, Mass., by the Puritans, 1620, and Baltimore by the Irish, 1632. Other settlements followed

along the North Atlantic coast, and not until late in the seventeenth century was there an actual settlement made in Louisiana, and that was at Adayes, near Natchitoches, a quiet little Indian village in 1694, when the Islanders arrived from the Canaries. After the death of De Soto, Muscaso ascended Red River, but beyond noticing the Indian occupants of the valley, he left no other record. In 1694 a few members of the colony of Islanders, with a few Spaniards and Mexicans came hither. In 1714 St. Denys located a few French Canadian families on the island of Natchitoches, and in January, 1717, M. De la Motte took possession of the place. In 1717, when De la Harpe returned to the post he found Commandant Blondel in charge and was so well pleased with the condition of affairs, that he wrote to Father Marsello, then superior of the Texan Missions, assuring him that his people could find all kinds of European goods at Natchitoches. Darby, in his history (published in 1817), speaks of Natchitoches in latitude 30° 40' on the right bank of Red River. In March, 1823, a fire originating in the old church destroyed sixty-five of the old buildings. Coulon de Villier and Roujot were commandants prior to 1774. Vaugine and other officers, referred to in the general history of the parish were here, but the kindest and ablest of the French or Spanish officials was St. Denys, whose name will be forever identified with the settlement and progress of this portion of Louisiana, for to him is due the crushing defeat of the bloodthirsty Natchez at this post in 1731.

In previous pages many direct references are made to the early land owners around the post, and even lot buyers in the town are named. Incidents in its progress from 1731 to the fire of 1823 are unobtainable, save in a legendary or uncertain form, but the ecclesiastical history is not wanting for in no place can be found a more perfect record than in the archives of the old parish house of the present Cathedral. From the settlement of 1714 to 1724 the mission was attended from Adayes by Rev. Anthony Margil or missionary priests.

The first baptism recorded is that of Francois Gaspar Barbier, September 3, 1724, by the Capuchin friar, Francois Balliss. Brothers Luis de Quintanillo and Maximin were here in 1729; Rev. Campe, a capuchin, in 1730, and in 1734 Father Pierre Vitry, a Jesuit, took charge of the parish. Revs. Jean Francois, Marmoulet, Archange, Barnabie, Ragobert, Eustache, Amé, Valentin, Anassthase, Varnird and Iufant, all capuchins, administered the sacrament of baptism prior to 1765. Father Stanislaus came in 1765, and was succeeded in 1775 by Father Luis de Quintanillo and he, in 1783, by Rev. Francois de Caldar. Father Dalvaux came in 1786 and, with Revs. De Veles and Pavie, administered the old parish until the close of 1796, when Father A. D. Sedella came, but Father Pavie was rector in fact up to August, 1807, when Rev. L. Bubst was appointed. Rev. J. Huerta was here in 1810, and J. M. Sora in 1811, as assistant priests—all capuchins. In April, 1813, Rev. J. Francisco Magnes was appointed and remained until August, 1822, when the church was without a pastor (the buildings were burned March 29, 1823).

On October 8, 1814, the claim of St. Francis Church was presented to the commission. Louis Buard established the fact that for eighty years the priests, wardens and singers of St. Francis held those lands, and that no other ones ever made establishment thereon, as church lands were held sacred. The claim for four and four-tenths arpents of land on the right bank of a small bayou near the village was reported favorably. Prior to this, on December 13, 1811, Rev. Father Dagobert deeded to the police jury of Natchitoches, 118.18 acres without consideration.

In 1778 Andre Rambin purchased a lot in the town from Poiret, also Charles Paire, Nicholas Lauve, and others named in the general history.

Capt. Isaac Wright who, in 1824, commenced steamboating between Natchez and Natchitoches, states that there was a large Mexican trade carried on there. The Mexicans would come in with hundreds of pack mules, loaded with specie, buffalo robes, tongues and peltries and return with dry goods and notions. In 1826 he and Capt. Gurney came down the Rigolet du Bon Dieu in a skiff. It was then a small bayou about thirty feet wide

and continued so until 1832, when the waters cut a wide channel. Up to that time Cane and Little Rivers were the navigable streams, forming this part of Red River. Loggy Bayou was at the foot of the great raft and there, in 1832, 500 or 600 Norwegians, in charge of Dr. Baum, were landed.

Postlewait's Salt Works, at the Saline, were established in 1805 and a large salt trade was carried on between this and Mississippi points, but years before this the Indians from the Mississippi came hither at stated times to procure salt.

In 1836 a merry company passed through Natchitoches: David Crockett, John Featherston, "Happy" Johnson, Ephriam Tully and Matthew Despallie. In describing the last named, the gambler, Greene, says: * * * "He was a villainous bully. He drew on me at Alexandria, in 1833, but I was expecting it, and shot him with a derringer. I hurried away, supposing he was killed, and was assisted in my escape by J. Madison Wells' father, who kept me at his plantation for several days. I am not sure whether it was Matt, or his equally bad brother, who was killed by ex-governor Wells." Rezin P. and James Bowie were residents of Opelousas Parish. Nassau, or Little Nas, a native of Natchitoches, who slept outside the Alamo during the battle of March 6, 1836, was the only male who escaped the fate of the besieged. Mary Britton and her infant were spared by the Mexicans.

The United States Land Office at Natchitoches was established July 7, and opened October 12, 1838, by Receiver Benoit Laurents and Register Patrick O. Lee. William Parmer made the first entry—the southwest quarter of Section 13, Township 7, Range 11, Natchitoches. W. T. Walmsley was register in 1843. In November, 1842, John Tucker signs the receiver's books, followed in July, 1847, by J. M. B. Tucker. John F. Payne was register in 1847. In June, 1849, Hugh Y. Waddell was commissioned register. John La Place was receiver in September, 1849, followed in September, 1853, by J. B. O. Buard; J. B. Cloutier, register. Thomas C. Hunt was in office, as receiver, in the fall of 1855, and in July, 1860, John La Place was reappointed receiver and S. M. Hyams register, succeeding W. W. Lester, special agent. In 1862 Mr. La Place surrendered the office to Felix Metoyer, appointee of the Confederate land commissioner. In July, 1867, Col. D. Seigler, register of the Natchitoches Land Office, returned, and later the old archives were brought hither. Receiver Lancaster also arrived during this month.

In June, 1871, J. Jules Bossier was appointed receiver and H. C. Myers register, and in June, 1874, A. E. Lemee was commissioned. John La Place, who served in the office during his father's administration, re-entered the office in 1882, and is the present deputy. L. H. Burdick succeeded Myers in July, 1872, and served until August, 1875, when L. Duplex took charge. In May, 1885, W. E. Russell was commissioned register, and in February, 1888, Willis Holmes succeeded him. On August 25, 1890, L. Duplex was reappointed register.

On March 5, 1839, B. St. Amans, S. M. Hyams, G. W. Russ, H. A. Ely and A. C. Surlls qualified as trustees of the town; M. R. Anail, clerk; W. L. Tuomey, attorney; Henry White and C. F. Rains, constables and collectors, and S. M. Hyams, surveyor. (No records 1840 to 1868.) In 1861 Felix Mettoyer was mayor. The council elected in April, 1868, comprised Theodore Schuman, mayor; Joe Ezernack, Jacob Israel, Henry Burns (colored), W. Brady (colored), John Genoe and Hugh McKenna, councilmen. Burns and Brady resigned rather than take the oath of office. Later that year A. E. Lemee, secretary and treasurer; and W. H. Carver, Jacob Israel, Joseph Ezernack and J. M. B. Tucker were trustees. The brick culvert and dirt bridge on Second street, over Bayou Amulet were constructed this year by Keyser & McKenna at a cost of $990, while in 1869 other structures were authorized. Philip Myers was mayor in 1870, and J. W. Little, constable, vice L. Hanson, resigned. The sum of $100 was appropriated to establish a telegraph line between this town and Alexandria. J. Ezernack, J. R. Williams, W. D. Harkins and A. Perini were councilmen, while in 1871, Tilman Watkins, E. Phillips, John Genoe and Samuel Parsons were trustees. Col. William M. Levy was appointed

agent of the town to negotiate with the New Orleans & Pacific Railroad Company for building the road via Natchitoches. The law suit growing out of the election of mayor this year entailed a small expenditure. Edward L. Pierson was declared mayor by the district judge, and in September the following named citizens were appointed delegates to the Shreveport Railroad Convention: W. M. Levy, W. H. Jack, Col. R. E. Burke, E. L. Pierson, A. E. Lemee, C. Chaplin, Jr., and C. F. Dranguet. In March, 1872, a night police force was established, and the question of raising $1,000 by special tax to purchase hose for the fire-engine was ordered to be submitted to the people.

Natchitoches was incorporated as a city by the Legislature July 5, 1872. The first meeting of the new council was held July 22, E. L. Pierson, mayor; J. A. Ducournau, M. H. Carver, Emile Rivers, Edmond Atkinson, John Genoe and J. C. Trichel, councilmen; A. E. Lemee, secretary and treasurer; C. Chaplin, Jr., attorney; J. H. Cosgrove, assessor, collector and chief of police, and Charles Hamlin, physician. John B. Levy was mayor in 1873; F. McDaniel, chief of police and J. H. Cosgrove, collector. Later, W. H. Redmond was appointed to this office; J. F. De Vargas, secretary and treasurer; C. J. Smith, chief of police; L. H. Burdick, of The Red River News, printer, and A. E. Lemee, mayor. J. F. De Vargas was mayor in 1874; C. F. Dranguet, 1877; Willis Holmes, 1879; Dr. R. S. Calves, 1884-90.

John La Place was elected clerk in 1874; W. H. Barbes, 1878; C. V. Porter, 1881; C. E. Greneaux, 1880. In August, 1881, J. H. Cosgrove was appointed chief of the fire department, and Willis Holmes, assistant chief; W. P. Morrow was chosen assessor in 1874; Lem. Greneaux, 1877; W. E. Russell, 1879; J. W. Little was marshal in 1877; F. P. Raggio, 1879, and W. S. Greneaux is the present marshal.

E. F. Fitzgerald was appointed postmaster in September, 1862. In September, 1866, this office was reopened by the United States, with George Monroe, postmaster; Cloutierville, with Oliver Brosset; Campti, with Reiny Lambre. R. W.

Taliaferro was postmaster in 1867. In 1868 Rufus Tabor was incumbent, keeping the office in the old Walmsley building. J. F. de Vargas held the office in 1875. Charles Le Roy and W. D. Harkins held the office successively. The Widow R. E. Burke held the office for two terms prior to 1885, Mrs. Sudduth took possession in February, 1885, with J. E. Breda, deputy. He succeeded Mrs. Sudduth in July, 1890, and is the present incumbent.

The first fire was that of 1823, which destroyed the second church building and sixty-five houses. In 1838 the second fire swept away the third church building. A few small fires are recorded prior to 1864, when the town was saved from the fury of the Federal troops by Bishop Martin.

The fire of April 19, 1881, destroyed property valued at $148,385, of which $55,900 worth was insured. It originated in the old Fontenot Hotel, purchased a short time before by Frank McDaniel, who promptly insured it for $7,000. Two blocks were destroyed, the owners of property being C. Chaplin, H. Walmsley, H. Bath, A. Prudhomme, Nelken Lecompte, George Kile, Joseph Henry, —— Payne, —— Shaffrach, J. Johnson, J. Ducose, Bullard & Campbell, Hugh Walmsley, Levy & Phillips, H. Litchenstein, Ducournau & Breda. The office of the Vindicator, the property of J. H. Cosgrove, was destroyed, with valuable files, State and National reports, and library. McDaniel was charged with incendiarism, and lodged in jail. The Fontenot House was a tall three-story building, which was at one time the jail.

The Cathedral Church of St. Francis is one of the historic landmarks of the United States. It was old when the immortal Declaration of Independence founded a great nation, and still a few miles away was the older church of San Miguel. In a former page the history of this church down to 1823 is given. After the fire of that year the work of rebuilding was entered upon, and in 1726 a new house of worship was completed in rear of the parish cemetery. In 1825 Revs. Anduze and Martin came in 1826; Rev. L. Dussausoy and J. B. Blanc came in 1827. Rev. A. Mascaroni was here at this time. Rev. E. D. Haurd came in

1833, Father Franciar being also here, and the latter remained in 1839, when Father V. Yamey took charge of the parish. In 1840 Rev. T. Alabau, P. C. M., Rev. E. Giustiniani and Father Pascual were here. Rev. R. W. Stehle came in 1842; J. M. Maynard in 1844. Father Figari, a missionary, assisted Rev. Giustiniani in 1847, and with Rev. L. C. M. A. Verrina and R. Pascual were priests in 1848. In June, 1849, Rev. A. Andrieu became pastor. In August, 1850, Rev. Aug. Martin with Frederick Cuney, assistant priest, were here. The latter was succeeded by Father Gelot in 1851, and in 1852 P. F. Dicharry, V. G., came. (He remained until 1887.) Rev. Y. Yaneau, of Marksville, L. Gergaud, who died at Shreveport in 1873, and J. M. Beaubien performed baptismal ceremonies here in 1855. Fathers F. Levouzet and Ch. Lebour in 1856; Y. M. Le Connait, J. L. Galop, C. Sorrentini and J. Gentille were here before the war. Father F. Martin came in 1862, and with Father Levouzet were here up to 1873, when the latter died at Shreveport. Father Martin remained until 1878 with Father Dicharry, vicar-general. That year Rev. A. Andries took Father Martin's place, and in 1889 Rev. A. Piegay came as assistant priest. In 1887 Father Andries was appointed vicar-general and acting secretary of this extensive diocese. The churches of the diocese in the parishes treated in this volume are as follows: St. Francis Xaviers, Alexandria, Rev. L. Minard; Sacred Heart, Pineville, Rev. R. Dumas, rector; Bayou Moreauville, Rev. P. E. Simon, Big Bend; St. Joseph's, Marksville, Rev. A. Chorin; Bayou Bourbeaux, Bayou Cie, Bayou Dolle; Mansfield, Bayou Pierre and Kingston, attached to the Carmelite monastery; Bayou Pierre and Prairie River, attended from Cloutierville; Bellevue, St. Johns, of Big Island, attended from Pineville; Campti, Rev. E. Armaud (succeeding Father Poullain); Clear Lake; St. John the Baptist, at Cloutierville; Rev. J. M. Beaulieu, Cotes D'Afrique; Cottonport, Rev. J. Rechatin; St. Vincent's, Fairfield, Rev. Gloster, attendant from Fairfield; Keatchie, attended from Fairfield, N. J. Roulleaux; Fairmont, attended from Pineville; Homer and Minden, attended from

Shreveport; Ile Brevelle (colored) and Old River, Rev. F. Grosse; KeKouen, attended from Natchitoches; Lecompte, attached to Alexandria; Plancheville, Rev. L. Gallop; Shreveport, Rev. Joseph Gentille; Spanish Lake, attached to Many; Spanish Town, attached to Bayou Pierre; Spring Creek, to Alexandria; Tiger Island, Natchitoches. In the whole diocese are fifty-three churches and chapels, and a population of about 30,000 persons.

The division of New Orleans diocese was recommended in 1852. Shortly after this recommendation was carried out, and Rev. Augustus M. Martin elected first bishop of the new diocese of Natchitoches July 29, 1853. He found in all Northern Louisiana a Catholic population of about 25,000, seven churches, four priests and the educational house of the Sisters of the Sacred Heart. On his death, September 29, 1875, there were sixty churches, together with the educational and charitable institutions of the Daughters of the Cross, referred to in the history of Caddo, and the Sisters of Mercy. Rev. F. X. Leray, a historical character in the history of Mississippi, was elected bishop in 1877, and had for his diocese all of Louisiana north of latitude 31°. In 1879 he was appointed coadjutor of New Orleans, but controlled Natchitoches as administrator apostolic, and on the death of Archbishop Perchi in December, 1883, became administrator of the whole State. He was soon after elected archbishop of New Orleans, and on March 19, 1885, the present bishop, Rt. Rev. Anthony Durier, was consecrated at St. Louis Cathedral, New Orleans.

Trinity English Protestant Episcopal Church was established May 23, 1841, by Rev. John Burke. It appears that on March 27, 1839, Bishop Polk visited the town, and on the 30th held the first Protestant services here at the court-house. He revisited the town February 21, 1841, and appointed Mr. Burke to this mission in May following, Mrs. Walmsley suggesting such appointment. The officers appointed May 23, that year, were S. M. Tibbetts, S. W.; F. Williams, J. W., succeeded by E. O. Blanchard, William Hunter, Lewis G. De Russy, Joseph G. Campbell, Victor, Adolph and Ambrose Sompayrac, George W. Lewis, D. M. Heard, Alfred Bludworth, Daniel H. Vail, Martin Fearing and Thomas H. Airey, vestrymen; Thomas P. Jones, clerk, succeeded by E. Hollis. (In December, 1841, the Methodist preachers entered this field, holding services in the court-house). Mr. Burke attended the little societies at Greenwood, Shreveport, Alexandria, Donaldsonville, Fort Jesup, Baton Rouge and Franklin, up to 1844, when he resigned. In 1843 a church building was erected here through the efforts of the first pastor. In December, 1844, Rev. Elijah Guion came here, and remained until June, 1848. For five years the pulpit was filled by visiting preachers, or by the rector of Alexandria. In July, 1853, Rev. Thomas S. Bacon arrived; the corner-stone of the present brick church was placed April 28, 1857, and the house was completed in 1858. Prior to this a silver eucharistic service was presented by Gen. De Peyster, of New York, and a tablet to the memory of his daughter was placed in the sanctuary, on the left of the altar. Mr. Bacon served the churches of this mission until April 12, 1861, when he resigned, leaving a Mr. Binet to take charge. In April, 1865, a Confederate chaplain, Rev. David Keer, succeeded Mr. Binet, but in March, 1867, the pulpit was found vacant, and the bishop appointed a lay reader. In March, 1870, the pastor of the Shreveport Church came here by appointment, but in December, 1870, Rev. Charles Ritter was appointed rector, and served until April, 1871. Rev. John Sandels came in April, 1872, and remained until his death, in October, 1874. From 1878 to 1883 Rev. Charles A. Cameron was pastor; then the pulpit was vacant for about two years, when Rev. M. T. Turner began his periodical missionary visits. In May, 1886, Rev. R. H. Prosser began his monthly visits, and in May, 1887, Rev. W. T. Douglass succeeded him. The church is now without a pastor, but the registers or records are safe in the possession of Mrs. Sullivan, one of the oldest members. The seats or pews were sent hither from Illinois, years ago, while the organ, built in Baltimore, was placed here in 1871. The bell was presented by Gen. De Peyster. The congregation is made up of thirty families.

Union Lodge No. 21, A. F. & A. M., was

chartered in 1818, and continued in existence until 1828. Phoenix Lodge No. 38, A. F. & A. M., was chartered October 6, 1836, with Samuel P. Russell, master; William Long, S. W.; William P. Jones, J. W.; W. F. Tabor, secretary; S. B. True, treasurer; J. M. Coons, S. D.; B. F. Chapman, J. D., and J. Holmes, tyler. Meetings were then held in Mason's Hall. The masters of this lodge since that time are named as follows: S. P. Russell, 1838; W. P. Jones, 1840 (presided as temporary master in 1839). There is no record of meetings in 1841–43; B. V. St. Amans, 1844; P. A. Morse, 1845; A. Seegar, 1846; Frederick Williams, 1847; J. B. Smith, 1848; S. M. Hyams, 1851; J. B. Smith, 1853; J. H. Stephens, 1854; J. B. Smith, 1855; John R. Williams, 1856; T. Hunter, 1857; J. B. Smith, 1858; John S. Levy, 1862; William Payne, 1863; F. Metoyer, 1864; C. Chaplin, Jr., 1867; J. E. Breda, 1868; S. M. Hyams, 1869, but Philip Myers presided generally; C. Chaplin, Sr., 1870; S. W. Kile, 1871; C. Chaplin, 1873; Thomas P. Chaplin, 1875; C. Chaplin, 1876; J. R. Williams, 1880; M. H. Wilkinson, 1882; Thomas P. Chaplin, 1886; C. Chaplin,. 1887; Adolph Kaffie, 1888; J. H. Cosgrove, 1889, and Dr. Z. T. Gallion, 1890. The secretaries of the lodge are named in the following list: James L. Gillispie, 1838; W. R. Speight, 1839; D. H. Boult, 1840; J. B. Smith, 1846; John F. Payne, 1847; D. H. Boult, 1849; Horatio Sibley, 1850; William Payne, 1851; D. F. Tabor, 1852; William Payne, 1853; T. Hunter, 1856; William Payne, 1857; W. P. Morrow, 1861; C. Chaplin, Jr., 1862; J. W. Norris, 1863; L. Caspari, 1864; C. L. Walmsley, 1865; William Payne, 1866; Ed Phillips, 1870; T. P. Chaplin, 1876; Dr. R. S. Calves, 1880; Phanor Breazeale, 1889, and Crokette K. Jones, 1890. The lodge numbers at present forty members with property valued at $8,000.

Cloutierville No. 110 was organized at the mouth of Cane River in 1852; Kissatchie Union No. 195, at Kile's Mills, in 1868, surrendered charter in 1880; Lake Village No. 205 dates back to 1869. It is now known as No. 86 with headquarters at Saline since 1874.

Natchitoches Lodge No. 89, K. of P., was instituted June 7, 1889. The officers installed in July, 1890, were: H. M. Hyams, C.; C. H. Levy, V. C.; J. E. Breda, P.; R. S. Calves, K. of R. and S.; H. M. Levy, M. of E., and N. Smith, M. of A.

The Thirteen Club elected the following named officers in June, 1890: J. S. Stephens, Jr., president; J. C. Trichel, Jr., V. P.; Clarence Pierson, secretary, and Simeon Simon, treasurer. This club has elegant quarters in the Review Building.

The Free Sons of Israel of Natchitoches were incorporated under the act of March 30, 1871. The object of this association was to subscribe funds to be employed in the erection of a synagogue and keep the burial ground in good order.

In 1879 the Methodist Episcopal Church building was erected, Rev. T. J. Hough being then preacher. The Baptists began their building that year during the pastorate of Rev. V. G. Cunningham, but pending its completion held services in the Fireman's Hall. The Baptist, Methodist and South African colored churches were in existence.

The Lutheran Benevolent Society was chartered December 7, 1882, with King Mickelbury male director; Mary Badgers, female director; Ad. Witherspoon, Hubbard Sharp, John Goings, Andrew Murdock, William Yarbrough, G. W. Duncan and Joseph Bennett, trustees. The officers included 12 male, and 12 female stewards and preachers; 3 marshals, 12 pilgrims and 12 mourning women.

In June, 1879, Rev. Walters, of the African Baptist Church, attempted to erect a church in the center of Buard Street, although the street had been open for thirty-five years.

Rev. Darius Logan, presiding elder of the African Methodist Church for the district from Natchitoches to Washington, was stationed at Colfax in 1883.

St. Joseph College was established in 1856 by Bishop Martin, at Natchitoches, in the buildings formerly built and occupied by the Sisters of the Sacred Heart, in 1846. Miss Tauzin (living), Josephine Geanty (deceased), Augustinia Deslouschs (living), and Aurelia Anty, now Mrs. Jules Normand were the first pupils in 1846–47. In September, 1888, five sisters from the Convent of

Divine Providence, San Antonio, Tex., arrived at Natchitoches for the purpose of establishing a day-school. The old convent buildings were restored. The State Normal School was established by the legislative act of 1884, which provided for an annual grant of $6,000. The buildings were erected by the Sisters of the Sacred Heart for educational purposes; but were purchased by the people for the purposes of this State school. The grounds embrace 105 acres. Dr. Edward Sheib was president of the normal school faculty. The school opened November 1, 1885, with thirty-six students, among whom were Della Ezernach, Edgar Tharp, Albert Dietrich, Elisha Breazeale, Millie Hughes, Maude Breazeale, Bertha Bahn, Pauline Haller, Bertha, Annie and Samuel Levy, Mary C. Sullivan, Cecile Deblieux, Nena Kearney, Emma Tessier, Hannah Aaron, Kate L. Trichel, Sam D. Kearney, Richard Percy, G. W. Barnes, Robbie Barnes and Madison R. Lay, all of Natchitoches Parish; Benny Rosenthal, of Alexandria; W. L. Ford, of Winn; Florence and Fannie Coffee, of De Soto; Lizzie Fortson, of Caddo; Lelia Hightower, of Homer, and Ida Corbett, of Spanish Lake, were also on the list of first pupils. About this time a presentation of 2,000 books was made to this school by John Morris, of New Orleans. The faculty in 1889 comprised Thomas D. Boyd, A. M., president, professor of psychology; A. L. Smith, methods and general pedagogue; Charles H. White, natural sciences; Miss Mary E. Washington, geography and calisthenics; Miss Mary Odalie Ezernack, physiology and hygiene; Miss Lizzie Carter, language; Miss Nellie Hughes, history; Miss Emma Oswalt, arithmetic; Miss Annie Burris, music, and Misses Emma Oswalt and Bessie Russell, principals of the practice school. C. H. Ling, of Cornell University, and R. L. Himes, of the Pennsylvania Normal, were added to the faculty in September, 1890.

The Bank of Natchitoches was incorporated in July, 1890, with the following named stockholders: H. M. Hyams, 1 share, $100; H. Safford, 1 share, $100; J. H. Cosgrove, 5 shares, $500; L. Levy, 1 share, $100; P. F. L'herisson, 1 share, $100; J. C. Trichel, 1 share, $100; Hill & Jones, 1 share, $100; J. A. Ducournau & Son, 1 share, $100; H. Kaffie & Bro., 5 shares, $500; Henry M. Levy, 1 share, $100; S. Nelkin, 2 shares, $200; M. L. Dismukes, 1 share, $100; D. C. Scarborough, 2 shares, $200; M. H. Carver, 1 share, $100; L. Caspari, 1 share, $100; D. P. Doak, 250 shares, $25,000; Thomas Doak, per D. P. Doak, 50 shares, $5,000; W. C. Doak, 50 shares, $5,000; Joseph Henry, 5 shares, $500; J. W. Cockerham, 1 share, $100; J. S. Stephens, 3 shares, $300; Phanor Breazeale, 1 share, $100; H. P. Breazeale, 1 share, $100; P. S. Prudhomme, 1 share, $100; Z. T. Gallion, 1 share, $100; Mat. Hertzog, per A. E. Lemee, 3 shares, $300; J. Alphonse Prudhomme, per A. E. Lemee, 3 shares, $300; A. E. Lemee, 105 shares, 10,500; C. E. Greneaux, 1 share, $100.

The Building & Loan Association was organized in March, 1890, with W. H. Jack, president; David Pierson, vice-president; D. C. Scarborough, attorney; C. K. Jones, secretary and treasurer, and Messrs. Stephens, Lemee, Hyams, Asher and Porter, directors.

The Louisiana society of Sons of the Revolution was organized May 16, 1890, with William H. Jack, president; T. J. Cross, secretary; W. H. Pipes, treasurer, and Jacob McWilliams, registrar. There are thousands of descendants of the men who fought with Rochambeau and Lafayette in the State, whose names should be enrolled on the records of this association.

The Southern H. & B. Association was organized in March, 1890, with J. C. Trichel, senior president; H. Simon, vice-president; G. L. Trichel, secretary and treasurer; Chaplin, Breazeale & Chaplin, attorneys. and C. S. Searing, local agent.

The Home Co-operative Cotton Seed Oil Company was incorporated February 14, 1890, the articles of association being signed by D. Pierson, J. S. Stephens, C. Chaplin, Charles H. Levy, D. C. Scarborough, J. C. Keyser, P. F. L'herisson, J. C. Trichel, A. E. Lemee per J. C. Trichel, M. L. Dismukes, N. T. Smith, S. Nelkin, R. L. Caspari, C. V. Porter, G. L. Trichel, D. A. Blacksher, Clarence Pierson and E. E. Buckner.

The Union Brick Manufacturing Company was

organized April 3, 1890, through the efforts of J. H. Cosgrove and C. K. Jones. The work of construction was begun in the summer, and in September the brick yards were completed and the first brick burned.

The Natchitoches Ice Company was organized October 15, 1890, with A. E. Lemee, president; A. Kaffie, secretary and treasurer, and the following board of directors: A. E. Lemee, Adolphe Kaffie, P. F. L'herisson, H. Simon and J. A. Ducournau, Jr. The company is organized with a capital stock of $10,000, 100 shares at $100 each, and has for its object the manufacture of ice, cold storage and bottling business.

The Red River Hedge Company (limited) was successfully organized in Natchitoches on September 3, 1890, by Col. George Moorman. The following are the officers and directors of the institution: Col. A. E. Lemee, president; Capt. A. E. Sompayrac, vice-president; J. A. Prudhomme, second vice-president; J. T. Trichel, treasurer; H. M. Hyams, secretary; J. H. Hill, general manager; D. C. Scarborough, attorney for the company. Among the directors are M. J. Cunningham, J. C. Trichel, Hon. L. Caspari, Gen. J. H. Cosgrove, J. T. Wallace, J. E. Deloche, Capt. C. E. Greneaux, E. J. Gamble, A. R. Cockfield, S. Nelson and others.

The opera house was opened October 2, 1887, Charles Gayarre lecturing on Mirabeau and the French Revolution.

The Natchitoches Opera House Company was organized in April, 1890, with D. C. Scarborough, president; J. C. Trichel, Sr., vice-president; P. L. Asher, secretary, and J. S. Stephens, Jr., treasurer; H. M. Levy, C. V. Porter and Dr. Z. T. Gallion, directors.

The hotels are the Normand, the Prothro, Mrs. Garza's and the new Adams House. The present Normand House was erected by Edouard Cloutier in 1858, at a cost of $22,000. During the war he sold this property to H. Schuman for Confederate money. The Ambroise Lecompte residence, now occupied by the United States offices' bank, and the Adams Hotel, is one of the oldest, as it is the largest, of the old residences of the city. The residence of Richard Hertzog is another of the large residences of olden times. There are two other large brick residences, one now owned by Matthew Hertzog and the other by Joseph Henry, which came down from early days.

The Natchitoches Land & Railway Company was incorporated November 23, 1885, with L. Caspari, W. H. Jack, D. W. Kile, A. E. Lemee, David Pierson, D. C. Scarborough, J. A. Ducourneau, Jr., and H. B. Walmsley, corporators and members of the first board of directors.

In June, 1887, the ordinance providing that a 5-mill tax be levied for ten years as a grant to the Natchitoches Railroad Company was adopted, and in August of that year work on the Tap Railroad was begun. In September W. E. Westerfield was superintendent of construction, Engineer Varnum was in charge, Parker was contractor, and Burns, engineer. In December the first excursion train passed over the road. In October, 1889, the following named directors of this railroad company were elected: L. Caspari, Joseph Henry, A. E. Lemee, W. J. Behan, W. B. Ringrose and H. H. Baker.

In 1883 "The Rogers," Capt. Grant, and "The Lilia," Capt. Teal, were engaged in the Cane River trade between its mouth and Natchitoches. In 1884 Capt. Teal's new boat was launched at the mouth of Cane River and named "The John Teal." "The Ranger," Capt. Wood engaged in this trade in 1885, and in April, 1886, the "Marco," Capt. H. McKnight, ran up the river.

The Merchants & Planters Protective Union was organized August 5, 1880, with L. Caspari, president; H. A. Walmsley, V. P.; A. Ducournau, secretary, and Jules Ducasse, treasurer. S. W. Kile, J. A. Prudhomme, J. J. McCook, S. Nelkin, J. H. Stephens, J. D. Stelle (Sabine) and M. H. Levy, directors.

Prudhomme is located on Old River, where the Natchitoches Railroad connects with the Texas & Pacific Railroad. It is in the midst of a wonderfully productive country, convenient to the parish seat. The chances for an important railroad town in the future are fair for the bed of the ancient Lake Ocassee.

Robeline, named after one of the early settlers, is a modern railroad town. As related in the history of this parish and Sabine, settlements were made close by as early as 1694–1711. Joseph Clark, an hospital steward at Fort Jesup, resigned and selected lands northeast and southwest of the present Robeline depot on which to build a log house. He settled at Fort Jesup about 1823, and married a woman at that post. James H. Gallion bought land southwest of the railroad except thirty acres above the present depot, which was entered by Judge Chaplin in 1881 or 1882. The Chaplin family may be said to originate at Fort Jesup, and when Mrs. Clarke died, Judge Chaplin became heir to the property. Clark's log house tavern stood where A. Dover resides, and J. H. Gallion's log dwelling where W. M. Cook's dwelling is, and his log store-house where L. Daniel's store is located. James E. Keegan settled three miles west in 1858, W. A. Ponder five miles west in 1853, and J. H. Cox close by, preceded them. Rauscheck, a Russian, who was discharged at Fort Jesup, located three miles southwest, and Philip Wagley resided on the site of the city, near Lake Clark. Stokers and other pioneer families of Sabine located along the old Mexian trail, but comparatively little progress was made until the railroad was built. In 1881 the New Orleans & Pacific Railroad survey was made and the road built. May 1, that year, Robeline was surveyed for C. Chaplin, and additions made by N. Stamper, but not until September were town lots staked. James E. Keegan moved his large home from the plantation into the new town; K. B. Wilson opened a saloon opposite James McCook's store of later days; N. A. Stamper's store-room was built in August, 1881; Hughes & Carter's grocery was opened soon after, and they were followed by Hopkins & Barber, and John Decker. C. J. Smith opened the second saloon; William Edwards the first livery; M. Brown the third hotel, and Mrs. Howe the fourth; James McCook's dry goods store was established later, and Walter D. Hopkins opened the railroad office; but in December, 1881, he vacated the office, leaving $1,500 to be accounted for. The year 1882 brought several new traders hither. The Gays

opened a general store, A. E. Cassady a drug store, Nash & Sons, L. Daniel and the Lees general stores, and B. D. Loper a saloon. In 1883 general stores were opened by G. J. Cook & Co., M. C. Fisher, W. W. Page and Mrs. E. C. Lovett, a livery stable by T. E. Dodd and a grocery by Martin Brown. The older traders made many improvements. Hill & Caldwell's cotton market store, John Blake's large store, Cox & Thomas' and the Lindsey store were all brought into existence. In 1884 Stamper's steam mill and gin was constructed, and Hogue entered the firm of Gay Brothers. During this year the business center began to change from the Boulevard to Texas Street. In 1883 the academy was erected and school opened in March, by R. W. Freeman, but prior to this one F. Truly taught school in the new town. The old public school building erected in 1888 is now used for the purposes of public and private academy. It is proposed to erect a new house on a lot offered by F. C. Blacksher. In September, 1890, J. E. Keegan, M. F. Buvens and F. C. Gay were appointed a committee to secure teachers, and F. C. Blacksher, L. B. Gay and W. W. Page to secure pupils for the new school; W. C. Cox presided, with J. E. Buvens secretary. The officers of the board are J. B. McCook, president; M. F. Buvens, secretary, and W. W. Page, treasurer. September 1, Prof. J. Fuller Hailey was engaged to teach.

The register of the Methodist Church at Robeline dates back to June 14, 1883, when Rev. Ben. Jenkins, Jr., the Freemans, Mrs. L. Collier and Mrs. M. F. Burdick signed the record book. R. A. Davis, Mrs. S. L. Carter, the Caldwells and Mrs. Presnell signed later that year. Mr. Upton succeeded H. Capers, and Rev. A. D. McVoy, Jr., succeeded Rev. R. S. Isbell as pastor. The present number of members is sixty-five. The church building was erected during Mr. Isbell's administration. The Colored Methodist Church was established in 1884 by Rev. H. Wallace.

The Baptist Church dates back to 1884, when the house of worship at Spanish Lake was moved to Robeline. Rev. W. M. Reese was the first pastor.

In 1888 a lot on which to erect a Catholic

Church building was purchased. Moneys were subscribed for this purpose, and in the fall of 1890 definite steps were taken to erect a house of worship. Since the beginning of Robeline, services have been held here once every month by Father Aubree, of Many.

The first meeting of the council of Robeline was held March 14, 1883, under charter of February 1, 1883. J. E. Keegan was then mayor with C. R. Lee, L. B. Gay, J. M. Moorman, J. V. Nash and L. Daniel, councilmen. In 1884 N. A. Stamper was mayor with J. B. Clifton, L. H. Burdick, M. C. Fisher, W. W. Page and B. D. Slay, councilmen. They were followed by L. Daniel, mayor; J. E. Keegan, J. B. Clifton, W. C. Cox, J. H. Caldwell and G. J. Cook, in 1886 and 1887; L. Daniel, in 1888; W. C. Cox, in 1889, and J. E. Keegan, in 1890. L. Daniel was first clerk, succeeded by J. B. Clifton, G. J. Cook and E. M. Lindsey, who has served from 1886 to the present time. In 1886 M. H. Carver, W. A. Ponder, M. Brown, H. Manhein and E. M. Lindsey were councilmen; I. H. King replaced Carver in 1887; W. M. Prothro, J. E. Keegan, R. W. Freeman, M. F. Buvens and E. M. Lindsey were councilmen in 1888. In 1889 G. L. Jackson took King's place, while in January, 1890, W. W. Page, F. C. Blacksher and J. F. Carter with M. F. Buvens and E. M. Lindsey form the council. The latter is also secretary and treasurer. The town is without debt and claims a little money in the treasury. The State census places the population at 415.

The first postmaster at Robeline was N. A. Stamper, in August, 1881. The office was then named Leolia after his daughter. On October 6, 1882, when J. M. H. McCook took possession of the office, it was known as Robeline.

The officers of the W. C. T. U. in August, 1888, were Mrs. James H. Hill, Mrs. W. C. Cox, Mrs. R. W. Freeman, Mrs. R. S. Isbell, Mrs. John Dunkleman and Mrs. J. H. Caldwell, in the order of Union rank. Little or nothing was accomplished by this society, but in 1890 a reorganization was effected with Mrs. R. W. Freeman, president; Mrs. Belle Carter, secretary, and Mrs. John Dunkleman, treasurer.

Cloutierville was founded in 1822 by Alex. C. Cloutier, with the object of making it the seat of justice for the new parish, which he petitioned to have established. The prospects were fair enough to warrant the erection of a large house for parish purposes, and also a large church building for Catholic worship, at that time the only worship known in Louisiana. [Vide general history.]

Marthaville is credited with only 290 people, but since the school attendance numbers 135 this must be far short of the actual population. It is probably 350 to 400. There is a large saw-mill and planing-mill here, which ship 2,000,000 feet of lumber per year, the trade principally being in Texas. They have a capacity of 25,000 feet per day, and are always running. The timber is at the door, and there is enough to run the mill for years. The school is the official pride of the town, though as a business point it is a very promising one. The town was first settled by the Rains family in 1851 and in 1852 others came into the neighborhood, such as the Crumps and Berrys. Prior to 1851 the Crumps and Berrys located one mile distant from the present town, and in 1852 the Baptists, Methodists and Presbyterians established Mount Pisgah Union Church. In 1853 a school-house was constructed at Marthaville, and in 1855 a post-office was established with J. J. Rains, master, and the name given in honor of his wife. Here also was the stage station of the Alexandria and Shreveport stage line as established that year. In 1857 a daily mail service was established. During the Bank's invasion a half-hour's battle was fought here with the Confederate troops under Green. From 1881 to 1883 G. W. Small, the first merchant here, carried on a large trade. The town was incorporated in 1884. In 1883 J. J. Rains became his partner. In 1882 the Bonds & Jordan store was built, but in 1883 the house was burned. J. J. Rains did business here in 1882–83, but in the latter year established a store at Negreet with J. W. Law, manager, and one at Broadwell's with W. A. Oliphant, manager. J. T. Hanson & Co. established a store here in 1884. H. E. Hanson was first railroad agent in 1881, followed by Charles Hanson in 1884. The saw-mills of Hanson & Brazier and J. J. Rains, Berry & Ingram's brick kilns, Waugh & Gentry's shingle-mill and the old Rains gin were early industries.

Grant's Point is the modern name given to the point at the mouth of Cane River. Frank Beaudry established a store here in 1865, as successor of the old *ante-bellum* French store of Madame Boulard. Owing to some difficulty with the people she was driven out. This action led to a suit against several persons in Grant Parish, and this suit led to a verdict for $5,000 damages against Meredith Calhoun. Morentine & Calhoun established their store on the Rapides bank of Cane and Red Rivers in June, 1865. They were followed by Morentine & Rachal and L. C. Serr & Co. T. Monk Wells, son of J. Madison Wells, located on Natchitoches bank, opposite Colfax, in May, 1883, where he proposed raising sugar cane. His store was on the Rapides bank of Cane River.

Provencal is an incorporated town of about 400 inhabitants. Joseph H. Stephens is mayor, justice of the peace and member of the parish school board. Eight years ago there was no town here. Then the store of Stephens & Gregory was opened. In 1883 Samuel Nelkin established his store here. The former firm purchased the town site in 1886 from Green & Brogan, the original owners, for whom it was surveyed. In 1886 the Methodist Episcopal Church house was erected, and in 1889 the Baptists erected their building. Where the lands have not been cleared they are covered with a heavy growth of beech, ash, oak, pine, gum and other trees useful for house-building or furniture. Four saw-mills and planing-mills, with a capacity of 140,000 feet per day, are constantly turning out rough and dressed lumber for shipment abroad. Two other saw-mills, with a capacity of 15,000 feet per day, are right at the town.

In July, 1890, the Provencal Land & Improvement Company was organized, among the members being the following named: Joseph Levy, S. Nelkin, J. T. Myrick, J. C. Wiggins, Mrs. Annie Crain, J. C. Nalley, S. E. Nalley, T. W. Hawthorne, W. R. Gibbs, D. W. Hall, D. McCorquedale, S. Moses, J. M. Killen, J. A. Ellzey, S. G.

Long, A. T. Foster, J. D. Salter, J. F. Carroll and J. C. Thomason. The fire of November 21, 1888, resulted in the destruction of property valued at $15,000. It originated in the Commercial Hotel, then owned by Dr. J. D. Addison, and spreading to the Stephens & Gregory bar-room, Brown's Hotel, John Trichel's small building and S. Nelkin's store, swept them all away. Immediately after the fire the work of rebuilding was entered upon, and to-day the general stores of S. Nelkin, Joseph Levy, R. W. Gregory, W. W. Farris, D. W. Hall & Co. and M. W. Carroll tell of its progress. The hotels of Mrs. Israel and Dr. A. J. Roquemore are well ordered hostelries.

Grand Ecore was surveyed in 1836 for Samuel Russell, and in 1854 was selected as the starting point of the mail coaches for Shreveport. In August, 1880, a post office was established with H. Manhiem, master.

The De Russy Cemetery, on the Grand Ecore Road contains some old-time obelisks. The Alexander lot close by was tenanted in 1855, during the yellow-fever epidemic.

Campti is one of the oldest towns on Red River. In 1827 it was the outfitting point for the upper country—Claiborne and Arkansas. In 1805 Francois Grappe was appointed interpreter by the Natchitoches Indians in selling a portion of their old Spanish grant of 1790, on Lac de Mure above Campti to Hypolite Bordelin. The latter paid $90 for this grant. The United States commissioners did not confirm Bordelin's claim, holding that the grant to Chief Tomac in 1790 was only provisional.

In 1864 Banks troops destroyed every house at Campti except R. Raphael's store on Front Street. This was burned in 1888. The Campti fire of January 30, 1874, destroyed the Coughlin buildings, then occupied by Raphael & Brother. For years prior to April, 1884, J. G. Readheimer was postmaster at Campti. That month L. Perot was appointed by the Republican administration, but in 1885 Mrs. McDaniel was commissioned. Marion Cauley's saw mill, above Campti, is the only manufacturing industry on the Coushatta and Natchitoches road.

In 1864 the residence of A. Lecomte at Magnolia plantation was destroyed by the Federal troops. In July, 1878, Matthew Hertzog the present owner, captured a white mocking-bird in the ruins. This plantation is one of the oldest as it is one of the largest in Louisiana.

Traditions, dating back to the last century, govern, in a measure, the Creoles of to-day. The war into which they were led by politicians, brought ruin to some of the oldest families, and the era of plunder, introduced after the failure of the Rebellion, humiliated, if it did not destroy, the high spirit of the others. Young women, educated in the great convent schools of the land, young men, taught in the colleges of the Eastern States and France—all raised up in elegant luxury, and with expectations as large as their desires —had replaced their parents in the control of the South. To such the vicissitudes of social change were unknown until the blithe of civil war fell upon their country, and withered up the social and industrial systems which they had known from childhood. The war days passed away, and the Creoles had to adopt the new order of affairs or die of inactivity. The greater number were equal to the emergency and entering the race for progress, buoyant as only Creole can be, won by earnestness and honor where experienced men failed through chicanery. With all this success, the changed condition of affairs is evident. Where the homes of prosperous planters of former days stood, is now the forest. The overseer and the slaves are memories. Men of to-day, who thirty years ago had promise of inheriting great wealth, labor in commercial or professional circles, always genial like their fathers, and proud like them. A few plantations exist under the old names, such as "Magnolia plantation," and farms resembling those of old obtain; but the romance of olden days is gone.

The State officers of Louisiana, who resided in Northwest Louisiana at the time of appointment or election, or who have since such appointment or election become residents, are named as follows: Thomas O. Moore, governor, 1860–64; James Madison Wells, acting governor, 1864–66, and governor 1866–68; Henry M. Hyams, lieutenant-governor,

1860–64, and Charles W. Boyce, president *pro tem.* of the Senate, 1864; John M. Sandige, speaker of the House, 1854–55; W. W. Pugh, 1856–59; Charles H. Morrison, 1860–61; Mortimer Carr, 1870; John C. Moncure, 1879, and Henry W. Ogden, 1884. Aristides Barbin, Henry B. Kelly and W. A. Strong served as secretaries of the Senate; Peter J. Trezevant and C. M. Pegues as clerks of the House; H. A. Bullard was Secretary of State in 1838, and W. A. Strong, 1877–84; Isaac E. Morse was attorney-general, 1853–55; A. S. Herron elected in 1865, but removed by Federal authority; James C. Egan, 1880–84, and Milton J. Cunningham, 1884–88. In 1850–52 Charles E. Greneaux was State treasurer, and Robert A. Hunter, 1855–59; Louis Bordelin served as auditor in 1850–54; Col. W. H. Jack is present superintendent of education; Henry A. Bullard was appointed judge of the Supreme Court in 1832, and served until 1845; George K. King was appointed in 1846; James G. Campbell was elected, and served until 1854; Josiah L. Cole, 1855–59; Thomas T. Land, 1858–62; Albert Voorhies, 1859–62; Thomas C. Manning (appointed), 1863–64; William P. Hyman (chief justice), 1865–68; R. B. Jones (associate justice), 1865; Thomas C. Manning (chief justice), 1877–80; William B. Egan (associate justice), 1877–80; William M. Levy, 1880–86; Thomas C. Manning, 1882–86, and Lynn Boyd Watkins, 1886–98; Thomas C. Manning was subsequently appointed United States minister to Mexico; George R. King was one of the judges of the court of errors and appeals in criminal matters during its existence from 1843–52; J. C. Moncure and A. B. George were appointed judges of the circuit court of appeals for the First Circuit in 1880, and A. B. Irion and J. M. Moon for the Third Circuit. Alex Borman is judge of the United States District Court for Western Louisiana.

The presidential electors from Northwest Louisiana since the position became an elective one in 1828 are named as follows: Placide E. Bossier (D.) 1828, W. H. Overton (D.) 1832, Placide E. Bossier (D.) 1836; Seth W. Lewis (W.) 1840; Thomas W. Scott (D.) 1844; James G. Campbell (W.) 1848; Thomas O. Moore (D.) 1852–56; William M. Levy (D.) 1860 (no vote cast for President in 1864); W. F. Blackman (D.) 1868; Thomas C. Manning and A. H. Leonard 1872 (vote of Louisiana not counted); W. A. Seay (D.) counted out, and A. B. Levissee (R.) counted in; Oscar Joffroin, of Avoyelles (R.), was also elector this year, 1876; Thomas C. Manning (D.) and W. H. Jack (D.) 1880; J. D. Watkins and W. H. Jack 1884.

The representative in the Confederate Congress from Northwest Louisiana was Henry Marshall, of De Soto.

Henry Boyce was elected to the United States Senate in 1866, but was not admitted. Henry M. Spafford was treated similarly in 1877, and died the same year, while Thomas C. Manning was denied his seat in the Senate in 1880.

The representatives of the district of Northwestern Louisiana in Congress were Thomas B. Robertson, XIIIth, XIVth and XVth Congress; Thomas Butler, XVIth; Josiah S. Johnson, XVIIth, and W. L. Brent, XVIIIth Congress. The XIXth Congress claimed two representatives from Louisiana, W. L. Brent and Edward Livingstone, who also served in the XXth. The XXIst Congress had three Louisianians enrolled on the list of members, H. H. Gurley, W. H. Overton and Ed D. White. In the XXIId were H. A. Bullard, Philemon Thomas and Ed D. White, all of whom served also in the XXIIId; Henry Johnson, E. W. Ripley and Rice Garland represented the State in the XXIVth and XXVth; Ed White, T. W. Chinn and Rice Garland, in the XXVIth; John B. Dawson and John Moore represented Central and Northern Louisiana in the XXVIIth; Dawson, of the Third District, and Bossier, of the Fourth District, in the XXVIIIth; John H. Harmanson and I. E. Morse, in the XXIXth, XXXth and XXXIst; A. G. Penn and John Moore, in the XXXIId; John Perkins, Jr., and Roland Jones, in the XXXIIId; T. G. Davidson and John M. Sandige, in the XXXIVth, XXXVth and XXXVIth Congress (not represented in the XXXVIIth, XXXVIIIth and XXXIXth; J. P. Newsham, Fourth and W. Jasper Blackburn, Fifth, in the XLth and XLIst Congress; Alex Bowman, *vice* James McCleary,

deceased, and Frank Morey, XLIId; G. L. Smith and Frank Morey, XLIIId; William M. Levy and W. B. Spencer, XLIVth; J. B. Elam and John S. Young, *vice* J. E. Leonard, deceased, XLVth; J. B. Elam and J. F. King, XLVIth; Newton C. Blanchard and J. F. King, XLVIIth, XLVIIIth and XLIXth. The former was re-elected in 1890. The Sixth District was represented in the XLVth Congress by E. W. Robertson; A. S. Herron was in the XLVIIth, and on his death E. T. Lewis was elected; Alfred B. Irion represented the Sixth in the XLIXth Congress, of which Congressman Price is now representative, and Congressman Boatner represents Northwestern Louisiana.

Josiah Adams, one of the successful planters of Louisiana, came originally from North Carolina, where he was born May 11, 1838. His parents, Briant and Pollie (Holdin) Adams, were also natives of North Carolina, and of nine children born to them four are now living, two residing in this State and two remaining in North Carolina. The father was very successful as a farmer, took an active part in the building up of churches, schools, and society in general, and was called to his final home in 1861, his wife having died in 1856. They were members of the Baptist Church. Josiah received his education in the country schools of his native State, and at the age of eighteen years decided to start out on his own responsibility, and accepted a position as overseer of a plantation. In January, 1858, he was married to Miss Juliania Bason, and their union was blessed with twelve children, the following now living: John Q., Christena, Richard, Benjamin, Roselia, Lora and Lucy. In the early part of 1882 his wife died, and on November 16 of the same year he was united in wedlock with Mrs. Clarlia (Forteneau) Ginger, she having had four children by her first marriage, two of whom died in infancy and the other two, Adam C. and Johnson, are living. She had no children by her second marriage. Our subject now owns 680 acres of land, 175 under cultivation, has a farm well stocked, also a mill and cotton-gin with all the latest improvements.

He formerly held a membership with the Farmers' Alliance. He and his wife worship at the Catholic Church. He is a liberal contributor to all public enterprises, and one of the representative citizens of this parish.

John N. Armstrong, well known as one of the enterprising planters of Ward 4, Natchitoches Parish, was born in Madison County, Ohio, July 5, 1849. His parents, Barnie L. and Mary (Rogers) Armstrong, were natives of Ohio and Tennessee, respectively, the father being born in Ohio on November 1, 1821, and the mother in Memphis, Tenn., on January 6, 1827. They were married October 4, 1847, and this marriage resulted in the birth of eleven children, two living: Alexander B. and John N. The father was a planter; he was also a senator in the Arkansas Senate in 1860. He is still living, and resides in Memphis, Tenn., his wife dying on December 23, 1888. In religion they worshiped with the Cumberland Presbyterian Church. Our subject was educated in the University of Virginia, and at the age of twenty-one began life for himself as a planter, owning a well-stocked farm of 474 acres, a steam gin, and a grist-mill. Emigrating to Louisiana in 1876, he was here married to Miss Lizzie Butler, a native of this State, who bore him five children: Lula, Jennie, Mary, Lizzie Nye and Barney. He is a promoter of all good for the welfare of his country.

Mason F. Atkins is a man whom nature seems to have intended for a planter, for he has met with more than an average degree of success in pursuing that calling, and is the owner of a good and well conducted plantation of 550 acres, on which he has resided since 1885, his residence being on Cane River, about five miles below Natchitoches. He gives considerable attention to stock-raising and trading, and makes a specialty of growing grass for hay, selling in 1889 over 2,000 bales. He was born in the Green Mountain State, December 7, 1845, to John and Abigail Atkins, and when about thirteen years of age he left the shelter of his parents' roof and went west as far as Michigan, but after remaining there until 1867 he removed to St. Charles, Mo., and from that time until about 1880

he was engaged in steamboating on the Mississippi, Missouri and Ohio Rivers, and was considered one of the best steamboat men of his day. He came to the parish of Natchitoches in 1881, and settled near Campti, but four years later came to his present farm. He was married in 1872, his wife being Miss Alice Boal, who was born in Missouri, and an interesting family of three children has been born to them: Medora, Lizzie and Maggie May.

John W. Babers is another honest, progressive and successful agriculturist, and, although his plantation comprises only 366 acres, he has 220 acres under cultivation, the yield from which, owing to its admirable management, is much larger than on many more extensive tracts. It was purchased in 1888, and is situated on the right bank of Cane River, and is a piece of land of which any one might well be proud to possess. Mr. Babers was born near Meridian, Miss., October 31, 1853, to A. J. and Elizabeth (Stokes) Babers, who were born in Winn Parish, La., and Mississippi, being sixty-five and fifty-eight years of age, respectively. John W. Babers is the eldest in a family of eleven children, nine of whom are living, and his youthful days, in addition to being spent in the common schools, were given to farm work. He came with his parents to Louisiana in 1865, and settled in Bienville Parish, but removed to Winn Parish in 1873, but has been a resident of his present farm since the fall of 1889, on which he expects to make his future home. His marriage to Miss M. E. Watson took place in 1876, she being a native of Claiborne Parish, La., born in 1858. To their union seven children have been born: William A., Lula, Lee A., Nettie, Pearl, Ella Jack and Mary M. Mr. Babers and his wife are earnest members of the Methodist Episcopal Church, and in his political views he is a Democrat, and socially belongs to Montgomery Lodge No. 168 of the A. F. & A. M.

J. L. Barbee is one of the leading and most successful planters of Nachitoches Parish, and is especially well known in Ward 6, of which he has been a resident for a number of years. He was born in Sabine Parish, La., on April 23, 1848, to Leslie and Argarine (Dulliam) Barbee, they being born in North Carolina and Georgia, in 1812 and 1818, respectively, their marriage taking place in 1837. The father emigrated from North Carolina to Alabama when a youth, and in 1842 they emigrated to Louisiana, settling in Sabine Parish, where he still resides. He followed the planting business for a number of years, after which he turned his attention to merchandising, a calling he followed for some eighteen years, after which he retired from business. He is a member of Sabine Lodge No. 75, of the A. F. & A. M., and he and his wife are members of the Presbyterian Church. He has always been a Democrat, politically since 1856, prior to which time he was a Whig, and from 1867 until 1868 he represented Sabine Parish in the State Legislature. The immediate subject of this sketch was educated in the common schools of Sabine Parish, and in 1872 he began business with his father, becoming associated with him in his mercantile establishment, at the time of their retirement being worth at least $20.000. In 1880 Mr. Barbee took for his companion through life Miss M. A. Carter, their union taking place on November 20, she being a native of Louisiana, born on May 18, 1861. To them five children have been born: Joseph L., A. V. (living), and three other children who died in infancy. Mr. Barbee is now following the occupation of planting, and owns land to the amount of 3,800 acres, of which 500 acres are under cultivation, well stocked and improved with good buildings, among the latter being an excellent mill and cotton gin. Mr. Barbee is a member of the Farmers' Alliance, and he is a man who takes an active part in building up churches and schools, as well as taking an active part in all other worthy enterprises. He is one of the substantial men of the parish, and as a law-abiding and public-spirited citizen has not his superior in this section.

Very Reverend Jean M. Beaulieu, who has been pastor of St. John's Roman Catholic Church at Cloutierville, La., for the past thirty years, was born in France, on January 10, 1832, and received his literary education at St. Meen. His theological training was at Rennes. He came to America with Bishop August Martin in 1854, being then a sub-

deacon, and was ordained priest at Natchitoches, La., on May 28, 1855. For a year he acted as assistant priest in the parish of Avoyelles, and in the latter part of August, 1856, he took charge of St. John's Catholic Church at Cloutierville, where he has been pastor ever since. This church is more than fifty-five years old, having been founded between 1830 and 1835, and for a great many years it was visited by priests from Natchitoches. In 1847 Father H. Figari became its pastor, and in 1850 Father G. Guy took charge of it, continuing to be its pastor until 1856. The church was rebuilt by Father Beaulieu in 1870, and its present dimensions are 50x90 feet. Its present membership is about 1,500. Under the pastorate of Father Beaulieu the church has had a very prosperous career.

Victor Sanguinet Benoist has devoted his attention to mercantile pursuits in this parish for many years, and the reputation he has acquired for honesty and upright dealing is above reproach. He was born in Cloutierville, La., January 30, 1838, to Charles Francis and Suzette (Rachal) Benoist, who were born in St. Louis, Mo., and Natchitoches Parish, La., in 1800 and 1808, respectively, the former being a son of Charles Francis and Catherine (Sanguinet) Benoist, the former being a Canadian by birth, and the latter a native of St. Louis, Mo., and the grand-daughter of Dr. Conde, who was a surgeon in the French army at Fort Chartres in 1755. The mother of Mr. Benoist was a daughter of Louis Julian and Madam (Lavespere) Rachal. He was descended from a family of some nobility in France. His grandfather, Jacques Louis Benoist, the son of Antoine Gabriel Francis Benoist, "Le Chevalier," was born in 1744, emigrated into Canada, and married in the Soumande family in 1765. Charles Francis and Suzette (Rachal) Benoist were married in Natchitoches Parish, La., about 1824, and became the parents of eight children, the subject of this sketch being the sixth in order of birth, and the only one now living. The names of the others are Amanda, Julia, Charles F., Clemence, Jules, Alphonse, Suzette and a daughter that died in childhood. The father of these children died of yellow fever in 1853, and their mother in 1869. The subject of this sketch spent his boyhood in Cloutierville, which place has been his home thus far. At fourteen years of age he entered the St. Louis University, a Jesuit institution, which he attended nearly two years, after which he entered Georgetown College of the District of Columbia, which he attended two years. He then returned home, and in 1862 was married to Mrs. Marie Celine Cloutier, who was born on Cane River, in Natchitoches Parish, to Neuville and Clara Prudhomme. Soon after the close of the war Mr. Benoist opened a mercantile establishment at Cloutierville, which he has conducted ever since, keeping an excellent general line of goods, and treating his customers with fairness and courtesy. His patronage is exceptionally large, but fully deserved, for he is one of the honorable business men of the parish. His marriage has resulted in the birth of seven children, as follows: William R., Neuville, Felix, Suzette, Clemence, Victor Sanguinet and Ludwick, all of whom are living except Felix, who died September 20, 1890. Mr. Benoist, his wife and children are consistent members of the Catholic Church, and he is a man in whom the public has the utmost confidence, being thoroughly reliable in every respect, and a man whose word is considered as good as his bond. Mr. Benoist's paternal grandmother, Catherine Benoist, was born in St. Louis, Mo., February 2, 1781, a daughter of Charles and Mary Ann (Conde) Sanguinet, the former being a son of Simon Sanguinet, who was a leading merchant of St. Louis for a number of years. Mary Ann Conde was a daughter of Augustus and Mary Ann (La Ferne) Conde, the Doctor, a son of a wealthy merchant of Bordeaux, France. The Doctor came to America about the middle of the eighteenth century, as an army surgeon, with the rank of major, and was stationed at Fort Chartres. In 1762 he married, his wife being a daughter of Bardet La Ferne, surgeon at Mobile. In 1765 he located in St. Louis, Mo., where he practiced medicine until his death, in 1776, leaving two children, Constance and Mary Ann, the former of whom married Patrick Lee, and the latter Charles Sanguinet.

Samuel Bernstein, an old and highly respected citizen of Ward 9, Natchitoches Parish, La., was born in Prussian Poland, June 21, 1816, to Julius and Bertha Bernstein, who were also born there becoming the parents of the following family: Samuel, Isaac, Robert, Gustav, Philip, Maurice, Augusta, Rebecca, Adolph, Mary and Joseph. Robert, Gustav, Rebecca and Adolph, died in Prussia, but the rest came with their parents to America, since which time the parents and Augusta have died, the death of the latter occurring on September 19, 1853. Mr. Bernstein died in Kingston, N. Y., March 17, 1868, and his wife in the same place January 7, 1876. The subject of this sketch was the first of the family to cross the ocean, this being in 1842. Philip came next in 1845, followed by Isaac in 1847, by Maurice and Augusta in 1850, and the parents with Mary and Joseph in 1857. Isaac and Mary reside in Kingston, Maurice resides in Winnfield, Winn Parish, La., and Joseph in Coushatta, Red River Parish, La. Samuel Bernstein learned the tailor's trade in his native land, and was there married in 1842, to Miss Charlotte Yachetsky, and came immediately with her to America, embarking at Hamburg July 27, and after a voyage of sixty-two days landing at Castle Garden, New York. They made their home in the city of New York until the fall of 1845, when they came to New Orleans which place they reached September 27. In the spring of the next year they removed to Little Rock, Ark., and in the fall of the next year to Pine Bluff, returning in the spring of 1848 to Louisiana, locating in Rapides Parish, and for five years resided on Little River and five years in Alexandria. In 1858 he removed to Montgomery, Grant Parish, where his wife died June 3, 1888, soon after which Mr. Bernstein removed to a farm which he owns in Ward 9, Natchitoches Parish, a part of which he had purchased in 1863. He now owns a good farm of 200 acres, the greater part of which is under cultivation. He is a member of the Hebrew Church, and in politics is a Democrat. During the greater part of his residence in this country he has been engaged in merchandising, this extending over a period of forty-eight years. Although in the seventy-fifth year of his age he is hale and hearty, and would readily pass for a man many years his junior. His brother, Philip, who also resides in this parish, was born April 10, 1827, and came to America on the vessel "Shenandoah," and for a few years made his home in New York City. He then came to Louisiana and located in Rapides Parish, but in 1858 went to Grant Parish, and on July 12, 1859, was married in Montgomery, to Miss Rosalie Marks who was born in Gnesna, Prussia Poland, May 10, 1840, to Marcus and Rena Marks, the latter of whom died October 3, 1860, in Prussia, and the former still resides in that country. She came to America in 1857, and in 1887 removed with her family to Natchitoches Parish and located in Ward 9, where he now resides. He and his wife have had a family of eight children as follows: Albert M., Henry, Augusta, Julian, Rudolph, Nettie, Arnold and Bertha, all of whom are living with the exception of Augusta, who died at the age of twenty-two months. Albert M. (is a physician and a graduate of a New Orleans Medical College, being now a resident of Montgomery), Henry (graduated in a New Orleans law college and is a prominent member of the bar of Winnfield). The parents of these children are members of the Hebrew Church, and in politics the former is a Democrat. Both Samuel and Philip Bernstein, and the family of the latter, are among the best citizens of this locality and have a large circle of warm friends. Samuel is a Royal Arch Mason, which order he joined in New Orleans, February 11, 1866. Philip is also a member of Montgomery Lodge No. 168, having been made a Mason in 1860.

Charles Bertrand, planter, Cloutierville, La. Mr. Bertrand, an energetic and worthy citizen of Ward No. 10, Natchitoches Parish, is one of the leading farmers of the community in which he lives. He was born on Cane River, three miles below Cloutierville, in this parish, February 24, 1843, and his father, whose name is also Charles Bertrand, was born in France June 16, 1815. The latter came to America in 1837, first located in St. James Parish, La., and in 1839 removed to Natchitoches Parish, where he was married, in 1842, to Miss Mary F. Rachal, who bore him the following children: Charles, one who died in infancy, Fran-

cois, Eloise, Harriet and Anna. Harriet is the only one besides our subject now living. The mother died in 1855 in France, whither the parents removed with their children in 1851. In 1856 the father, with three children, returned to America, but Charles did not return with him, although he came over in 1861. In September of that year he entered Company C, Eighteenth Louisiana Regiment, and served in it until August, 1862, when he entered Company D, Third Louisiana, with which he remained until the close of the war. He was captured at Vicksburg, but was at once paroled. From the war he returned to Natchitoches Parish and engaged in merchandising at Cloutierville. He was married, in 1866, to Miss Lise Woods, daughter of Richard and Clementine (Rachal) Woods, natives of Tennessee and Louisiana, respectively. Mr. Bertrand removed, in 1869, to the plantation he now occupies, two miles northeast of Cloutierville, where he has ever since been engaged in farming. His extensive plantation contains 300 acres, with 170 acres under cultivation, and everything about the place indicate to the beholder an industrious and enterprising owner. Mr. and Mrs. Bertrand have had eight children, viz.: Florentine, Charles, Leopold, Francois, Woods, then a son died unnamed, Harriet and Clemence (twins). Only Leopold and Woods are now living. Mr. and Mrs. Bertrand are members of the Catholic Church, and are much esteemed citizens of their community. In his political views Mr. Bertrand affiliates with the Democratic party.

P. F. Bouis, one of the foremost and most successful business men in Natchitoches, was born in this city on May 18, 1836, and is the son of P. V. and Emelie (Chamard) Bouis. The father was born in France and crossed the ocean to America in 1835, and located at Natchitoches. His death occurred in that city in 1837, when only thirty-five years of age. The mother was born in this parish in 1815 and is still a resident of Natchitoches. P. F. Bouis, the youngest of three children born to his parents, two of whom are now living, was reared and educated in this city. When but twelve years of age he started out to fight his way in life, and had made quite a beginning when the war broke out. In 1861 he joined Company C, Second Louisiana Cavalry, and served until the close of the war. The same year he was married to Miss Mary M. Hartman, a native of Natchitoches, born in 1847, and the fruits of this union have been five children: Edward, Louis V., Stella, Oscar, and Leo. In 1866 Mr. Bouis entered the employ of Mr. J. A. Ducournau, and with him has since continued, a period of twenty-four years. He is Mr. Ducournau's chief clerk, and is a gentleman of unusual good business acumen. He is a Democrat in his political preferences, and is a representative of one of the old families of the parish.

H. P. Breazeale, editor and proprietor of the Natchitoches Enterprise, is a native-born resident of this city, his birth occurring on November 13, 1856, and although a young man, his career thus far has been both honest and praiseworthy. The parents of Mr. Breazeale, Winter W. and Adeline (Prudhomme) Breazeale, were natives, also, of Natchitoches Parish, the father born on September 5, 1827, and the mother in 1835. She died here in October, 1878. The paternal grandmother of our subject is still living in this city, and was born in this State on January 8, 1808. Her father, William Winter, came to Natchitoches in about 1816, and about the first of this century obtained a grant of 3,000,000 acres of land in Arkansas from the Spanish Government. He died where Little Rock now stands. H. P. Breazeale is the eldest of eleven children, ten of whom are living, and was educated in the schools of Natchitoches. He worked on the plantation until twenty-two years of age, and then in 1879 came to Natchitoches, where for one year he filled the position of deputy sheriff. After this he was deputy clerk of the district court for a short time, and in the fall of 1882 he was elected clerk of the police jury and parish superintendent of public schools, which offices he has since held. He is popular with all, kind and courteous in his intercourse with his fellow-men, and is always willing to aid any enterprise for the good of the parish. In 1888 he established the Natchitoches Enterprise, and this he still continues. This paper is found to be a welcome visitor in the numerous homes into which it enters, and is a newsy, spicy sheet. Mr. Breazeale was married in 1886 to Miss Cammilla Leacht, a native of Vicksburg, Miss., born on January 10, 1865. They have three children: Hopkins P., Winona and Cammilla. Mr. Breazeale is a member of the Catholic Church, and in his political views is a Democrat.

Dr. Alexander P. Breda, physician and surgeon, Natchitoches, La. Among the many practitioners of the "healing art" in Natchitoches Parish, deserving of special mention is Dr. Breda, who was born in Natchitoches on December 19, 1837, and who is a son of Dr. John P. and Marie Helmina (Dranguet) Breda. [See sketch of J. Emile and J. E. Breda.] Dr. Breda is the eldest of a numerous family, and in addition to a common-school education he attended the Western Military Institute at Drennon Springs, Henry County, Ky. This school was broken up in 1853 from yellow fever, and Dr. Breda returned home. He began the study of medicine in 1855 under the dictation of his father, and in 1859 he graduated from the medical department of that far-famed and well-known institution of learning, the University of Louisiana. He began at once the practice of his profession in Natchitoches, and here he has since continued. In 1862 he was filled with a natural desire to assist the Confederacy and enlisted in Company "C," Second Louisiana Cavalry, under Col. W. G. Vincent, and was detailed as medical assistant. Later he was commissioned assistant surgeon of the Seventh Louisiana Cavalry, and thus continued until the close of the war. He was formerly an Old Line Whig, and voted with that party until 1856, and since 1868 he has been an ardent Republican. He is a member of the Masonic fraternity. Dr. Breda has been a resident of this parish for fifty-three years, and thirty-one years of that time he has practiced his profession. He is a physician of recognized ability, and is a well-posted man.

J. Ernest Breda, attorney, Natchitoches, La. Mr. Breda, a man of marked character, and more than ordinary prominence in the affairs of Natchitoches Parish, is the third of a very large family of children born to Dr. John P. and Marie Helmina (Dranguet) Breda. The father was born in France on April 6, 1808, and died May 1, 1882, in Natchitoches. He studied medicine in the Baltimore Medical College, and afterward practiced his profession in that city in partnership with Dr. Skinner. He came to Shreveport, La., in 1835, and in 1838 came to Natchitoches, where he practiced his profession until his death. The mother was born in Natchitoches on April 10, 1818, and now resides in the parish where she has made her home for forty-five years. J. Ernest Breda was born in Natchitoches, on September 25, 1841, received a common-school education, and for four years previous to the war studied medicine. On August 9, 1862, he joined the Beazeale Battalion of Natchitoches Rangers, Confederate States army, and remained in the service until June, 1865, when he took the oath of amnesty. On April 1, 1864, he was taken prisoner by Capt. Inwood, of the New York Zouaves. After the war Mr. Breda continued the study of medicine until January 31, 1866, and on February 1 of that year he began the study of law, being admitted to the bar in August of the same year. In January, 1870, he began the practice of law in Natchitoches, and in January, 1872, he formed a partnership with N. A. Robison, who died the same year. In January, 1873, Mr. Breda was appointed district attorney for the then Ninth Judicial District, which was then composed of five parishes, viz.: Natchitoches, Sabine, Grant, Union and Rapides. He served in that position until November, 1874, when he was elected parish judge of the parish of Natchitoches. November, 1876, he was elected district judge of what was then the Seventeenth District. Mr. Breda is one of the best lawyers in this district, and has shown good judgment and heart enough not to make his office an engine of inhumanity and injustice. He was married on December 29, 1873, to Miss Elcey Hertzog, who was born in this parish on December 28, 1852, and who is the daughter of Henry and Laure (Lecomte) Hertzog. Five children are the fruits of this union: Elmira, Edmee, Emma, John P. and Joseph E. Mr. Breda was formerly a Whig in his political views, but is now a stanch

Republican. He joined Phoenix Lodge No. 38, A. F. & A. M., in 1864, and Natchitoches Lodge No. 89, of which he is president. He is one of the representative men of this city. The first vineyard ever set out or attempted here was in 1856, by Dr. J. P. Breda, who put out about one-half acre, or 1,300 vine cuttings, and in the following year about 5,000 vines. In 1858 he set out 7,000 vines besides replacing missing ones, and in 1859 he set out over 25,000 vines more. In 1860 he set out over 25,000 besides replacing and thus had about 25 acres in vines. He, at the same time, had planted an extensive peach orchard, containing over 3,000 trees, for making peach brandy. The first crop of wine was pressed in the summer of 1861, and from a field of about three acres sixty barrels were obtained, of forty gallons each, or 2,400 gallons of wine. In 1862 late frosts reduced the crop to only thirty barrels, and owing to wet weather and mildew, the crop was only forty barrels in 1863. In April, 1864, the orchard and vineyard were entirely destroyed by Bank's army, who burned all fences and camped on the ground. These vines were of European variety. The second attempt was made to raise grapes by Dr. J. P. and J. Ernest Breda, in the fall of 1874, when they set out 2,450 cuttings on one acre. In 1875 they set out the same number and in 1876 set out three acres, or about 8,000 vine cuttings, all American varieties. The first crop in 1878 from an acre and a half, yielded forty barrels of forty gallons each, or 1,600 gallons of very fine wine, all of which was lost during the political troubles. J. Ernest Breda now has about 200 vines of select varieties suitable for this latitude and climate and will continue setting out vines yearly until he re-establishes the old vineyard know as Cote Breda. Mr. Breda has made 200 gallons of peach brandy to an acre of four year old trees.

J. Emile Breda, postmaster, Natchitoches, La. Mr. Breda needs no introduction to the people of Natchitoches Parish, for he is a native-born resident of the same and although young in years he has become prominently identified with its interests. He was born on July, 5, 1858, and is the youngest of nineteen children, four of whom are now living, born to the union of Dr. J. P. and Marie Helmina (Dranguet) Breda. The father was born in France on April 6, 1808, and died in Natchitoches in 1882. He came from his native land to the United States about 1830, settled in Baltimore, Md., and there studied medicine in the Baltimore Medical College. Subsequently he practiced his profession in that city in partnership with one Dr. Skinner and remained there until about 1835 when he came to Natchitoches. Here he practiced his profession until his death. The mother of our subject was born in Natchitoches on April 10, 1818, and now resides in this city. Her family was one of the earliest in this part of Louisiana. J. Emile Breda was educated in Natchitoches, and for about five or six years after finishing his education he was engaged in farming. He was then appointed United States deputy collector of internal revenue of the Thirteenth District of Louisiana, under George Drury, and held that position for about nine months, when the Thirteenth District was abolished. After this, for about eight and a half months, he was assistant postmaster under Mrs. E. Suddeth, postmistress at Natchitoches, and then began clerking for Levy & Kaffie with whom he continued for twenty-three months. From 1887 to 1889 he was engaged in agricultural pursuits. In politics he is a Republican, and July, 1889, he was appointed postmaster at Natchitoches by President Harrison, taking possession of the office on July 27 of that year. Mr. Breda is a good business man, and his character is above reproach. He was married on February 11, 1885, to Miss Marie Emee Tauzin, a native of Natchitoches, born in 1866. They have two children: Marie Blanche and Marie Emee. The family are members of the Catholic Church.

James Madison Burkett, planter, Robeline, La. This gentleman is one of the prominent and substantial agriculturists of Ward No. 6, Natchitoches Parish, La. He was originally from Jackson Parish, La., born on June 18, 1845, and was the son of George Washington and Ann (Cannon) Burkett, the father born on February 17, 1815, and the mother on April 12, 1817. The parents

were married prior to the year 1838, and to their union were born ten children, James M. being fifth in the order of birth, and five of whom are now living. Their names in the order of birth are as follows: Mary Frances, Jesse Allen, George Washington, William Jasper, James Madison, Thomas Benton, John Norvel, Josiah Newton, Margaret Elizabeth and Isadore Jane. Those deceased are Mary Frances, Jesse Allen, George W., William J. and Margaret Elizabeth. The mother of these children died in 1869, and afterward the father married Mrs. Armecy Hendrick, who is still living. Mr. Burkett, however, died on January 13, 1881. The paternal ancestors of Mr. Burkett (our subject) were formerly from South Carolina. His parents were married in Lawrence County, Miss., and in about 1843 or 1844 they removed to Louisiana, locating in Jackson Parish. In about 1849 they removed to Bienville Parish and in the fall of 1857 they removed to Natchitoches Parish, in which both spent the remainder of their lives. The early life of James M. was therefore spent in the parishes of Jackson, Bienville and Natchitoches. In the fall of 1863 he entered the Confederate army and continued in service until cessation of hostilities. Returning to the parish of Natchitoches he has resided in it ever since, giving his attention to farming. He located on his present property in Ward 6, on Spanish Lake, eight miles north of Robeline in 1872, and on September 26 of that year he was married to Miss Isabella Mahala Carroll, of Natchitoches Parish. To them have been born seven children, who are named as follows: Anna Elizabeth (deceased), born October 11, 1873; James Clifford, January 19, 1876; Claudie Idel, March 23, 1878; Zuella, March 10, 1880; Daniel Winfred, November 19, 1883; Mabel, August 30, 1887, and Amy Dora, January 2, 1890. Socially Mr. Burkett is a member of the Farmers' Alliance, and in politics he is a Democrat. He owns 300 acres of land and a comfortable home. He and Mrs. Burkett are members of the Baptist Church.

L. R. Burnside, a native of Mississippi, was born in Neshoba County December, 1857, the oldest child of John and Martha (Jones) Burnside, the father a native of South Carolina, born in 1808, and the mother of Alabama, born in 1833. They were married in 1854. The father was a planter, and emigrated from South Carolina to Alabama at an early day, locating in Pickens County, where he resided a short time, and then emigrated to Mississippi, commenced farming in Neshoba County, and resided there until his death, which occurred November 22, 1871. His widow is still living on the old home place. Lake Burnside was named after a brother of his. He was a member of the Masonic and Pattsburg, Miss., fraternities, and was a Royal Arch Mason, held the office of justice of the peace for a number of years, and his widow is a devout member of the Baptist Church. L. R. Burnside was educated in the private schools of his native county, and at the age of twenty years decided to work on his own responsibility, and engaged in farming, which he conducted until 1882, when he emigrated to Louisiana. In 1877 he married Miss Rosanna T. Fox, a native Mississippian, but she died January 20, 1890, leaving two children, Robert H. and Emmet, to mourn their loss. March 23, 1890, he was married again to Miss Jane Graham, a native of Alabama. She is a member of the Baptist Church. Although he started out with little, he has, through energy and perseverance, succeeded in establishing a merchandising business valued at $12,000, and also owns 183 acres of land, 121 acres under cultivation. He is a member of the A. O. U. W., and a liberal contributor to all public enterprises.

Capt. Woodson B. Butler is one of the successful planters of Natchitoches Parish, born December 7, 1840. His parents, John W. and Julia A. (Hailey) Butler, were natives of Virginia and Ohio, respectively, the former born in 1809 and the latter in 1821. They were married in 1840, and of the ten children born to them four are now living. The father, one of the noted physicians of this State, began to practice in 1832, and continued for about twenty years, when he retired much to the regret of his many patients. In connection with his practice he conducted farming, took a very active part in politics, has held the office of land commissioner for two terms, and was also State senator. He died March 21, 1886, mourned not only by his family, but also by a large circle of friends, his wife having preceded him May 1, 1875. Woodson B. was educated in the Centenary College, later became overseer of his father's farm, and held this position for six years, when he went into the merchandising business with his father. In 1861 he was called upon to serve his country, and entered the Confederate army as a private under Gen. Ben McCullough in Company G, Third Louisiana Infantry; took part in the battles of Elk Horn, Iuka, Corinth and Vicksburg, where he was taken prisoner, paroled and returned home. Later he re-entered the army, was sent to Shreveport to do post duty, and was there at the time of the surrender. So faithfully did he serve his country that, in May, 1862, he was elected to the captaincy of his company. Upon returning home he turned his attention to farming, and now owns 175 acres of good land, sixty-five acres improved. His farm is well stocked, and contains a steam gin-mill and grist mill. In 1878 he was united in marriage to Miss Bettie Williams, a native Georgian. Two children blessed their union: John W. and Bessie L. The latter passed from life August 3, 1882. December 1, 1883, Mrs. Butler was called to her long home, and in July, 1887, our subject took for his wife Miss Carrie Campbell. They have three interesting children: Maggie L., Annie L. and William B. Being one of the representative citizens of this parish, he was appointed a member of the police jury, and held this position for two terms.

Monroe F. Buvens, a popular young business man and merchant of Robeline, La., owes his nativity to Many, Sabine Parish, La., where he was born on December 28, 1862. The parents, John G. and Sarah A. (Dendy) Buvens, were born in Belgium in 1829, and Alabama in 1832, respectively. John G. Buvens accompanied his father, Peter, to America when he was about twelve years of age and located with him at Many, La., being among the first settlers of that place. There both the grandfather and father spent the remainder of their days, the latter dying at the age of fifty-two years. By occupation the father was a farmer. He was an upright, worthy man, and one who led a life of industry. He acquired considerable means, most of which he lost, however, by the burning of his house shortly before his death, which occurred in 1871. His wife, Sarah A. Dendy, to whom he was married in about 1853, survived him about five years, dying in 1876. Monroe F. Buvens was the eighth in a family of ten children, of whom four sons and three daughters are now living. He spent his boyhood and youth in his native town, received his early education there, and when eighteen years of age he entered the employ of his brother-in-law, John Blake, a native of Ireland, who came to America when fourteen years of age, and who became a prominent merchant of Many. Our subject clerked for Mr. Blake from May 1, 1880, until February, 1885, and then the latter established a branch store at Robeline, La., of which Mr. Buvens became manager. In August, 1885, Mr. Blake died, after which Mr. Buvens assumed the management of Blake's store at Many, the business being conducted under the name of Mrs. John Blake. In January, 1886, Mr. Buvens consolidated the two stores at Robeline, and of the one thus formed he continued as manager until January 1, 1889, at which time he associated himself with his sister, Mrs. Blake. They have since owned the business jointly, the firm name being M. F. Buvens & Co. Mr. Buvens is pleasant and agreeable in his intercourse with the public, and throughout his business career in Robeline he has not only acquired a large patronage but also a circle of warm friends. The business of this firm occupies a good two-story building, 40x66 feet, both floors of which are well stocked with all kinds of general merchandise. Under the able management of Mr. Buvens the establishment has enjoyed a very prosperous career, and is now one of the leading stores of Robeline. Mr. Buvens was married on June 26, 1884, to Miss Ella F. Hogue, eldest daughter of A. H. Hogue, of Many, La. Their marriage has resulted in the birth of three children: Robert Elmer, James Monroe and Annie Kathleen, all living. Mr. and Mrs. Buvens are consistent members of the Catholic Church, and as such are highly esteemed. Mr. Buvens is a Democrat in politics, and in 1883, or when twenty-one years of age, he was appointed by the governor returning officer for Sabine Parish, serving in that responsible position for about two years, or until his removal to Robeline, necessitated his resignation. In January, 1888, he was elected a member of the city council of Robeline, and in January of the following two years he was re-elected. He is therefore now serving his third term. He is secretary of the recently organized Robeline Public and Private Academy, and is also secretary of the Anti-Lottery League of Robeline. Mr. Buvens is a young man of good habits, and he possesses every qualification necessary for a successful business man.

Monroe W. Carroll, a prominent lumber manufacturer and dealer of Provencal, La., was born in the parish of Natchitoches, seven miles southwest of the city of Natchitoches, on January 8, 1860, and when thirteen years of age he accompanied his parents from Natchitoches Parish to Beaumont, Jefferson County, Tex., remaining there with them until 1881. In September, 1878, he entered Roanoke College, of Salem, Va., attended two years, and, in October, 1880, entered Eastman's Business College, of Poughkeepsie, N. Y., from which he graduated in the early part of 1881. He then returned home, and in March of that year engaged in the saw-milling business at Nona, Tex., where he continued, doing a good business, until September, 1885. While there he was a member of the firm of the Nona Mills Company, of which he was general manager. In January, 1886, he returned to Natchitoches Parish, and at once established a large saw-mill at Provencal, which he has owned and operated ever since. The daily capacity of this mill is 45,000 feet, and he employs about fifty men. Mr. Carroll was married on June 23, 1887, to Miss Lula Prothro, of Mount Lebanon, Bienville Parish, La., and they have two children: Monroe W. and an infant daughter, Lula Pearl. Mr. and Mrs. Carroll are members of the Baptist Church, and are highly respected in the community in which they live. In politics he adheres to the Democratic party. He is at present a member of the city council at Provencal, and during the four years of his residence at Nona, Tex., he served as postmaster at that place, being the first officer of that kind. Mr. Carroll is thoroughly familiar with every detail of the saw-milling business, and he has shown himself to possess a large amount of inventive genius as well. He invented an improvement for locomotive engines, receiving a patent upon it January 21, 1890, and while his patent, on account of its recent invention, is not in general use, it is in successful operation at Mr. Carroll's mill, bidding fair to become a useful and valuable invention. Mr. Carroll is an enterprising and progressive young man, and is made of the kind of material calculated to make life a success. He is recognized as a man who is thoroughly reliable, upright and honorable. Mr. Carroll is the fourth of nine children, four sons and two daughters now living, born to the union of Frank L. and Sarah J. (Long) Carroll, natives of Alabama and Georgia, respectively. The parents were married in De Soto Parish, La., in about 1852, and are now living at their home in Waco, Tex.

Americus V. Carter, a prominent and honored citizen of Natchitoches Parish, who resides two miles northeast of Robeline, is a native of Amite County, Miss., born November 2, 1839. He was the son of Isaac F. and Margaret (Holden) Carter, both natives also of the Bayou State, the former born in Pike County and the latter in Amite County. The paternal grandparents of our subject, William and Jemima (Cole) Carter, were natives of South Carolina and the great-grandfather, Isaac Carter, was a native of the Old' Dominion. The maternal grandparents, Thomas and Elizabeth (Flannigan) Holden, were born in South Carolina. The parents of our subject were married in 1838, and reared a family of four children, three sons and a daughter, whom we will now name in the order of their birth: Americus V., William O., Elizabeth A. and Thadeus A. Elizabeth A. died in July, 1889, leaving a husband and five children. The father of Mr. Carter died in February, 1853, and his mother in 1878. When Americus V. was about one year and a half old, his parents removed to Louisiana and located in Natchitoches Parish, on a plantation ten miles west of the city of Natchitoches and four miles east of his present home. He attended the parish schools, prepared himself

for college at Bellewood, Sabine Parish, and when eighteen years of age he entered Mount Lebanon College, of Bienville Parish, which he attended during the years 1857 and 1858. He was married September 20, of the last-named year, to Miss Martha Ponder, daughter of Silas and Lucitta (Darden) Ponder, and sister of the late Hon. William A. Ponder, of this parish. After his marriage Mr. Carter engaged in farming for himself, and this has been his principal occupation all his life. In 1862 he entered the service of the Confederate army, in Company E, Second Louisiana Cavalry, as a second lieutenant, and served until the cessation of hostilities, being promoted to first lieutenant during that time. He was in the battle of Franklin, and was in numerous skirmishes. At the time of Bank's raid, and while engaged in attempting to drive him back, Mr. Carter was captured at Henderson's Hill, Rapides, and was held a prisoner for about four months, being exchanged in July, 1864. He had previously been captured in 1862, at Burwick City, but was paroled a day later. From the war he returned home and resumed farming, his home then being on Spanish Lake. In 1870 he removed to his present property, where he has resided ever since, and where he has a beautiful and comfortable home. Besides farming he has given some attention to merchandising and journalism. During the year 1885, and also the year 1887, he owned and conducted a general store in Robeline. In 1884 he bought the Robeline Reporter, of which his son, I. F. Carter, was editor and he proprietor until January, 1886, when he sold it to Dr. J. H. Canningham. Mr. Carter was the editor of the Reporter in 1887, when it belonged to a stock company. In September, 1889, he and his son, Ponder S. Carter, purchased it, and under the name of Carter & Son, they conducted the paper until 1890, when they sold it to S. C. Presiey. Mr. Carter helped to survey Robeline, and he built the first house in that city. He has since erected several other residences, and is the owner of considerable property in town. By reason of the above facts he is called "the father of Robeline." Mr. and Mrs. Carter have seven children living as follows: Bessie, Isaac

F., William E., Ponder S., Lillian Lee, Thadeus A. and A. Everly. Mr. and Mrs. Carter are members of the Baptist Church, and in politics Mr. Carter is strictly Democratic. He served as a member of the parish police jury from 1877 until 1880, and four years later he was reappointed to that position, serving in that capacity ever since. During the entire time he has been a member of that body he has been chairman of its finance committee, which is evidence of the complete confidence reposed in him by the people of the parish. He was made a member of the Democratic Central Committee of the parish in 1872 and has served constantly ever since. He has also held the position of returning officer of the parish since 1884. Mr. Carter is one of the representative and leading citizens of Natchitoches Parish, and no one is more favorably or extensively known. He is an active and prominent worker in the Farmers' Alliance.

Dr. Thadeus A. Carter, physician, Robeline, La. Dr. Carter, a physician of acknowledged merit in Natchitoches Parish, and a prominent and honored citizen of Robeline, La., was born in the parish of Natchitoches, ten miles west of the city of Natchitoches, November 22, 1851. He was initiated into the duties of the farm at an early age, and received his primary education in the parish schools. In 1871 he entered Shelbyville College, at Shelbyville, Tex., and here attended six months, after which he spent about two years on his father's farm. In 1873 he began the study of medicine, under the direction of Dr. C. Cunningham, of Natchitoches. He studied with him about one year, and in the fall of 1874 entered the Tulane Medical College, of New Orleans, in which he took two full courses of lectures, graduating in March, 1876. He at once began the practice of his profession in Natchitoches Parish, and here he has been actively engaged ever since, being now one of its most prominent physicians. In 1881 he located in Robeline, and he is now the leading physician of that place. Dr. Carter was married October 3, 1877, to Miss Sarah L. Smith, daughter of Robert E. Smith, of Natchitoches, and the fruits of this union were five children: Mason T., Silas E., Norwood W., Laura L. and Eva T. All are living, with the exception

of Laura L., who died at the age of one year. Mr. Carter is a member of the Baptist, and his wife a member of the Methodist Episcopal, Church. The Doctor devotes his entire attention to his profession, and he has built up a wide reputation as an able physician and skillful surgeon. He has a wide acquaintance, and in every circle of life, whether of a social, religious or professional character, his standing is of the best. He and wife have a large number of friends, and are highly esteemed by all. The Doctor is a stanch Democrat in his political preferences. The father of Dr. Carter, Isaac F. Carter, was born in Covington County, Miss., and removed to Louisiana, locating in Natchitoches Parish in 1840. He spent the remainder of his life in this parish, and was one of the substantial and leading planters. He died in 1853. The mother, whose maiden name was Margaret U. Holden, was born in Amite County, Miss., and was there married to Isaac F. Carter, whom she accompanied to this parish. About one year after the death of Mr. Carter, she was married to Hon. W. A. Ponder, late State representative from Natchitoches Parish. She died in 1879, and Mr. Ponder in 1890.

Isaac F. Carter, attorney, Robeline, La., is a prominent attorney, and one who contributes to the strength of the Louisiana bar, a native of Natchitoches Parish, La., having been born ten miles west of the city of Natchitoches on June 9, 1863, and is the son of Americus V. and Mattie J. (Ponder) Carter, who are old and honored citizens of Natchitoches Parish. The father is also a native of that parish (see biography). The grandfather, Isaac F. Carter, a native of Mississippi, located in Natchitoches Parish in 1840, and there passed the remainder of his days, his death occurring in 1856. He was a farmer by occupation, and although he was in very moderate circumstances when he located here, he accumulated a large estate, and when he died was one of the wealthiest planters and slave owners of the parish. The mother of our subject is a sister of the late Hon. W. A. Ponder, of this parish. Isaac F. Carter passed his youthful days on his father's farm, and received his early education in the private schools in the vicinity of his home. At nineteen years of age he entered Keatchie College, of De Soto Parish, which he attended two years, and then started out as a school teacher. This pursuit he continued for ten months, teaching a private school near Provencal, La., and about the same time he commenced teaching he began studying law, all his leisure time being devoted to it. At the close of his term of school he entered the office of Judge D. Pierson, of Natchitoches, and under his direction pursued his legal studies for one or two years, at the expiration of which time, upon the solicitation of friends, he located at Robeline, where he accepted the office of justice of the peace. At the same time he entered upon the practice of law. This was in the fall of 1884, and from attending to his official and legal duties he, in the early part of his residence in Robeline, had some experience in the newspaper business. On January 1, 1885, he took charge of the Robeline Reporter, and acted as editor and manager one year. In the fall of 1887 he resigned the office of justice of the peace to devote his whole time to his law practice, having been admitted to the bar in the preceding July, and since that time the practice of law, and business pertaining thereto, has received his undivided attention. He is in possession of a lucrative practice, and is an able and brilliant attorney. In the spring of 1890 he purchased a large and handsome farm which adjoins the city of Robeline on the north, and which contains 350 acres. He is now giving his personal attention to its management. Mr. Carter was married on November 2, 1887, to Miss Josie L. Carter, eldest daughter of John J. Carter, of Minden, La., and their marriage has resulted in the birth of two children, Lucile and Isaac F., both living. Mr. and Mrs. Carter are members of the Baptist Church, and are active workers in both the church and Sabbath-school, Mr. Carter having served for many years as superintendent of the Sunday-schools at Robeline. He is at present president of the Union Sabbath-school Convention. In politics Mr. Carter is a Democrat. He is a young man of ability, and one whose prospects for the future are bright. He and wife have a large circle of friends, among whom they are very popular.

Harmon Carter, marshal of the city of Robeline, La., and a worthy citizen of that place, is a native of Natchitoches Parish, La., born about ten miles south of the present site of Robeline on October 11, 1859. His father, Harmon Carter, Sr., was born in the Bayou State, and at the age of eighteen years came to Louisiana, where he resided for several years in Natchitoches Parish. He was married at the age of twenty to Miss Martha Ann Estes in the above mentioned parish, and with her removed to Sabine Parish in the fall of 1861, or when our subject was but two years of age. In 1868 the mother died in Sabine Parish, and two years later the father married Miss Sarah Ann Addison, who died in June, 1873. He survived her only a few months, his death occurring in December of the same year. By occupation the father was a farmer. He served in the Confederate army throughout the entire Civil War, first as a private, later as a courier, and finally as a lieutenant. He was a brave soldier, and served the Confederacy faithfully and well. Harmon Carter, Jr., remained on his father's farm in Sabine Parish until after the death of the latter, and in 1874 returned to Natchitoches Parish, having ever since resided in the vicinity of Robeline. His chief occupation has been that of a farmer. In August, 1883, or shortly after the town was founded, he located in Robeline, where he has remained ever since. Aside from farming, for the past six years, Mr. Carter has served in several different official capacities. In April, 1884, he was elected constable, and he has served continuously ever since, having been re-elected in 1888. During the entire time he has held the last-named office he has also served in the capacity of deputy sheriff. Since January 1, 1890, he has also held the position of city marshal at Robeline, and in all positions he has made a good officer, discharging his duties in a skillful and efficient manner. Mr. Carter's marriage was consummated on February 17, 1881, to Miss Nettie J. Wagley, of Natchitoches Parish. Their marriage has resulted in the birth of four children: William Harmon, Bessie Lee, Floy Belle and Sallie. All are living except Bessie Lee, who died at the age of two and a half years. Mr. and Mrs. Carter are members of the Baptist Church, and in politics the former is a Democrat. Both are much-esteemed citizens of the community.

Hon. Leopold Caspari, president and general manager of the Natchitoches Railroad Company, was originally from France, where his birth occurred July 28, 1830, and is a son of David and Charlotta (Baruch) Caspari, natives also of France, the father born in 1800 and the mother in 1802. The parents both died in their native country, the former in 1876 and the latter in 1844. Hon. Leopold Caspari, the eldest of six children, three now living, was educated in the land of his birth, and served two and a half years as an apprentice in a dry goods store prior to the Revolution of 1848. In 1849 he came to the United States, settled in Natchitoches Parish, La., and embarked in merchandising at Cloutierville, where he continued until 1858, after which he removed to Natchitoches. There he carried on merchandising and farming very successfully. In 1861 he joined the Pelican Rangers No. 1, and entered the ranks with the title of second lieutenant. Subsequently he was commissioned captain and served the Confederacy faithfully and well for nearly four years. Mr. Caspari was one of the leading spirits in the building of the railroad from this town, and has been president of the road since its construction. He is one of the most enterprising men in this part of the State. He affiliates with the Democratic party in his political views, and in 1884 was elected to the General Assembly from this parish and re-elected in 1888. In 1884 he was instrumental in passing a bill for the establishment of the State Normal School at Natchitoches. During his legislative career he took an active part. For eight years he was a member of the public school board, and for four years was officially connected with the State Normal School, and he has ever been interested in all enterprises for the good of the parish. He was married, in 1862, to Miss Amanda Woods, who was born in this parish, and who died in 1883. Nine children were born of this union: Richard L., Samuel, Joseph, David, Emanuel, Charles, Gustave, Julia and Dora. Mr. Caspari is a member of the A. L. of H., the K. of P., and of the B'nai Brith, a Jewish order. He is a first-class citizen and representative man of this part of the State.

Landry Charleville is an influential business man of Cloutierville, Natchitoches Parish, La., his birth occurring in the town in which he now resides June 10, 1827, being a son of John Baptiste and Aurqra (Rachal) Charleville, the former of whom was born in St. Louis, Mo., about 1802, and the latter in Natchitoches Parish, La., in 1810. The father came to this State and parish in 1825, making the entire trip on horseback, and was here married soon after to Miss Rachal, who bore him a family of thirteen children, ten reaching maturity, and two sons and two daughters now living. The father of these children, who was a son of Joseph Charleville, a native of Tennessee, died of yellow fever in 1853, having been a farmer throughout life, leaving at the time of his death an estate valued at $25,000. His widow survives him, and has remained a widow since his death. She is now past eighty years of age, and makes her home with her son Landry. The paternal grandfather of the subject of this sketch moved from New Orleans to St. Louis, Mo., when that place contained only two houses, and near that city he subsequently died in 1849. His wife's maiden name was Victoria Verdon, and she also was a native of New Orleans. Her mother, who was a very wealthy lady, was the owner of a line of keelboats, upon which she made several trips to St. Louis, each trip occupying about three months and being devoted to carrying merchandise to that city. Her husband came to this country from France. Following is a copy of a notice of the death of Mr. Charleville's grandmother: "Died, on Friday, January 16, 1863, at 7 o'clock P. M., at the residence of her grand-daughter, Mrs. Eliza O'Flaherty, Victoria Charleville, aged eighty-two years and ten months. She died a true Christian, and was universally beloved. Mrs. Charleville was the widow of Joseph Charleville, formerly a well-known citizen, who deceased eighteen years since. She was born in St. Louis, and lived there all her life, of course, witnessing strange mutations in appearance of the city, and great changes in its social aspects and in the governments to which it has been subjected. She had seen French and Spanish lieutenant-governors, and lived under all the Presidents of the American Republic, who thus figured in its annals. She was a lady of estimable character, and leaves a numerous family of children, grand and great-grandchildren to lament her loss.'' Landry Charleville's maternal grandparents were Louis Julian and Melanie (Lavespere) Rachal, both of whom were born in the parish of Natchitoches, La. In 1837 Landry Charleville was sent to St. Louis to attend school, and there he remained a student in an establishment managed by David H. Armstrong (who afterward became a United States Senator) for one year, after which he secured a position in a store, and as early as seventeen he was doing a small grocery business in the above mentioned city. Later he resumed clerking, and thus continued until the latter part of the Mexican War, when he resigned his position and entered the United States service in the company commanded by Capt. Koskiloski. After four months' service the war closed and he was discharged at Fort Leavenworth and went back to St. Louis, where he resumed clerking. A year later he engaged in business for himself as a manufacturer of, and dealer in, clothing, and in March, 1850, he came to Coultierville, La., where he remained six months, returning at the end of that time to St. Louis, where he remained until 1853, engaged chiefly in the clothing business. In that year he returned to Cloutierville, returning once more to St. Louis the following year, where he purchased a clothing house on the corner of Washington Avenue and Third Street. In 1856 he sold out and spent a short time in Kentucky, after which he again came back to that town and opened a wholesale and retail grocery store on Broadway, in what is known as the Llewellyn Building. In the latter part of 1858 he established a grocery at Montgomery, La., the following year being spent in traveling throughout Texas and Louisiana. He again engaged in business at Montgomery, and upon the breaking out of the Civil War he entered the Confederate army in Capt. Phillip's company,

Whart Adams' cavalry, composed of Louisiana, Mississippi and Alabama men, but after the battle of Shiloh he retired from active service on account of his age and entered the Louisiana State service, occupying a position in the treasury department, where he remained until hostilities ceased. During this time he was also extensively engaged in buying and selling negroes and cotton, and after the war closed he engaged in mercantile pursuits in Cloutierville, to which his attention has since been given, much of his time being also devoted to dealing in land and live-stock. In this line he does the most extensive business in Natchitoches Parish, and his general mercantile establishment is very largely patronized. His business transactions have been attended with good results, and he is now the owner of several tracts of valuable land. Mr. Charleville was married March 4, 1850, to Miss Pauline Du Prey, who died in 1887, having borne five children, all of whom are deceased. Mr. Charleville is a Democrat, politically, and is one of the most active and enterprising business men and public-spirited citizens in this parish.

Lamy Chopin, merchant and farmer, Chopin, La. This prominent business man and influential citizen of Natchitoches Parish, was born in the parish in which he resides on February 19, 1850, being the son of J. B. and Julie (Benoist) Chopin. The father was a native of France and came to America in early manhood, locating in Natchitoches Parish, La. Both parents are now deceased. The home of Lamy Chopin has been in Natchitoches Parish nearly all his life. When twelve years of age he went to France, where he spent six years in school, and when eighteen years of age he returned to America, where he has since devoted his attention to merchandising and farming. He now owns a large general store at Chopin, a station on the Texas & Pacific Railroad, and he has been located there ever since the road was built, or for a period of about eight years. He is also the owner of the old Chopin plantation, which contains 4,000 acres, and upon which the town of Chopin is built. It was formerly the McAlpine plantation, and upon it Mrs. Harriet Beecher Stowe spent some time while writing her famous novel, Uncle

Tom's Cabin. Mr. Chopin was married on January 16, 1878, to Miss Cora Henry, daughter of Hon. Joseph Henry, of Natchitoches Parish. They have one child, a daughter, named Eugenie. Mr. Chopin and wife are consistent members of the Catholic Church, and in politics the former is a Democrat. He has served as a member of the board of police jurors of his parish for three years, from 1877 to 1880, and from 1885 he has been postmaster of his town which is called Chopin. Mr. Chopin has made substantial improvements upon the old plantation, and he now has a beautiful and comfortable home. He is a well-informed man and one who possesses an excellent capacity for business. He and wife rank among the best citizens of the parish.

Anglo P. Cockfield is a prominent young planter and stockraiser of the parish of Natchitoches, his home being on Beulah plantation, ten miles southeast of the city of Natchitoches, but his birth occurred in Williamsburg County, S. C., January 5, 1852, being a son of William H. and Hannah Cockfield, they, as well as their parents, being also born in that State. Both paternally and maternally, Mr. Cockfield is of Irish descent, was one of a family of nine children born to his parents, there being one son and four daughters now living, the names in the order of their birth being as follows: Letitia Everett, Ladson Hartley (deceased), Justin Compere (deceased), Anglo Puritan, Tustin Level, Belton Theodocia, Lily Corinne, and William Ebeneezer Joseph (deceased). The father of these children, who was a farmer by occupation, died in 1880, but the mother is still living, her home being in Williamsburg County, S. C. The subject of this sketch spent his boyhood, youth and first years of his manhood in his native county upon his father's farm, but on July 17, 1877, left home for the purpose of coming to Natchitoches Parish, La., his arrival here dating the 23d day of the same month. He at once purchased the farm he now occupies, which is situated ten miles south of Natchitoches, and which contains 629 acres, and is known as Beulah plantation. It is well improved with good residence, and is one of the largest and best plantations in the parish. In 1887 he erected

a fine large barn, and his property is otherwise admirably improved with good fences and thirteen cabins, and 300 acres are in good cultivation. It is bounded on the east by Red River, and is one of the highest plantations between Monette Ferry and Grand Ecore. Mr. Cockfield is the owner of two other good plantations, one of 260 acres on Cane River, and one that contains about 400 acres on Little River, two other smaller tracts being also in his possession, and these together with the plantation on which he lives, amount to 1,700 acres. Some idea of his industry and good management can be gathered when the fact is known that he brought with him from South Carolina less than $400. He has worked hard and is now one of the leading planters of the parish. Notwithstanding the amount of hard labor he has performed, he is well preserved and would readily pass for a man ten years his junior. His marriage, which took place February 23, 1883, was to Miss Marcia Cockfield of this parish, and to them four children have been born: Taney Autun, Le Roy Akron, Moma Eble, and an infant son, Stanley Forno. The eldest child is dead. Upon his home plantation Mr. Cockfield is conducting a first-class store, in which is kept all kinds of plantation supplies, and here also a post-office has been established, which has been named Roy, in honor of his eldest son, and of which he is postmaster. He is a member of the Masonic order, and in politics is a devoted Democrat. He is an enterprising young man and possesses in an eminent degree, those qualities which are necessary to success. He and his wife have a large circle of friends, by whom they are very highly respected.

J. H. Cosgrove, editor and proprietor of the Democratic Review, at Natchitoches, owes his nativity to Claiborne Parish, La., his birth occurring on April 29, 1842, and is the son of Hugh Cosgrove, who was born in County Cavan, Ireland, in 1796, and who died in California in 1864. The elder Cosgrove came to the United States in 1835, and from 1836 to 1841 he engaged in the drug business in New York City. From there he moved to Minden, La., and was there engaged in the same business until 1844, when he came to Natchitoches.

Here he carried on the same business until 1855, when he went to California. His wife, whose maiden name was Miss Mary Ann Burke, is of Irish ancestry, and was born in Montreal, Canada. She now resides in Terrell, Tex. Her father, Peter Burke, was born in County Mayo, Ireland, and was the third son of Sir Walter Burke. Peter Burke died not long ago when in the one hundredth year of his age. In the fall of 1854 J. H. Cosgrove entered the Texas Masonic College, at Larissa, Tex., a Cumberland Presbyterian school, and graduated from the same in July, 1857. He then returned to Natchitoches and on September 1 of that year he entered the mercantile house of Walmsley, Carver & Co., remaining with the same until August, 1860, when he went to Gilmer, Tex. There he had charge of the office and books of Wright & Beasley until April 19, 1861, when he enlisted as a private in Richardson's Cavalry Company, from Marshall, Tex., Confederate States Army. He was afterward transferred to Company C, Fourth Texas Infantry, Hood's Brigade, Army of Northern Virginia, and served in all the engagements of that army from May, 1863, to the close of the war. He was three times wounded. He was a brave, true soldier, and served the Confederacy faithfully and well. He was married on February 14, 1867, to Miss Julia A. Johnson, a native of Natchitoches, who was educated at the Mansfield Female College, and who is one of the leading women of this point. Five children are the fruits of this union, viz.: Louise, born on November 9, 1872; Burdette, born June 7, 1875; Annie, born November 12, 1877; Eddie Burke, born January 13, 1882. From 1874 to 1882 Mr. Cosgrove edited, owned and published the People's Vindicator, and since 1888 he has been publishing the Democratic Review. Under his efficient management the paper has proved a decided success, and its editorial policy has been directed by a man of good judgment. Its reputation as a representative journal of this portion of the State is well established. In politics Mr. Cosgrove is a Democrat of the liberal school, and believes in protection. In 1880 he was appointed brigadier-general by Gov. L. A. Wiltz, of the Fifth Special Military District of Louisiana, and

in 1882 he was made a Mason at Natchitoches Lodge No. 38. He has held only two civil offices, first as printer of the Constitutional Convention in 1879, and in December of the same year he was elected a member of the Lower House of the Louisiana Assembly. He was chairman of the committee on public printing, also acting chairman of the committee on New Orleans City affairs, and was a member of the committee on ways and means. As a soldier Mr. Cosgrove was gallant, and always found in the discharge of his duties, and as a legislator he took a leading part. In fact his superior intelligence and extended knowledge of men and affairs is recognized by all, and he is one of the leading men of the State.

Dr. Penn Crain. Prominent among the successful professional men of Natchitoches Parish is the subject of this sketch, born in the parish of Rapides, July 4, 1838, the son of Col. Robert A. and Elizabeth (Wood) Crain, the former a native of Fauquier County, Va., and the latter of Charles County, Md. Only three of the eight children are now living, and residing in this State. Col. Crain's principal occupation through life was that of a planter. He emigrated to Louisiana in 1817, after which he served as colonel by appointment from the governor of the State. He located in Bayou Rapides, residing there until his death, which occurred September 27, 1852. Being one of the honored and law-abiding citizens of this State, he was chosen legislator for one or two terms. He and his wife were members of the Episcopal Church. Dr. Crain received his early-education in Virginia. He served in the Confederate army during the entire war. He then re-entered the medical department of the University of Louisiana, where he graduated, and received his diploma in 1866, commencing his practice in North Louisiana May 14, 1878. He was married to Mrs. Virginia Terrett, nee Sompayrac, she having three children: George A., James P. and Burdett A., by her first husband, and to this union were born two sons, Robert A. and Alfred P. Socially Dr. Crain is a member of the K. of P., and is also an active member of the State Medical Association. His wife is a member of the Episcopal Church.

Charles Frederick Crockett, operator and station agent of the Texas & Pacific Railroad at Robeline, La., was born in the province of New Brunswick, Canada, April 13, 1860, and his parents, William and Mary (Deniston) Crockett, were natives, respectively, of Ireland and Canada. The father died in 1876, but the mother is still a resident of Canada. Charles Frederick Crockett attained his growth on a farm in Canada, and received a good common school education. At the age of nineteen years he began the study of telegraphy, mastered this in due time, and at the age of twenty he was employed as operator and relief agent on the Inter-Colonial Railroad, of Canada, continuing there two years. In 1882 he was tendered a position by the Texas & Pacific Railroad, which he accepted, and he first became operator at Provencal, La. Between two and three months later he was transferred to Boyce, where he was both operator and agent until January, 1884. In that month he was transferred to Robeline, where he has been both operator and agent ever since. Mr. Crockett was married on April 25, 1883, to Miss Jennie B. Hunter, of Boyce, La., and this union has resulted in the birth of three children: Charles William, Annie Mary and Walter Henry. Annie died when fifteen months old. Mr. and Mrs. Crockett are members of the Methodist Episcopal Church. Mr. Crockett is a pleasant young gentleto-meet, and is a skillful operator.

Hon. Milton J. Cunningham, attorney at law. In giving a history of Natchitoches Parish, La., the name of Mr. Cunningham deserves honorable mention, for he has always been industrious and public-spirited, and has ever aided enterprises which tend to the interests of his section. Although just in the prime of life, he has made his way to the front ranks among the energetic attorneys of this parish, and, owing to the attention he has always paid to each minor detail of his work, and to his able management of all cases which have come under his care, he has won a wide reputation as an able, talented lawyer. He was born in what is now De Soto Parish, La., March 10, 1842, to J. H. and Ann (Buie) Cunningham, who were born in South Carolina and Mississippi in 1810 and 1812, and died in Natchitoches Parish, La., and Homer, La., in 1886 and 1850, respectively. The father was a lawyer and physician, and for a period of twenty-six years he was a member of the Natchitoches bar, being exceptionally able and talented. Hon. Milton J. Cunningham is one of twelve children born to his father's first marriage, of which family five are now living. He was educated in the schools of Homer, and in 1858 began teaching the young idea, a calling he continued to follow until 1860, when he entered the law office belonging to his father, where he remained a student of law until 1861. The opening of the Rebellion caused him to cast aside his books to enter the Confederate service, becoming a faithful soldier until the close of the war, in the Second Louisiana Infantry. He resumed the study of law after his return home, and attended a course of lectures, being admitted to the bar in January, 1866, after which he began practicing in Natchitoches, and here and in the city of New Orleans he has followed his calling ever since, being one of the leading lawyers of the State. He is a stanch Democrat in politics, and in 1872 was elected district attorney, but was counted out by the Republicans. In 1875 he was appointed district attorney of the Seventeenth Judicial District, and served about ten months, making an efficient official. In 1878 he was elected a member of the Louisiana General Assembly, and the following year a member of the Constitutional Convention. In 1879 he was elected to the State Senate for a term of four years, and while a member of that body made a faithful and able legislator. In 1884 he was elected attorney-general, and served with distinction for four years. Since 1888 he has devoted his time and attention to his practice, and besides his office here, also had one in New Orleans. He has occupied the front rank in his profession for almost a quarter of a century, and by his long practice and study his position is so well established that it is conceded by competent judges that he ranks among the highest civilians. His success at the bar has been attained rather by the force of native talent and culture than by tact. Close and attentive to business, abstemious in all his habits, laborious in research, he has never permitted the interests of his clients to suffer, and 'as he always thoroughly prepares his cases, he is rarely taken by surprise. Clients rely implicitly on his word, as well they may, and he fully deserves the reputation he has obtained among the attorneys of the South. He was married in 1866 to Miss Thalia Tharp, who died in 1872, leaving three children: Milton J., Jr., John H. and William T. In 1874 he was married to Miss Anna Peyton, of New Orleans, who died in 1878, having borne two children: Ida G. and Milton C. Mr. Cunningham's third marriage took place in 1880, his wife being Miss Cecile Hertzog, of Natchitoches, who died in 1886, a family of four children having been born to her union with Mr. Cunningham: Sidney, Ivy, Charlotte and Laura.

Mrs. M. E. Curry resides on a beautiful and valuable plantation of 1,500 acres, situated twenty-two miles southeast of Natchitoches, on the Red River. She was born in the southeastern part of Missouri, being a daughter of Judge John F. Ross, who was a Kentuckian by birth, his wife, whose maiden name was Anna Lee, being also a native of the Blue-Grass State. Mrs. Curry was reared to womanhood in the State of her birth, the most of her education being also acquired there, and for some time she was an attendant of St. Vincent's Convent, where she acquired a thorough education. In 1876 she came to Louisiana, and after spending two years in Rapides Parish she came to Natchitoches Parish, where, in 1878, she was united in marriage to Augustus I. Curry, a South Carolinian by birth, who came to this parish in his boyhood. He was a gentleman who possessed many worthy traits of character, and his death, which occurred in 1882, was lamented by all. He left no children. During her entire married life, and also her widowhood, Mrs. Curry has resided upon the same farm. Her home is one of the most beautiful country seats in the parish, and is situated on the west bank of Red River, which at this point forms a crescent. In front of her residence is a beautiful natural grove, and this, together with artificial improvements, makes it a most desirable place at which to live. Mrs. Curry is an

intelligent and cultured lady, and is very highly respected and esteemed by her numerous acquaintances and friends.

Lambert Daniel, merchant, Robeline, La. Mr. Daniel is one of the most successful merchants in Natchitoches Parish, and his thrift, enterprise and ability have procured for him the success that always attends those virtues. He was originally from Alabama, his birth occurring in Monroe County September 14, 1855, and is a son of Joseph L. and Amanda M. (Daily) Daniel, both natives of that State. The parents were married December 8, 1852, and their union was blessed by the birth of eight children, five of whom were sons, and all of whom are living. The youngest is now seventeen years of age. They are named as follows: Josephine I., Lambert, Emma A., John P., Laura A., Larkin O., Lee and Anson W. The mother of these children died on October 16, 1884, and their father is a resident of Moss Point, Jackson County, Miss. Lambert Daniel spent his early days in his native county, and when fourteen years of age he accompanied his parents to Sabine Parish, La., where he assisted on the farm. It not having been his good fortune to have the advantages of school privileges during his boyhood, he, when twenty years of age, with money he had earned himself, went to Many, Sabine Parish, La., and there entered a private school taught by Prof. Packer. There he pursued his studies about three months, after which he returned home, and for three years he assisted his father and brothers to cultivate the farm. About the time he returned home he purchased a small farm in the vicinity of the old home place, and during the three years he was at home he also cultivated this, and with the profits paid for the land. Not satisfied with the education that he already possessed, late in the spring of 1879 he went to Pleasant Hill, La., and there attended for three months a private school taught by Prof. T. C. Armstrong. Returning home again he next became engaged in teaching a school on the Sabine River, in Sabine Parish, La., where he remained five months, and gave up this position to enter the employ of Mr. J. D. Stille, of Many, La., as salesman, collector and book-keeper. This gave him a good knowledge of business. In January, 1882, he resigned his position, sold his farm, and took the money he had thus received to invest in merchandise for himself at Robeline, La. He has conducted a general store at that place ever since, and he is now the leading merchant of the town. Beginning at the start in a small way, his business has grown until it has reached mammoth proportions. His stock when he began consisted only of groceries, hardware and crockery. In addition to this he carries a line of dry goods, clothing, boots and shoes, hats and caps, furniture, stoves, saddlery, flour, wagons, agricultural implements and drugs. In fact, he has a great deal of everything necessary to the domestic economy of this section that money can buy. His present building, which he erected in 1889, is a two-story, iron-roofed structure, 50x75 feet. Mr. Daniel is a courteous and accommodating man, and has built up a large patronage. He is widely known, not only as a successful business man, but as an upright, honorable citizen. Besides his business interests at Robeline he owns a one-half interest in a general store at Marthaville, La. Mr. Daniel was married on March 15, 1882, to Miss Caroline Gay, of Many, Sabine Parish, La., and they have had four children, all now deceased. Mr. Daniel is a stanch Democrat, politically, and in 1885 he was elected mayor of Robeline, and re-elected to the same position in 1888, serving two terms of one year each. While holding that position he discharged his official duties in a manner which gave entire satisfaction to the public and in a manner which won for him the confidence of all. Mr. Daniel is pre-eminently a self-made man, having started for himself with only a pair of willing hands and a mental capacity to direct them, and with these gifts he has made his way in life, reaching a point of substantiality and influence of which any man might be proud. He has a large circle of warm friends by whom he is highly respected and esteemed. His business amounts to about $50,000 per annum. He ships each year 1,200 to 1,500 bales of cotton and employs three men.

Lark O. Daniel, attorney, Robeline, La. Mr. Daniel is a young legal practitioner, who is steadily and surely making his way to the front in his profession of law, and as a prominent and useful citizen. He is well versed in law, and has all the attributes essential to a successful career at the bar and in public. He owes his nativity to Monroe County, Ala., born March 16, 1866, and is the son of Joseph L. and Amanda (Daily) Daniel, a more extensive mention of whom is made elsewhere in this work. When Lark O. Daniel was six years of age his parents removed to the State of Louisiana, and located at Many, Sabine Parish, where he was reared to mature years, and where he received his early education. At sixteen years of age he took up the vocation of a teacher, as a temporary pursuit, and he taught three terms, all in Sabine Parish. About the time he began teaching he also entered upon the study of law, and during the time he was in the school-room, he spent the leisure time he had in the evenings in this study. His preceptor during the first two years was Hon. J. Fisher, late State senator from the Fourth District. He subsequently pursued his legal studies under the direction of Judge D. Pierson, of Natchitoches, and in August, 1887, he was admitted to the bar at Shreveport. Meanwhile, in 1884, he had entered upon the practice of law at Robeline, and while his familiarity with the law at that time fully entitled him to admission to the bar, he could not legally be admitted on account of his age. He has been engaged in the active practice of his profession at Robeline ever since, but aside from this he is also deep in merchandising, having won for himself a widespread reputation as a merchant. Although he began on a comparatively small scale in merchandising four years ago, his business has assumed mammoth proportions, all the result of his agreeable manners and the confidence that the people have in him. His business amounts annually to about $60,000, and his trade extends over a large part of Louisiana, Texas and Arkansas. Mr. Daniel was married on February 11, 1886, to Miss Mary F. Collier, of Shreveport, La. In politics Mr. Daniel is a Democrat. He takes a great interest in local politics, and his influence for his party is not only exerted in its private councils but also upon the stump.

He is a young man whose brilliancy, push and progressiveness can not but enable him to achieve marked success. Though he is now but twenty-four years of age he has already won a place in legal circles, and in the commercial world of which any man might be proud.

E. V. Deblieux, one of the foremost planters and wide-awake merchants of Natchitoches, was born in this city January 11, 1820, being the son of Alexander L. and Euphrosine (Tauzin) Deblieux. His father was a Frenchman by birth, but was raised in this country, coming when eleven years old to Augusta, Ga., remaining in that State until 1800, when he immigrated to Louisiana. In 1815 he was first sergeant in a muster roll, which marched to New Orleans. After the disbandment of this organization he returned home and entered into the mercantile business, receiving, in the meanwhile, an appointment to the United States Mail Department, which he held for four years. He made a visit to France in 1835. On his return to America he again settled in New Orleans, opening a commission business there, which he conducted for two years, when he returned to Natchitoches, remaining here till his death in 1869. To him and wife (who was also a native of Louisiana) were born six children, two of whom are living and reside in Natchitoches Parish. The mother of this family died in 1842. The senior Deblieux was actively alive to the growth of his parish, being particularly interested in the upbuilding of churches, schools, and society in general. He and his wife were believers in and worshipers of the the Catholic faith. The principal of this sketch received his early training in France and Louisiana, and being left to his own resources, in 1837 he settled upon an 800-acre plantation, and is now the owner of 600 acres, and engaged in planting and merchandising. May 22, 1849, he married Aurora Metoyer, of Louisiana, who died September 25, 1853, leaving to his care the following family: Alexander L. and Aurora (deceased). He was again married, in 1855, to Julie Prudhomme, also of Louisiana, and to this marriage have been born nine children, eight of whom are living: Marie (deceased), Leon, Camille, Jefferson, Stella, Ma-

tilda Valery, Julie and Lestan. His second wife died January 18, 1889, in full communion with the Catholic Church. Alexander Louis Deblieux was commissioned auctioneer in 1823 and 1825, quartermaster of the Eighteenth regiment of militia in 1825, and postmaster at Natchitoches in 1818. E. V. Deblieux is a veteran of the Mexican War, in which he served as second lieutenant.

Marcus L. Dismukes, attorney at law, Natchitoches, La. Mr. Dismukes is a leading member of the bar of Natchitoches Parish, and a member of the firm of Jack & Dismukes. He was born in Shelby County, Tenn., on January 26, 1851, and is a son of Thomas H. and Mary Jane (Hager) Dismukes, natives of the Old Dominion, the father born in 1802 and the mother in 1812. The parents moved to Arkansas in 1854, and settled in Columbia County, where the father carried on agricultural pursuits for some time. He died in Fayette County, of that State, in 1879, but his widow is still living and makes her home at Louisville, Ark. Marcus L. Dismukes, the fifth of ten children born to the above union, seven of whom are still living, received his education in the common schools and under the tuition of Prof. William C. Jack, who is one of the most scholarly men of this country. Mr. Dismukes began teaching at the age of nineteen years and continued that occupation until 1877, when he came Natchitoches. Here he began the study of law in the office of William H. Jack, and was admitted to the bar in 1879. He began practicing his profession here in 1881, and in the following year formed a law partnership with William H. Jack which now continues. He has been successful from the very beginning and now ranks among the prominent lawyers of Natchitoches Parish, or this part of the State. In politics he adheres to the Democratic party. Mr. Dismukes was married in 1880, to Miss Katie C. Jack, a native of Arkansas, born in 1857, and the daughter of Prof. W. C. and Catherine (Welborn) Jack. To Mr. and Mrs. Dismukes have been born four children: Mary, Ada Ruth, Marcus L., Jr. and Charles H. Mr. Dismukes is a member of the A. O. U. W., L. of H., and K. of P., Natchitoches Lodge No. 86. Jack

& Dismukes is one of the leading law firms of Northern Louisiana.

Jared S. Dixon, merchant and planter, Natchitoches, La. Among the many prominent and successful citizens of Natchitoches Parish, who are not only prosperous in their business relations, but who are esteemed and respected for their many good qualities, stands the name of Jared S. Dixon. He was originally from Bossier Parish of this State, his birth occurring on May 6, 1860, and is the son of J. M. and Lizzie (Dalrymple) Dixon. The father was born in the southern part of Louisiana in 1827, and died at Franklin, La., in 1863, from the effect of wounds received while in the army. He was a member of the Third Louisiana Cavalry. The mother was a native of South Carolina, born in 1840, and died at Collinsburg, La., in 1876. Of the two children born to their union, Jared Dixon is the elder in order of birth. He received a good education in the common and public schools. In 1885 Mr. Dixon came to this portion of Natchitoches and began opening a plantation eleven miles northwest of this city. He established his store in 1886. He now cultivates about 1,000 acres of land, and is making a success of agricultural pursuits as well as his mercantile business. He is a Democrat in politics, and in 1877 was instrumental in establishing Egypt post-office of which he was appointed postmaster. Egypt is now connected with Natchitoches by telephone, which was built by Mr. Dixon, in January, 1890. In 1882 he joined Rocky Mountain Lodge, K. of P., in Louisiana, and was transferred to Dixie Lodge and subsequently to Natchitoches Lodge No. 89, of which he is now a member. He is one of the substantial men of the parish.

Charles F. Dranguet, attorney, Natchitoches, La. Mr. Dranguet, one of the prominent legal lights of Natchitoches, is a native of this city, his birth occurring on April 10, 1834, and is the son of Benjamin F. and Victoria Celeste (Pauzin) Dranguet. The father was born in Rouen, Normandy, France, on April 6, 1777, and died in Natchitoches on April 6, 1837. The mother was born in the city of Natchitoches, or the port of Natchitoches, on December 25, 1795, and died here in 1871. The father came to Natchitoches from the West Indies in 1812, having gone to the latter place from France in 1794, on account of the French Revolution. By occupation he was a merchant. His marriage to Miss Pauzin took place on April 5, 1815. In the fall of 1814 he left here with a military company (although not then naturalized), to go to New Orleans, to join Gen. Jackson, and upon his arrival there he was selected by that general to guard the Crescent City. Charles F. Dranguet, the youngest of six children, only two of whom are living, first attended school in Natchitoches, and later entered the St. Vincent College, at Cape Girardeau, Mo., where he continued until 1854. He then returned home and taught school, which he limited to twelve pupils, all boys, who were well advanced. During this time he was studying law under John Blair Smith and Judge J. G. Campbell, and was admitted to the bar in 1859, after which he immediately entered upon his practice in partnership with Col. William M. Levy. This continued until the breaking out of the war, when Mr. Dranguet joined the Second Louisiana Cavalry, Confederate States Army, as a private in Company C, and about three months later was elected second lieutenant of Company D, Second Louisiana Cavalry. He served in this until the close of hostilities. Afterward he resumed the law practice, and this he has since continued. In 1871 he was appointed district attorney of what was then the Seventeenth Judicial District, by H. C. Warmoth, and in 1874 he was also appointed parish judge of Natchitoches Parish. In 1876 he was elected mayor of the city of Natchitoches, and filled that position ably and well. In politics he adheres to the Democratic party. He was married in 1859 to Miss Eliza Greneaux, a native of this parish, born in 1840, and to them were born nine children: Eliza, Benjamin F., Charles F., Jr., Laura, Lelia, Louis A., Edgar M., Stella and Oscar. Mr. Dranguet is a member of the Catholic Church, and is a representative of one of the old families of Natchitoches. The father of Mrs. Dranguet, Judge C. E. Greneaux, was born in Natchitoches in 1804, was parish judge, then clerk of the court, and was afterward appointed treasurer of the State of

Louisiana for three years, at the end of which time he was without opposition elected State treasurer. He died in Natchitoches in 1858. He was thoroughly a self-made man, and a very popular one.

J. A. Ducournau, the oldest merchant now residing in Natchitoches, was originally from France, his birth occurring on December 24, 1815, and he is the son of John B. and Mary (Rival) Ducournau, both natives of France. The father was born in 1785 and died in his native country in 1853, and the mother was born in 1793, and also died in France in 1823. From 1828 to 1845 the father was a resident of Louisiana, residing in the Crescent city and at Natchitoches. He was a well-educated man and a true French gentleman. J. A. Ducournau is the only living representative of his father's children. He was educated in France, and in 1834 emigrated to the United States, where he was for some time a resident of New Orleans. In 1839 he came to Natchitoches and the same year engaged in merchandising at the corner of Front and Church Streets, where he continued until the conflagration of 1881, when he was burned out. He then purchased his present business house on Front Street, and has since continued in business in this place, a period of over fifty years, with the exception of only a short time during the war. He has experienced all the troubles and business depressions of more than half a century, but has always been able to pay 100 cents on the dollar, which fact proves him to be one of the best and most careful business men in the South. He was united in marriage in 1849 to Miss Appoline Castenado, a native of New Orleans, and the result of this union was two children: Estelle (who was married to A. J. Planche), and J. A. D., Jr. The last named was born in Natchitoches, and educated at Spring Hill College, Alabama, and in 1881 became a member of the firm of J. A. Ducournau & Son. He was married in 1883 to Miss Lelia Sompayrac, a native of this parish. They have two children: Lucile and Louis. Mr. Ducournau, Jr., is a Democrat in politics, a member of the city council, and socially is a member of the American Legion of Honor. Our subject

is also a Democrat without question, was among the first who endeavored to secure a railroad to Natchitoches, being treasurer of the Natchitoches Railroad Construction Company, and is now treasurer of the State Normal School located here. He is a gentleman retiring in his disposition, and one who spurns notoriety. He is honest to a cent, and his word is as good as his bond.

Louis Dupleix, register of United States Land Office, Natchitoches, La. Mr. Dupleix was born in France on September 29, 1820, and is a son of Yoes and Marguerite (Lawalle) Dupleix, natives also of France, where they died at a good old age. Louis Dupleix is the third of six children, three now living, born to the union of the above worthy couple. He was educated in his native country at Dupleix Institution in Bordeaux which school was founded by his father. He came to the United States in 1841 and for a year and a half resided in New Orleans, after which he removed to LaFayette Parish, residing there about six years. In 1848 he came to Natchitoches and here he has since resided, esteemed and respected by all. While a resident of La Fayette Parish he was engaged in various occupations, teaching, merchandising and planting, and after coming to this city he still carried on merchandising and farming, carrying on the same for a year. After this for three or four years he was engaged in the newspaper business and owned the Natchitoches Union and the Natchitoches Times. Later he again returned to agricultural pursuits, continued this one year, and then embarked in the commission business in New Orleans. After this he followed farming until 1872, when he was appointed register of the United States Land Office at Natchitoches by Gen. U. S. Grant. This position he held under the administration of Grant, Hayes, Garfield and Arthur, and on May 19, 1890, he was appointed to the same position by President Harrison. Mr. Dupleix was married in 1843 to Miss Clemence Dugas, a native of La Fayette Parish, La. Her death occurred in 1886. In politics Mr. Dupleix was formerly a Whig, but is now a Republican. He is well educated, and is an upright honorable gentleman.

Thomas Jefferson Flanner has been a resident

of Natchitoches Parish, La., from his birth, which occurred March 27, 1854, and his earnest and sincere endeavor to succeed in life, especially in the occupation of farming, is well worthy the imitation of the rising generation. His father, Dr. T. J. Flanner, whose name was the same as his own, was born at Newbern, N. C., and his mother, whose maiden name was Pauline Roubien, was born in the parish of Natchitoches, La., upon the plantation now occupied by the subject of this sketch. The parents were married in 1850 and had three children as follows: Joseph, Thomas Boyce (deceased) and Thomas Jefferson. The father of these children died in the latter part of 1853, when the foul epidemic of that year was at its height. Dr. Flanner sacrificed his life at his post of duty a few months before the subject of this sketch was born. His widow survives him and makes her home with her youngest son, Thomas Jefferson. The latter spent his early life in his native town of Natchitoches, in the schools of which he received his early education. At the age of eleven he accompanied his mother to New Orleans, where he spent six months in a Jesuit college, after which he entered Springhill College, another Jesuit institution, which he attended one year. At the age of thirteen years he made a pleasure trip to Europe, remaining abroad for some six months, after which he returned to America and entered Georgetown College of the District of Columbia, remaining in the same for one year. He then completed a course in the commercial college of J. G. Lord, of New Orleans, after which he took a course in book-keeping in Soule Commercial College of the same city. For one year following this he was employed as book-keeper in a wholesale and retail hat house, and for six months clerked in a crockery establishment, both of New Orleans. He was then in the employ of an exchange broker a short time, after which he engaged in the pursuit of produce broker, continuing thus six months. In 1877 he returned to the parish of Natchitoches and took charge of the Reform plantation, sixteen miles southeast of Natchitoches, which he subsequently purchased and which he occupied and managed

ever since. It is situated on both the Breville Bayou and Texas & Pacific Railroad and Cane River and the Natchitoches Railroad, and its improvements are of the best, being one of the most complete in this respect of any plantation on the river, for over $10,000 worth of improvements have been put upon it in the last four years. It is well stocked with the best breeds of horses and cattle, among the former there being some excellent specimens of thoroughbred trotting horses and among the latter some magnificent specimens of the Jersey and Devonshire varieties. Mr. Flanner was married in 1880 to Miss Daisy Sers, who was also born in Natchitoches Parish. They have had five children, as follows; Josephine, Thomas J., Leo, Ricardo and Eugene of whom Thomas J., Leo and Ricardo, are dead. Mr. Flanner is a member of the K. of P. order and the A. L. of H., and in his political views is a conservative Democrat. In 1888 he was offered the nomination by his party for the State Legislature, and although this would have been equivalent to an election, he declined. He is a shrewd, intelligent, broadminded man who possesses great force of character, and much executive ability, and his views on political questions, as well as all the popular topics of the day, are considered sound. He is recognized throughout this section of the State as a man whose opinions are worthy the attention and consideration of all. He is strongly opposed to ring rule and corruption in every form, and by putting forth his greatest efforts against all such he has wielded a powerful influence for good. He is well known throughout this section of the State and the confidence and respect of all citizens are his.

Valery Gaiennie, deceased, owned one of the largest and best farms in Natchitoches Parish. He was born in New Orleans, June 2, 1816, and removed to this parish in 1835, at the age of nineteen, with his father, Gen. Francois Gaiennie, adjutant-general of Louisiana Militia, where he continued his farming pursuit. January 27, 1843, Miss Heloise Metoyer, a native of this parish and daughter of Benjamin and Aurora (Lambre) Metoyer, became his wife, their union being blessed by the following children: Amanda, Mathilda, Denis, Louise, Aurora, Heloise, Emeline and Valery, the third and last being deceased. As he is one of the representative citizens of this parish he was nominated to the office of police jury (before the war of 1861, an office of honor without salary). He died April 1, 1877, leaving a sorrowing family and many warm friends to mourn their loss. His widow is a very energetic woman, and after his demise undertook the management of the plantation, and has been very successful, now owning 700 acres of land, 250 acres under cultivation, and a farm well stocked. Her grandfather came to Louisiana at the time the French took possession, they being among the pioneers of the State. The family are all members of the Catholic Church.

E. J. Gamble, merchant and planter, of St. Maurice, La., is an excellent example of what can be accomplished through energy and perseverance, for he has won his way to his present position through his own unaided efforts. He was born in White County, Tenn., December 13, 1852, to Charles R. and Emily F. (Cameron) Gamble, the former of whom was born at Meigs County, Tenn., in 1829, and died at Sparta, Tenn., in 1859. His wife first saw the light of day in White County, Tenn., in 1834, and is now making her home in Putnam County, Tenn. E. J. Gamble is the eldest of their four children, two being now alive; was reared to the arduous duties of the farm, but was given the advantages of the common public schools, later completing his education, and spending two years at Chatata Seminary, in Tennessee, where he made the best of his opportunities. He became self-supporting at the age of thirteen years, but continued to earn his own living in Tennessee until 1873, when he came to Louisiana upon a borrowed capital of $45, settling in Natchitoches Parish, where he has since made his home. He is the owner of a good plantation in Ward 4, and has under cultivation 275 acres, but the most of his attention is given to general merchandising, at St. Maurice, his establishment being opened to the public in 1886. It is excellently managed, is well fitted up and has an extensive and lucrative trade. He has truly been the architect of his own fortune, and is

now worth about $22,000, all of which has been earned by good business ability, industry and far-sightedness. He was appointed postmaster of St. Maurice, in 1886, and is still filling the position in a very satisfactory manner. His marriage took place in 1875, and was to Miss Anna K. Harrison, who was born in Caldwell Parish, La., in the month of January, 1856, and has borne her husband four children: Harry P., Emma J., Sarah S. and E. Lillian. Mr. Gamble is a Democrat in politics and is one of the enterprising residents of the parish.

Louis B. Gay, dealer in wines, liquors and cigars, is a native of Sabine Parish, La., born January 22, 1855, son of Louis B. and Elizabeth (Nash) Gay, the birth of the former occurring in Georgia, and his death in Sabine Parish, where his mother also died. The latter's father, Valentine Nash, was one of the old settlers of Sabine Parish, and has now attained to the advanced age of ninety-five years, being one of the most highly esteemed residents in this section. Owing to the early death of his parents Mr. Gay was reared by his grandfather, Nash, and was given the advantages of the common schools in his youth. In 1880 he started out for himself, and opened a general mercantile establishment at Many, La., being in partnership with his brother, the firm name being L. B. and F. C. Gay. In 1881 they removed to Robeline, and here continued their business, taking A. H. Hogue as a partner, the name of the firm being Hogue & Gay Bros. After remaining associated for two years they dissolved partnership, and for five years Mr. Gay has followed his present calling, at which he is doing well. He keeps a large and excellent line of goods, and his house is at all times orderly and quiet. In 1880 his marriage with Miss Lulu Fox was celebrated, she being a native of Alexandria, La., and an intelligent and pleasant lady. Their family consists of four children, whose names are as follows: Lafayette, Louis B., Nena and Howard. As a Democrat Mr. Gay has always supported the men and measures of that party, and socially he belongs to Natchitoches Lodge No. 89, of the A. F. & A. M., and also belongs to the K. of P.

Thomas Gregory, general merchant, Provencal, La. Mr. Gregory is one of the influential citizens of Provencal. He comes of a long line of Virginian ancestors, his father, Richard C. Gregory, and his grandfather, also Richard C. Gregory, were both natives of the Old Dominion. The father was born in Lunenburg County and was married in about 1835 to Miss Martha Hamlin, a native of Nottoway County, Va. Her father, John Hamlin, was a native of Virginia. Mrs. R. C. Gregory is a sister of the late Dr. Charles Hamlin, of Natchitoches, La. The Gregorys were originally from England and the Hamlins from Wales. Of the nine children born to Richard C. and Martha (Hamlin) Gregory, four sons and three daughters are now living. The names of the children in the order of their births are as follows: Mary, Octavia, Thomas, Agnes, Richard W., Charles, William S., Mattie and Plummer. Those deceased are Mary and Charles. The parents of these children are aged respectively eighty and seventy-six years, and both are still living, residing in Lunenburg County, Va. Thomas Gregory was born in Lunenburg County, Va., May 3, 1842, was reared in Lunenburg and Nottoway Counties, and from the age of seven to nineteen years he attended the best schools and academies of those counties. He prepared himself for the University of Virginia, which he intended to enter, but by the time he was fully prepared the Civil War had broken out and he threw aside his books, resigned his hopes for a collegiate education and entered the service of the Confederate army, enlisting in Company G, Eighteenth Virginia Regiment, Gen. Pickett's brigade, of the celebrated Pickett's division A. N. Va., known as the Nottoway Grays, in 1861. Out of the 105 men which composed his company but one escaped being either killed or wounded. Mr. Gregory served in the first battle of Manassas, battle of Gaines' Mill, Frazier's Farm, Seven Pines, the second battle of Manassas, and the battle of South. Mountain or Boonsboro, Md., the last being on September 14, 1862. There he was severely wounded, and upon recovering he was transferred to the commissary department, in which he served at Blackstone, Va., until the end of the war. He then re-

turned home and gave his attention to farming, although during a portion of the time was connected with the sheriff's office of Lunenburg County. In 1870 he removed to Yazoo County, Miss., where he resided until 1880, being engaged as a school teacher, book-keeper, and as the partner of Col. R. M. Johnson, in mercantile pursuits. In 1880 he came to Louisiana and located in the parish of Natchitoches. In 1881 he formed a partnership with J. H. Stephens, in merchandising at Provencal, and the firm continued for nine years or until December 31, 1889. They founded the town of Provencal, and so long as they were in business there they were its principal merchants. In politics he is a Democrat, and is one of the prominent men of Provencal, having the respect and confidence of all.

Charles E. Greneaux is a prosperous and successful general merchant of the city of Natchitoches, and as he was born here on June 11, 1860, and here has spent his life, his many admirable qualities are known and appreciated, and his reputation as a man of business has remained untarnished. His parents, L. A. and Amelia (Lemee) Greneaux, were born in Natchitoches, La., in 1835 and 1837, respectively, the former's death occurring in New Orleans, La., in 1861. His grandfather, Judge C. E. Greneaux, was a native of Louisiana, who was at one time State treasurer of Louisiana, and an able and talented man. He died in Natchitoches about 1858, at a ripe old age. Charles E. Greneaux is the younger of two sons born to his parents, and is in every sense of the term a self-made and self-educated man. In January, 1881, he began the general mercantile business in this city, and as he conducts affairs on strictly honorable principles, and keeps a first-class establishment, he has built up a trade that extends throughout the surrounding country. He has always been prominent in the affairs of the parish, and on the Democratic ticket, of which he has long been a supporter. He was elected to the office of secretary and treasurer of the city of Natchitoches in 1888, and discharged his duties with faithfulness and undoubted ability. He is one of the directors of the Red River Ledge Company, interested in the Cotton Seed Oil Mill and the Bank of Natchitoches, and at all times gives the support of influence and money to enterprises which he considers worthy and that he thinks will benefit his section. He is captain of a company of Natchitoches State Militia, and he and his most estimable wife are worthy members of the Catholic Church. She was formerly Miss D. M. Piper, who was born in Louisiana in 1858, and to her union with Mr. Greneaux two children have been born: Alma and Irma.

Joseph Henry. Of the many foreigners who emigrated to this country, none is more worthy of mention than the above named gentleman. He was born in county Londonderry, Ireland, January 24, 1828, his parents, John and Martha (Criswell) Henry, being also natives of the Emerald Isle. They were married in 1826, were the parents of seven children, of which our subject is the only one now living. His father was very well educated, having graduated from Dublin University, Ireland, and emigrated to New York in 1839, coming from there to Texas in 1841, where he died shortly after, his widow following him in 1879. They were both members of the Cumberland Presbyterian Church. Joseph Henry was educated at a private school, and at the age of fifteen years began clerking for a firm in Natchitoches, remaining with them until 1855, when he began business for himself with a stock of $10,000, and in 1858 he sold out, his stock being valued at that time at $30,000. Later he turned his attention to farming, has been very successful, and now owns 4,000 acres of good land, of which 2,000 acres are under cultivation. His farms are well stocked; contain three cotton-gins and mills, and all the latest improvements. January 22, 1856, he was united in wedlock with Miss Ausita Roubieu, a native of this State, and a lady of considerable wealth, born January 30, 1832. Their union has been blessed with four children: Joseph, Cora, John H. and Samuel J., all living and residing in this parish. During the late unpleasantness between the North and the South he enlisted as a private in Company B, Second Louisiana Cavalry, under the command of Gen. Taylor and Col. W. G. Vinson, participating in the battles of Frankland, La., and Henderson Hill (where he was captured, taken to New Orleans, held there four months and then exchanged). Before the war he was considered quite wealthy, but on returning home, found not only his home destroyed, but himself in debt $18,000, which by hard work he has managed to pay, and also to accumulate his present fortune. October 15, 1866, he was called upon to mourn the loss of his wife, and January 19, 1869, he took for his second wife Miss Eugenie Chapin, also a native of Louisiana. He and his family are worthy members of the Catholic Church, is one of the most influential citizens of this parish and was chosen Senator of his State. He is at present known to be one of the largest taxpayers of this parish, and has settled on each one of his children a large plantation.

J. C. Henry, a prosperous planter of Natchitoches Parish, was born in this parish December 9, 1859, his father being Joseph Henry, who was born in county Londonderry, Ireland, January 24, 1828. See sketch of father). Our subject, after attaining his majority, began the world for himself by settling on a plantation of 150 acres, 100 of which were under cultivation, and by his indomitable will is now the possessor of 750 acres, 450 being thoroughly cultivated and stocked, and in connection with these is the owner of a gin and grist-mill plant equipped with all the modern improvements. In 1884 he was married to Emeline Gaiennie, a native of Louisiana, and to them have been born five children: Martha C. (deceased), Mable, Bessie, Cora (deceased), and Joseph H. Socially he affiliates with the K. of P. lodge; officially holds the office of justice of the peace, and is identified with the school board of Ward 4. In religion, he and family are communicants of the Catholic Church, and he is a member of the Farmers' Alliance, being president of Breazeale Union.

John H. Henry, a prominent young business man of Derry, Natchitoches Parish, La., was born in the city of Natchitoches on July 18, 1862, and is the son of Hon. Joseph Henry of the same parish (see biography). His boyhood was spent in his native town, and at twelve years of age he entered the Abingdon Male Academy of Virginia, which he attended three years. At the age of sixteen he entered the St. Louis University, a Jesuit institution, which he attended three years, and from which he graduated with honors at the age of twenty. Returning home he was, for a short time, engaged at farming with his father, and in October, 1883, he went to New Orleans, where he entered the employ of the firm of R. M. Walmsley & Co., cotton factors and commission merchants. He continued in the employ of this firm eighteen months and there laid the foundation for a good business education. In 1884, desiring to engage in a pursuit more agreeable to his health, he resigned the position and again returned to his home, carrying with him a fine recommendation from his employer Mr. Walmsley. He was at this time about twenty-one years of age, and upon the aniversary of his twenty-first birthday his father presented him with a plantation, which is located on Red River, in Ward 4, which was then valued at $5,000 and which he still owns. For three years following this he was engaged in farming in connection with his father. In February, 1889, he and his father established a general store at Derry, Natchitoches Parish, and our subject has ever since given his attention to its management. He carries a $4,000 stock of plantation supplies, and enjoys a very large patronage. Mr. Henry is a member of the Catholic Church, and in politics he is Democratic. He is a young man of good habits, and though his career has not been long he has the respect and esteem of all. By a judicious management of his father's present, he has increased his possessions until it is now double what it was. He possesses a courteous and accommodating manner, and is a gentleman highly popular with all classes.

James H. Hill, of the firm of Hill & Jones, dealers in machinery, and agents for life, fire and accident insurance, also dealers in real estate, is a native of Spaulding County, Ga., his birth occurring May 15, 1843. His parents, John G. and Emily (Lake) Hill, are natives of Georgia also, the father born in 1812, and the mother in 1818. By occupation the father was a life-long merchant, and was commonly known as "Black Jack Hill." He was a Mason of high rank, and one of the leading men of Georgia. He was one of the first settlers of Griffin, Ga., and the principal street in that city bears his name. He died beloved and honored, in his native State in 1852. The inscription upon his tombstone expresses the whole story—"A good man." The mother died in 1849. James H. Hill, the fifth of seven children, three of whom are now living, received his primary education in the common schools, and later attended Marshall College, Georgia. He came to Louisiana in 1858, located in De Soto Parish, and there continued until the breaking out of the war, when he joined the Army of Northern Virginia, under Gens. Lee and Jackson, and continued with this until the close of hostilities. He was captured only three days before the final surrender, and released in June, 1865. Returning to Natchitoches Parish after the war he embarked in the receiving, forwarding and wholesale grocery business, at Grand Coteau, La., which business was successfully conducted for six years, when he purchased a plantation on Red River, with a view of making a fortune out of cotton, at 25 cents a pound. This he continued for ten years, but the fortune came not. Then he embarked in the merchandising business, and recognizing the great need of improved machinery in farming, undertook to introduce them in his locality. In this he was successful. He abandoned farming in 1879, and engaged in his present occupation, in the meantime establishing the largest commercial house ever opened in Robeline. This, however, proved unsuccessful, being established in 1883, and closed in 1887. Since the last-named year Mr. Hill has been representing the great Gullet Gin Company, of Amite City, La., as traveling salesman, and through his influence said company has been handling all lines of machinery. In four years' sales this company has not lost over one per cent in bad debts, through the sales made by Mr. Hill. The firm of Hill & Jones now represents the great Gullett Gin Company, of Louisiana; the Mutual Life, of New York, and the following five insurance companies of New Orleans: Mechanic's & Trader's, Mutual, Sun, Crescent and the Home. The Red River Hedge Company, organized September 1, 1890, at Natchitoches, unanimously elected Mr. Hill as general manager of that company, contrary to his wishes, on account of so much other business. In politics Mr. Hill has been a life-long Democrat, and in 1885 declined the office of clerk of the Eleventh District Court, at the hands of Gov. S. D. McEnery, on account of the death of Clerk G. W. Kearney. Mr. Hill is at present a member of the parish school board, and for about five years was a member of the jury commission of the parish of Natchitoches, appointed by Judge D. Pierson. Mr. Hill is one of the best business men in this section. He was married in 1868, to Miss Mary R. Hyams, daughter of Col. Samuel M. and Emily (Prudhomme) Hyams, and niece of Ex-Gov. Hyams. To Mr. and Mrs. Hill were born nine children: Rosa, Samuel H., Adeline S., Bertha L., Cora L., James H., Eswell, Flowers and Matilda. Samuel H. is not twenty years of age, and is book-keeper in one of the largest wholesale houses in Shreveport, viz.: N. Gegg & Son. Miss Rosa is a graduate of the State Normal School, and is now one of the most successful teachers in the parish. Mr. Hill has been a Mason for twenty-five years, and is a member of Phœnix Lodge No. 38. He is also a member of the A. L. of H. and Natchitoches Lodge No. 89, of K. of P. He is one of the leading men of this part of Louisiana.

William R. Hollingsworth. The mercantile interests of this section have for some time been ably represented by Mr. Hollingsworth, who has also been engaged in conducting a plantation. General merchandising, of course, necessitates the carrying of a varied assortment of goods, and Mr. Hollingsworth carries a stock, the variety of which can not fail to satisfy every want of his patrons. He was born in De Soto Parish, of this State, October 15, 1856, being a son of W. W. and Sarah (McCracken) Hollingsworth, both Alabamians, the former dying in De Soto Parish during the war, his widow still surviving him, being a resident of Alabama. William R. is their only child, and during his boyhood he was given a common-school education, acquiring a thorough knowledge of the common branches. In 1874 he began to make his own way in the world, and two years later came to Natchitoches Parish, and in addition to planting, opened a mercantile establishment.

In January, 1890, he removed to his present place of business, and has since done exceptionally well in both his callings. On June 1, 1889, he formed a copartnership with S. E. Russ, Jr., and the firm has since been known as Russ & Hollingsworth. They have under their supervision about 1,700 acres of land, and are doing an extensive and paying trade, for they are live, energetic business men. Mr. Hollingsworth was married on November 30, 1881, to Miss Anna A. Hollingsworth, and by her has two children: Clarence W. and William R. On April 18, 1890, he was appointed postmaster of Allen, which place is about sixteen miles from Natchitoches, and has held the same, although a warm Democrat in his views. As a man of business he has done remarkably well, and as his property has been earned by his own efforts, he deserves much credit for his tact and enterprise.

E. E. Honmett, one of the seven children who blessed the union of Robert E. and Celia (Barker) Honmett, was born in Red River Parish, July 24, 1849, the former a native of Maryland and the latter of Texas. The father emigrated to this State at a very early day, settled in Red River Parish, where he opened up a farm. He was justice of the peace for fifty-six years, held the office of deputy sheriff, and being one of the enterprising and progressive men in this vicinity, took an active part in the building up of churches, schools, and all enterprises for the advancement of education and society. Socially he affiliates with the Masonic order, Bethany Lodge No. 241, is a Master Mason and a member of the Farmers' Alliance. His wife dying in 1856, he married Miss Dorphey Davis; they have eleven children. Himself and wife worship at the Methodist Episcopal Church. Our subject was educated at home, and at the age of twenty-one years decided to start out on his own responsibility, with nothing but energy and good will, and by perseverance has worked his way up until he now owns 140 acres, eighty acres improved and a farm well stocked, owning some fine Short-horn cattle. November 9, 1869, he was joined in wedlock with Miss Parlee Jones, a native Mississippian, born in 1844. To this union were born eleven children, seven living: Roger H., Lucy E.,

Eugene R., Clara L., Albert T., Callie I. and Leola M. He has held the office of justice of the peace for two years, himself and wife are members of the Methodist Episcopal Church South, and he is a liberal contributor to all public enterprises for the improvement of his country.

Henry M. Hyams, clerk of the district court for the parish of Natchitoches and one of its prominent citizens, has resided here the greater portion of his life, and it is but justice to say that there is not a man in the parish who possesses greater personal worth, or who is more substantial or progressive in his views than he. He is a son of Samuel M. and Emily E. (Prudhomme) Hyams, who were born in Charleston, S. C., and Natchitoches Parish, La., respectively, and grandson of Samuel M. and Eliza (Levy) Hyams, the former having been born in London, England. The mother of our subject was the daughter of John Baptiste Prudhomme, a native of France. The parents of Henry M. were married December 1, 1836, and became the parents of the following children: Henry M., Emily E. (wife of Charles N. Prudhomme, of Natchitoches Parish), Mary R. (wife of James H. Hill, of Robeline, La.), and Jackson D. (who was married to Miss Aurore Gaiennie, with whom he now resides on the Red River in Natchitoches Parish), these being the only ones now living. Those deceased are Samuel M., John P., Eleazar L. and Kosciusko. Samuel M. Hyams, the father of the immediate subject of this sketch, accompanied his parents from South Carolina to New Orleans when about fifteen years of age, and there received a collegiate education, and studied civil engineering. For a great many years thereafter he was United States deputy surveyor, and while engaged in this capacity he surveyed almost the entire State of Louisiana, and while following that pursuit met and married Miss Prudhomme, of Natchitoches. He soon after purchased a tract of land three miles from Natchitoches, and upon it he resided for several years, converting it into a farm. He served as captain under Gen. Taylor and Col. Peyton in the Mexican War, and it was while he was thus employed that the subject of this sketch was born August 8, 1846, at the home of his uncle,

Ex-Lieut.-Gov. Henry M. Hyams, who then resided in Rapides Parish, at whose home the mother was visiting. A few years after Mr. Hyams returned from the Mexican War he removed from his farm to Natchitoches, and it continued to be his home throughout the rest of his life. He was a life-long Democrat, and took a very active and influential part in political affairs, and for some time held the office of clerk of the district court (the same being now held by his son), sheriff, recorder and the office of register of the United States Land Office. He was the owner of large plantation interests and a large number of slaves. By the able management of his possessions he amassed a fortune, but the greater part of this he lost during the war. In the beginning of the Rebellion he organized a company in his home parish, and in this connection it should be stated that it was the largest company organized in the State. At New Orleans it was divided into two companies, which were lettered F. and G, and became part of the Third Louisiana Infantry, commanded by Col. Louis Hebert. Mr. Hyams was made lieutenant-colonel of the regiment, and served about two years, participating in two of the hardest-fought battles. He was then retired from the service on account of ill health, this, however, being contrary to his wishes, as he did not wish to leave his post of duty, but his constitution was unable to bear the constant privations and hardships of war, and reluctantly returned to his home. His combined energies were devoted to the Confederacy, which doubtless, had not a more enthusiastic supporter. By his side in the service were his sons, Samuel M., who was adjutant of his regiment, and John P., who was placed upon the colonel's staff. After the war Col. Hyams turned his attention to the practice of law, and owing to native ability he acquired a large practice, which he successfully managed until his death in 1869. He was a Royal Arch Mason, and as a man and citizen was above reproach. His widow survives him, being now seventy-six years of age. The subject of this sketch spent his boyhood in Natchitoches, and at the age of fourteen years he entered the Louisiana State Seminary, a military school at Alexandria, which was presided over by W. T. Sherman, and which he attended one year, a member of the freshman class. He left school for the purpose of entering the Confederate army, but upon returning home was persuaded by his father to remain at home two years longer on account of his youth. In 1863 he entered the military service of the ordnance department under Maj. Gaines, but in 1864 became a volunteer, enlisting for sixty days, during which time he held the rank of second sergeant, but acted as first sergeant. He subsequently spent some time with Lane's Texas Cavalry, and later, at the suggestion of his father, joined the Third Louisiana Infantry under command of Col. Samuel D. Russell, receiving the appointment of sergeant-major of the regiment, in which capacity he served until the war terminated. He returned to his old home in Louisiana, and for some three or four years he was employed as deputy clerk of the Supreme Court, deputy district clerk and deputy recorder. December 1, 1868, he was married to Miss Mathilde A. Gaiennie, of this parish, a daughter of Valery and Eloise (Metoyer) Gaiennie, by whom he is the father of the following named children: Eleazar L., Valery G., Emily Eloise, Mattie A., Denis J. and Mary Lucile, all of whom are living, the eldest of the family being twenty-one years of age and the youngest eleven. After his marriage Mr. Hyams turned his attention to farming, a pursuit he followed on Red River until 1885. In June of that year he was appointed by Gov. McEnery, clerk of the district court for Natchitoches Parish, and was nominated by his party for the same office in December, 1887, and elected in April, 1888, his present term expiring in 1892. Politically he has been a life-long Democrat, and has been one of his party's most active and enthusiastic supporters in this part of the State. He is a member of the Masonic lodge, is chancellor commander of the K. of P., and belongs to the A. L. of H. He is a Catholic in his religious views.

Hon. William Huston Jack. As an example of the usefulness and prominence to which men of character and determination will attain, we have but to chronicle the life of Mr. Jack, who is the intelligent and efficient superintendent of public instruction of Louisiana. He is a descendant of a long line of illustrious ancestry, and worthily fills his position in this line. At the commencement of the Revolutionary War, one of the worthy and patriotic citizens of Charlotte, N. C., was Patrick Jack, his great-grandfather a native of the Emerald Isle, who emigrated to America about 1730, and "pitched his tent" in the Old North State. His lineage is traceable to noble ancestors, one of whom was a ministerial sufferer in the reign of Charles II, in 1661. Col. William H. Jack is one of the most distinguished and talented lawyers of the South, and one of the most eloquent of her gifted bar. He first saw the light of day in Wilkes County, Ga., June 4, 1836, being the second son of Prof. William C. and Catherine Clara (Wellbone) Jack, the former of whom was born in Wilkes County, Ga., October 8, 1808, and died in Natchitoches, La., in November, 1886, having been a distinguished educator of this State. The mother of the subject of this sketch was born in Athens, Ga., September 23, 1818, and passed to her long home in the State of Arkansas in July, 1860. William H. Jack came from Arkansas to Louisiana in 1860, being then twenty-four years of age. After a considerable amount of preparation, both in the common and civil law systems, he began the practice of law in Natchitoches, where he has attained the highest rank in his profession, his reputation for ability, zeal and earnestness being fully recognized not only in Louisiana, but in the adjoining States. For several years he was associated in the practice of law with Judge David Pierson, and for legal ability and thorough knowledge of law, this firm had not its superior in the State. Mr. Jack's very superior mental endowments were practically recognized in 1863, when he was elected to the State Legislature, serving during 1863-64, and while a member of that body he was chosen chairman of judiciary committee, and although he was the youngest member of the House, and was known as the "boy member" he showed that he had the intellect and sound views that, as a usual thing, only mature years bring. During the dark days of reconstruction and the Radical-rule period in

Louisiana, Mr. Jack took a prominent and leading part against "Carpet-bag Government" and alien usurpation, and was inspired by no other motive than a love of country and a patriotic desire to see the government of his State restored to the hands of her people. During this period he was one of the advance men of the Democratic party, and his qualities of leadership were never more significantly displayed than in the arena of politics. He has been prominent in the councils of his party, and was one of the chief instigators of the famous Natchitoches revolt against the Kellogg government, and the mover of the Natchitoches resolutions, which required the Republican office holders to resign their trust into the hands of the people, and desist from further encroachments on their rights. The struggle against heavy odds was long and doubtful, but in 1876 the smoke of political conflict drifted away, which fact was owing to the skill and determination of such leaders as Mr. Jack. In 1874 he was elected district judge, but Gov. Kellogg refused to commission him on account of an alleged informality in the notice of the election, but really for political reasons and purposes. In 1880 and 1884 he was chosen as one of the presidential electors for Louisiana, and has always been deeply interested in State and National politics, and is regarded as one of the ablest, most active and indefatigable leaders of the party in this State if not in the South. In 1890 he was appointed by Gov. Nicholls, superintendent of public instruction of Louisiana to succeed Judge Breaux, promoted to the supreme branch, and his address delivered July 25, 1890, at Shreveport, before the Louisiana Educational Association, was a masterly and scholarly effort, and shows him to be in this, as in all matters, a thorough master of the situation, and fully equipped to admirably discharge the duties of this responsible position. In May, 1880, he was elected president of the Baptist State Convention of Louisiana, which body represents about 37,000 members, and this position has been conferred upon him by unanimous vote, at the several annual elections since 1880. The present finds this distinguished lawyer and orator enjoying the enviable position of being one of the represen-

tative men of his State, true to his convictions and earnest and sincere in all his deeds, a man to be respected and loved. He has been twice married, having six children by his first wife (Mary C. Whitfield), none by the last. His eldest daughter, Ida Lillian, is the wife of Judge W. P. Hall, of Mansfield. His second, Ada Whitfield, is the wife of M. H. Carver, Esq., of Natchitoches. His eldest son, John W., is practicing law in Dallas, Tex., and his second son, William H., is secretary in the superintendent's office at Baton Rouge. The other two children: Whitfield and Mary Kate, reside with him at Natchitoches. He was married to his present wife, Miss Ella G. McIntyre, an accomplished lady of Minden, La., about seven years ago, and in their home true-hearted, yet unostentatious, hospitality is displayed.

Edmond W. Jackson is a merchant and the owner of Maude plantation, which is just below Natchitoches, on the left bank of Cane River, and comprises 206 acres of fine farming land. This gentleman was born in Monroe County, Ga., on May 19, 1848, to Warren and Maria (Davis) Jackson, both Georgians, the father being drowned in Sabine Parish, La., in 1869, when about forty years of age, having been a planter by occupation. The mother died in De Soto Parish, La., in 1859, the year following her arrival in Louisiana. Edmond W. is the youngest of four living children, and was reared on a farm, receiving a common-school education. In 1869 he began life for himself as manager of his uncle's (Monroe Chapman) plantation, on Red Bayou, where he remained one year, the following year clerking for an uncle (H. J. Davis) at Pleasant Hill, La., receiving for his services $250 per annum. After remaining at this point until 1874, he then removed to G. W. Robinson's plantation, on Red River, where he remained for eleven years, a portion of the time receiving $1,200 per annum as compensation. Following this he was engaged in business for himself for some time in the same neighborhood, leasing the plantation of Mrs. Tally D. Brown, but in the fall of 1889 he purchased his present plantation, and at the same time opened a general mercantile establishment on the bank of Cane River. He has made his own way in life, and the property he has secured has come to him through his own untiring efforts. He is a Democrat, and a member of Phœnix Lodge No. 38 of the A. F. & A. M. Miss Lucretia Maude Foster became his wife in 1873, her birth having occurred in Alabama in 1855. The following children have been born to them: Eugene M., Edward F., William W., Joshua A., Howard H. and Sallie B.

Richard Ervin Jackson, M. D., is an able and scholarly physician of Natchitoches Parish, but now resides in Ward 9, on Red River, sixteen miles southeast of the city of Natchitoches. He was born in Graves County, Ky., September 23, 1836, to Hardy and Sarah (Little) Jackson, who were born, reared and married in Davidson County, Tenn., the former being a son of John Jackson, and the latter a daughter of John Little. Upon his father's side Dr. Jackson is the descendant of an emigrant from Ireland. His parents were married in 1822, and soon after removed from Tennessee to Graves County, Ky., becoming early settlers of that county. Hardy Jackson was twice married and his first marriage, which was to Miss Little, resulted in the birth of five children, all sons, of whom the subject of this sketch was the third. They are named as follows: John Milton, James Hardy (deceased), Richard Ervin, William Leftwich (deceased), and Robert Lockeridge. The mother of these children died in 1842, and about two years later their father was married to Mrs. Nancy Rutland, a widow who was a sister to his first wife. To them two children were born: Eliza Ann and Isaac, the latter dying in infancy. Eliza Ann now resides near Anson, Tex., and with her lives her mother who is once more a widow, Mr. Jackson passing from life in 1862. The subject of this sketch spent his early boyhood in his native county, and at the age of nine years, or in the fall of 1845, he accompanied his father and stepmother to what is now known as Limestone County, Tex., and a year later they removed to Louisiana, locating in Bienville Parish, five miles from the town of Arcadia. It was there that the father passed from life, and it was also there that Richard Ervin spent the remainder of his

boyhood. He first attended the common schools of Graves County, Ky., and Bienville Parish, La., and afterward entered an academy of Arcadia, which he attended one year, and a similar institution at Mount Lebanon, of the same parish one year. In 1858 he took up the study of medicine under the preceptorship of his brother, Dr. John M. Jackson, of Columbus, Ky., and remained with him a year and a half. In October, 1859, he entered the medical department of the University of Louisville, and in it attended one course of lectures. In the fall of 1860 he entered the New Orleans School of Medicine, in which he attended his second course of lectures, and from which he graduated in the spring of 1861. He at once located at Montgomery, La., but a month later the Civil War broke out and he entered the Confederate service, serving until the close. During the first three years he acted as assistant surgeon, the first eighteen months of that time being in the hospital service. During the last year he held the rank of surgeon. He served the Southern cause with devotion, and until the struggle was ended he consecrated his whole energy to the triumph and perpetuity of the Confederacy. At the close of the war he again located in Montgomery, where he was an eminently successful medical practitioner until 1876, when he removed to a farm about a half mile below Montgomery, on the opposite side of the river in Natchitoches Parish, which place he purchased in 1872, and which he has ever since occupied as his home. It contains 250 acres of exceptionally fertile land, and is in a fine state of improvement. Besides this he owns a tract of eighty acres on the opposite side of the river in Grant Parish. Since 1876 he has managed his plantation and practiced his profession, following the latter calling more for the accommodation of his neighbors than from choice. He is a very able and successful physician, being especially skilled in surgery, and did he desire it he could have an extensive and paying practice. He, however, prefers to devote the greater part of his attention to the management of his farm, this pursuit being more agreeable to his tastes and health. His marriage, which occurred on November 22, 1866, was to Miss Aurelia Townsend, who died October 3, 1877, leaving four children: Mildred (born October 1, 1867), Albert Sidney (born October 2, 1868), Elmo Murray (born November 19, 1869), and Jennie Perrin (born November 28, 1873). On November 14, 1885, the Doctor was married to Miss Lelia Pierson, of Natchitoches, who is his present wife. His first wife was a member of the Methodist Church, and he and his present wife are members of the Baptist and Episcopal Churches respectively. Dr. Jackson is a member of the Masonic fraternity, and in politics is a devoted member of the Democrat party. From the year 1880 until 1884 he served as a member of the State Legislature, having been elected by his party in the fall of 1879 as one of the representatives for Natchitoches Parish. Besides this he has held several other minor positions, among them being that of police juror. The Doctor is pleasant and agreeable in his manners, and he and his estimable wife have a large circle of warm friends.

Carroll Jones is a plantation owner of the parish of Natchitoches, La., but first saw the light of day in Sumner County, Tenn., April 4, 1815. When he was seven years old he was brought to Louisiana, and the remainder of his boyhood and his early manhood were spent in Rapides Parish. In his early manhood, although his principal pursuit has always been farming, he did considerable trading and speculating in live stock, and some of the horses he raised were the finest in the United States, being thoroughbred race horses that made names for themselves. He was successful in both farming and the live-stock business, and became one of the leading plantation owners of Rapides Parish. In 1869 he came to this point and located on his present plantation in Ward 9, eighteen miles southeast of the city of Natchitoches, which then contained about 1,200 acres of land, but since that time he has made adjoining purchases until he is now the owner of 1,500 acres. This plantation is splendidly situated, extending across the Cane River, and is sufficiently high to prevent overflow. For this reason it is very desirable, as well as for the fact that the improvements are first class.

Mr. Jones' residence is a large and commodious one, being 180 feet long by 80 feet wide. The yard in which it stands contains a fine cedar grove, and overlooking, as it does, the beautiful Cane River, it is one of the most beautiful country seats in the parish. It is also well improved in the way of fences and tenement houses. Mr. Jones is the owner of another plantation four miles farther down the river, which is valuable and in a good state of improvement. In the month of December, 1844, he was united in marriage to Catherine Clifton, who was born in Rapides Parish in 1829, and to them thirteen children have been born: Laura (born December 14, 1845), William C. (born December 24, 1847, and died August 17, 1870), Jerry M. (born October 14, 1849), Maria L. (born October 15, 1851), Rachel (born November 7, 1853, and died March 10, 1857), Matthew (born November 2, 1858), Martha (born October 8, 1860), Catherine (born July 15, 1863, and died May 26, 1864), Cora born December 18, 1865), Carroll (born February 22, 1867), Floresten (born April 12, 1869), Mary (born August 30, 1872), and Louis T. (born February 5, 1875). Mr. Jones, his wife and children are consistent members of the Catholic Church, and in politics he is a Republican. He is an honorable man, a liberal, upright citizen, and his home is recognized as one in which true hospitality is extended.

James W. Jones, president of the Farmers' Alliance of Natchitoches Parish, was born in Georgia, December 18, 1838, and passed his boyhood and youth under the parental roof. In 1859 he came to Louisiana, and settled in what is now Grant Parish, where he made his home until 1887, when he moved to his present place of residence in Natchitoches Parish, one and a half miles from the city. In 1861 he joined Company C, or what was known as the Winn Rifles, rose to the position of second lieutenant, and was a brave and efficient officer, serving until the close of the war. He was wounded at the battle of Vicksburg. Since the war he has been engaged in farming and has made a success of this occupation, as a glance over his well-kept place will clearly indicate to the beholder. He took a leading part in the Grange movement, and has always taken the same kind of interest in the Farmers' Alliance movement. In July, 1890, he was elected president of the last-named organization of this parish, and is eminently fitted for that position. He was married in the year 1863, to Miss Annie M. Dobbs, who was born in Marietta, Ga., in 1842. They have five children who are named as follows: Rowena, Lillie, James R., Hattie and Ernest W. Mr. Jones is a close adherent to Democratic principles, and socially is a member of the Masonic fraternity, Phœnix Lodge No. 38, of this city. He joined this society in Montgomery, La., and for about four years was Master of Lodge No. 168, of that place. He and Mrs. Jones are members of the Baptist Church. Mr. Jones was the eldest of four children, three now living, born to James and Harriet (Cooper) Jones, natives of Georgia and Virginia, respectively. The father died in his native State, in 1839, when about thirty years of age, and the mother also died in that State, in 1847, when about twenty-eight or thirty years of age. The maternal grandfather of our subject, Rev. John W. Cooper, was a minister in the Baptist Church for about thirty-five or forty years. He died in Georgia, in 1849, at the age of seventy years.

Joseph C. Keyser, brick contractor, Natchitoches, La. The parents of Mr. Keyser, J. C. and Elodiscia (Centina) Keyser, were natives respectively of Philadelphia, Penn., and Florida, and the latter was born in 1795. The father went to Florida at an early date, was there married, and died there of yellow fever in 1835. The mother still resides in Louisiana. Joseph C. Keyser (the youngest of six children, five of whom are now living, born to the above mentioned worthy couple), first saw the light of day in Escambia County, Fla., April 2, 1835. He received a common-school education, and in 1850 came to Louisiana. Since 1858 he has had his home in Natchitoches. He began learning the brick-mason's trade in New Orleans in 1852, completed it, and in 1861 he joined Company G, Third Louisiana Infantry, participating in the following engagements: Wilson Creek, Pea Ridge, Corinth, Iuka, the siege of Vicksburg and in numerous other engagements. After the war he returned to his trade, and has assisted in putting up nearly all the best brick buildings of this city. He was married in 1871 to Miss Josephine Raggio, a native of Natchez, Miss., and they are the parents of four children: Ellen, John, Hamlin and Paul. Mr. Keyser was formerly a Whig, but has been a Democrat since the Rebellion. He is a Mason, a K. of P. and is also a member of the A. L. of H. He is one of the reputable citizens of this parish.

Joseph H. Kile, brother of George W., whose sketch follows this, and a son of S. W. Kile, is also a native of Natchitoches, La., his birth occurring on May 18, 1852. He was educated in the schools of Natchitoches, and subsequently attended the State University at Baton Rouge, La. On November 24, 1876, he was married to Miss Cecelia Buvens, a native of Natchitoches, and to this union have been born seven interesting children: Lucile, Joseph F., Alice E., Camille L., Daisy C., May Pearl and Alma. In politics Mr. Kile, like his brother, affiliates with the Democratic party. Socially he is a member of the A. L. of H., Tioga Council No. 587, and is a K. of P. of Natchitoches Lodge No. 89. Mr. Kile is manager of the Natchitoches Opera House.

George W. Kile, grocer, Natchitoches, La. Among the most important industries of any community are those which deal in the necessaries of life, and next to bread and meat, nothing is more necessary than groceries. Natchitoches has many first-class establishments doing business in this line, prominent among the number being that conducted by Mr. Kile. This gentleman is a native of Natchitoches, born on October 5, 1854, and is a son of S. W. and Eliza B. (Power) Kile, natives of Kentucky and Ireland, the former born in 1822 and the latter in 1823. The parents moved to Natchitoches at least forty-five years ago, and were among the most eminently respected citizens of that city. The father was a man of push and energy, and as he started out in life with limited means, he had need of all his faculties to succeed. He was ever a hard worker, and believed in having all around busily employed. In his death, which occurred in 1888, Natchitoches lost one of her best men. Too much could not be said in his favor and naught against him. He was a member of the Masonic fraternity, Phœnix Lodge No. 38. He, learned the trade of blacksmith in St. Louis, and followed this during the early part of his life, but later engaged in merchandising. The mother is still living, and has been a resident of Natchitoches for nearly fifty years. Their family consisted of nine children, only two now living. George W. Kilé, the third in order of birth, of the above mentioned family, was reared and educated in his native city. His life has been that of a farmer for the most part, but he now has been merchandising for about four years. He is upright in all his dealings, and is deserving of the large and constantly increasing patronage of which he is in the enjoyment. As can be seen, the family has been long and favorably known here. They are, and always have been, stanch Democrats.

Judge George A. Killgore is a well-known and honored citizen of Natchitoches Parish, and has resided here but a few years. He was born in Union Parish, La., June 7, 1855, being the son of George A. and Eliza A. (Taylor) Killgore, the former a native of Georgia, and a son of Robert and Julia Killgore, and the mother a native of Alabama, and a daughter of Judge John and Jane Taylor. The marriage of George A. and Eliza A. Killgore was consummated in 1846, and resulted in the birth of five children: Mattie, Nettie, Mary, John and George A., of which family Mary died in infancy. George A. spent his boyhood in his native parish, attending the public schools until the age of fifteen years, then entered the Louisiana State University at Baton Rouge, which he attended two years, or until the institution was suspended. Soon afterward he entered Soule College, of New Orleans, from which he graduated in 1874, completing, in addition to other studies, a course in commercial law. Returning to his home in Union Parish, he took up the study of law properly under the preceptorship of Hon. George H. Ellis, of Farmerville, remaining with him two years, completing a full legal course, and in July, 1876, or just one month after his twenty-first birth-

day, he was admitted to the bar. He at once began practicing his profession in Farmerville, where he continued successfully until November, 1886. In 1878 he was elected judge of Union Parish, and he continued in that capacity until 1880, when the office was abolished throughout the State. It is a coincidence worthy of note that his grandfather was the first judge of the parish and he was the last one. He also served in several other important capacities while a resident of Union Parish, among them being that of parish attorney, which he held for several years. He was retained by the parish authorities as attorney in several very important cases, and discharged his duties in so admirable a manner that he won respect from all. In 1886, desiring to engage in an occupation more beneficial to his health, he came to this parish and located upon the Cashmere plantation, eight miles southeast of Natchitoches, situated on the Natchitoches Railroad and Cane River. He formed a partnership in the raising of cotton and live stock with Judge Alexander B. George, and with him is also joint owner in the Cashmere plantation, which is one of the most beautiful country seats in the State. Judge Killgore was married in February, 1879, to Miss Mollie Smith, who died in November, 1879, and in December, 1882, he wedded Miss Mittie Morton, his present wife, by whom he has three children: George Morton, Robert Oliver and Kathleen, of whom the eldest child died at the age of one and one-half years. Judge Killgore and his wife are members of the Baptist Church, and the former is a member of the K. of P. and the A. L. of H. He is a stanch member of the Democratic party, and he and his wife have a large circle of friends, among whom they are very popular.

D. R. Knight. Prominent among the leading men of Natchitoches Parish, La., and among those deserving special notice for their public spirit and energy, is the gentleman of whom this notice is given. He has been closely identified with the progress and development of this section for many years, and no more whole-souled gentleman can be found than he. He was born in Georgia, January 5, 1836, to Speer and Nancy (Carey) Knight, the former of whom died in Florida in 1844, and the mother in Louisiana in 1869. D. R. Knight is the youngest of their ten children, only two of whom survive. In childhood he went with his parents to Florida, where he lived until 1854, when he came to Louisiana and settled in what was then Rapides Parish, removing in 1885 to his present place of residence near Robeline. He followed the occupation of farming alone until 1889, when he added his saw-mill and cotton-gin, the two latter enterprises being very remunerative and the best arranged establishments of the kind in the parish. Mr. Knight is an energetic and straightforward man in every respect, and is genial and pleasant in his intercourse with his fellow-men. His marriage took place in 1869, the maiden name of his wife being Viola Eddleman, who was born in Mississippi, and to their union a family consisting of four children has been born: Ellen, Thomas, Maude P. and Daniel. Like the majority of the residents of this parish, Mr. Knight is a Democrat, and he has shown his approval of secret organizations by becoming a member of Sabine Lodge of the A. F. & A. M.

Adolph L. Lacoste, civil engineer and druggist, Natchitoches, La. This prominent and successful business man was born in Natchitoches, La., November 27, 1848, and is the eldest of three living children born to the union of Timothy and Olaudine (Faure) Lacoste. He first attended school in this city and here remained until fifteen years of age, when he went to Europe. From August, 1864, until August, 1868, he was a student at Bordeaux Lyceum, from which he graduated in 1867 with the degree of B. A., and in 1868 the degree of Bachelor of Science was conferred upon him. After this he returned home, and, after remaining there eight months, went back to Europe, where, in 1871, he was admitted to St. Etienne Mining School, from which he graduated in July, 1874. Until December of that year he was a draughtsman with an architect, and then he was for six years civil and mining engineer in the coal mine of Epinac, France. He returned to his native home in January, 1881, and here he has since resided. His first work on returning home was engineering the construction of the Natchitoches Railroad; and

after this he began surveying, which he still continues. Since February, 1890, he has also been engaged in the drug business, having registered by examination before the board as a pharmacist at New Orleans, on August 11, 1890. Mr. Lacoste has spent much time and money in fitting himself for the duties of life, and, on the whole, he may well be satisfied. He is a member of the Roman Catholic Church, and in politics is a Democrat. He is a well-educated and popular man. The parents of our subject were born in Louisiana, the father in St. James Parish on March 6, 1823, and the mother in Natchitoches Parish on January 1, 1823. Both are now deceased, the mother having died on September 1, 1880, and the father on June 18, 1890. They came to this city about 1840, and for about forty-seven years the father was a prominent druggist here. He was a man universally respected.

Alexis E. Lemee, receiver of the land office of Natchitoches, La., is a prominent and honored citizen of that place, and fully deserves the respect and esteem which he commands from all classes. He was born in the city in which he now resides on February 18, 1845, and has grown up among her people, winning the respect, liking and good-will of all with whom he has come in contact, but, notwithstanding the old saying that "familiarity breeds contempt," his case has proved the exception to the rule. His parents, Alexis and Eugenie (Lamarlaire) Lemee, were born on the island of St. Domingo in 1801 and in Baltimore, Md., respectively, the former removing from his native island in 1825 to the United States, and was married in Baltimore, Md., about 1830, soon after which they removed to New Orleans, La., locating the following year in Natchitoches, where Mr. Lemee spent the rest of his life, and where the mother is now living, an aged and venerable lady. For a great many years after locating in Natchitoches the father was cashier of the Union Bank of that place, a branch of a bank of the same name at New Orleans. He died in 1852. His wife was born in 1806, was a daughter of Gen. John Lamarlaire, who was a member of Gen. Jackson's staff at the battle of New Orleans. The subject of this sketch was the tenth of eleven children, seven of whom are living, the eldest being sixty and youngest forty-five years of age. Their names are as follows: Ida, Eugenie, Emma, Adolphe, Amelie, St. Ange, Cecile, Fanny, Antoinette, Alexis E. and Celina. Eugenie, Emma, St. Ange and Celina are deceased. Alexis E. Lemee entered Georgetown College, D. C., when fourteen years of age, in which institution he pursued a classical course for three years, completing the junior year. He then left college for the purpose of entering the army, and in March, 1862, was mustered into Company G, Twenty-sixth Louisiana Regiment, with the rank of sergeant, which company was commanded by Capt. Octave V. Metoyer. He served until the close of the war, taking part in the battles of Chickasaw Bayou and the siege of Vicksburg, besides numerous other engagements of less importance. He was twice promoted while Vicksburg was being besieged, first to the rank of first sergeant, and second to the rank of lieutenant. At the surrender of Vicksburg he was captured, but was paroled twenty-four hours later, and returned home. In 1864 he joined the Trans-Mississippi Department, with which he served until peace was finally declared, being mustered out of service as acting adjutant of his regiment. He returned to his Louisiana home, and in 1866 was appointed clerk of the Supreme Court of Natchitoches, in which capacity he continued until 1870. Three years later he was elected mayor of the town, and after serving one year was appointed by President Grant receiver of the United States Land Office at Natchitoches, in which capacity he has since served, discharging his duties in an able and dignified manner, complete satisfaction being given to all concerned. In 1876 he was elected treasurer of Natchitoches Parish, in which capacity he served until 1884, elected eight successive times. He is president of the Bank of Natchitoches, and is also prominently identified with numerous other enterprises, being a large stockholder in the Home Co-operative Cotton Seed Oil Company, Limited, of which he is secretary and treasurer. He is also a stockholder in the Natchitoches Railroad Company, being secretary and treasurer of this company also.

April 20, 1870, he married Miss Desiree Morse, who was born in Natchitoches in April, 1844, being a daughter of Peabody Atkinson Morse, a native of Haverhill, N. H. Mr. and Mrs. Lemee have had six children as follows: Alexis M. (born in February, 1871), Peter E. (born in May, 1873), Eloise (born in May, 1876), Daisy (born in October, 1877), Effie (born in October, 1879, and died in October, 1881), and Amelie (born in December, 1881). Mr. Lemee is a life-long and devoted member of the Democratic party, and is a member of the Roman Catholic Church.

Dr. Joseph A. Leveque. Among the widely known and most successful physicians of the parish is Dr. Leveque, who was born in West Baton Rouge, La., January 6, 1832, his father being Joseph A. Leveque, who was born in Assumption Parish, La., and his mother, Doralise Landry, a native of West Baton Rouge, she being Mr. Leveque's first wife, and the mother of six children by him, their names being Joseph A., Lize, Louis (deceased), Aloysia, Samuel and Justinian (deceased). When Joseph A. was a lad of ten his mother died, after which his father married again, his wife being Miss Bazilide Landry, a sister of his first wife. They have four children as follows: Evelina, Celeste, Benjamin, and May, and are now making their home at Lake Charles. The subject of this sketch spent his boyhood in his native town in the schools of which he received his early education. At the age of eleven years he entered St. Vincent's College of Cape Girardeau, Mo., in which he completed a full classical course, graduating at the age of eighteen. He at once took up the study of medicine, and for three years was under the preceptorship of Dr. Amzi Martin, of West Baton Rouge, after which he entered the Medical Department of the University of Louisiana, at New Orleans, in which he attended two courses of lectures. He next entered the Pennsylvania Medical College of Philadelphia, from which he graduated in 1855, at once entering upon his practice in the parish of Iberville, La., where his home continued to be until 1866. In 1861 he joined the Confederate army, for twelve months, acting as first lieutenant of the Fourth

Louisiana Volunteers, participating in the battle of Shiloh. In 1862 he was appointed surgeon of Col. Favrot's battalion, continuing to hold this position until the close of the war, discharging his duties in a loyal and patriotic manner to the Southern cause. In 1866, on account of the prevailing high water in the parish of Iberville, the Doctor came to this parish and located on Cane River, twelve miles southeast of Natchitoches, where he has built up a large and paying practice. He has been remarkably successful in the treatment of the cases that have come under his care, and fully deserves the widespread reputation he has gained. His marriage took place in 1863, his wife being Miss Theresa Kirkland, who was born in West Baton Rouge in 1841, to Vincent and Pauline (Hebert) Kirkland. The Doctor and his wife are the parents of two children: Lucy and Joseph M. Dr. Leveque and his wife are members of the Catholic Church, and he is a Democrat in his views. In every circle in life he has discharged his duties in a manner becoming a good and law-abiding citizen, and by his honorable, upright course he has won many warm personal friends.

Charles H. Levy. What is usually termed genius has little to do with success of men in general. Keen perception, sound judgment and a determined will, supported by persevering and continuous effort, are essential elements to success in any calling, and their possession is sure to accomplish the aims hoped for in youth. Mr. Levy possesses these attributes in an eminent degree, and a brief history of his career will not come amiss. He was born in Norfolk County, Va., August 18, 1837, and was the youngest of seven children born to his parents, of whom only three are living. His father, John B. Levy, was a Virginian by birth, but in 1870, thinking a change of scene would be beneficial, in more ways than one, to himself and wife, he came to Natchitoches, La., but the following year removed to Texas, his death occurring at Long View, in the Lone Star State, in 1877, when about eighty-nine years of age. His wife, whose maiden name was Emeline Butt, was a native of the Old Dominion, and passed from life at Long View, Tex., in 1875, when about seventy two years

of age. Charles H. Levy was given excellent advantages in his youth, and was educated in the Virginia Collegiate Institute at Portsmouth, Va. In 1855 he was so fortunate as to secure the appointment to an apprenticeship at the Government Navy Yard at Gosport, by Secretary of the Navy J. C. Dobbin, and during this service, in addition to attending to his duties, he attended a night school in Portsmouth, for the purpose of perfecting himself in mathematics, preparatory to entering the Engineer Corps of the United States navy, and in 1857 was examined by a board of naval engineers at Philadelphia, with very satisfactory results, and was appointed third assistant engineer in November, 1857, and in January, 1858, was ordered to the steam frigate "Colorado," to be attached to the West Indies or Home Squadron. He remained in the navy until June, 1861, in the meantime being appointed to the position of second assistant engineer. He resigned his position in the United States navy in 1861, and went South, receiving the appointment in June, 1861, of second assistant engineer of the Confederate navy, being promoted in 1863, to first assistant engineer, and the following year to chief engineer in the Confederate navy. He held this position very creditably until the close of the war, after which he came to the Pelican State, and settled in Natchitoches, which place has since been his home. From 1866 until 1879 he was engaged in farming, but in the latter year he was elected to the position of justice of the peace by the Democratic party, of which he has been a member all his life, and this office he has held with credit to himself and to the satisfaction of all concerned up to the present time. He has been an active member of his party in this parish, meriting, by his untiring services, the honorable recognition which he has received. He has always been a man of great self reliance, eminently fitted to stand alone, and his intelligent and charitable views on all subjects have won him friends innumerable. He belongs to Natchitoches Lodge No. 89, of the K. of P., and he and his worthy wife are members of the Episcopal Church. His marriage, which took place in 1868, was to Miss Emily A. Pierson, who was born in Natchitoches in 1849, a daughter of

Aaron H. and Margaret G. (Martin) Pierson. To Mr. and Mrs. Levy six children have been born: Lelia, William M., Charles H., Mahlon H., Clyde P. and Myrtle E. Mr. Levy and his wife are noted for their hospitality and kindly feelings toward all, and their home is a favorite resort for their many friends.

Henry M. Levy, dealer in general merchandise, Natchitoches, La. Mr. Levy, a successful and popular business man of Natchitoches, is another of the many prominent citizens of this parish who is of foreign birth, having been born in Russia on April 14, 1843. His parents were also natives of that country and both died there, the mother in 1843 and the father later. Henry M. Levy came to the United States when but eleven years of age, spent a short time in New York City, and then came to Louisiana, where he settled in New Orleans. There he resided nearly all the time until 1858, when he came to Natchitoches and until 1861 worked on the farm. He joined the first company that left Natchitoches to enter the army during the war and was with Levy's company, Second Louisiana Infantry, and was in active service until cessation of hostilities. He was wounded at both Chancellorsville and Gettysburg. In 1866 he began merchandising in this city, and in 1867 formed a partnership with Edward Phillips, this continuing until April 7, 1887. In 1889 he began the business again in this city, and is carrying it on very successfully at the present time. Mr. Levy was united in marriage to Miss Esther Phillips, a native of Liverpool, England, born in 1846, and their family consists of nine children: Bertha, Annie, Samuel, Edna, Edgar, Leola, Bessie, Paul and Mary. Mr. Levy is strictly Democratic in his political views. He is a member of Phœnix Lodge No. 38, A. F. & A. M., the A. L. of H. and the K. of P., Natchitoches Lodge No. 89. He is also a member of the Hebrew Society, I. O. B. B. Mr. Levy is one of the oldest merchants of the city.

Leopold Levy is one of the leading general merchants of Natchitoches Parish, La., and has succeeded in establishing a safe and remunerative trade, for his close attention to business, combined with a large and select stock of goods of the most reputable manufactures, together with the reasonable prices at which he disposes of them, have contributed largely to his success. He was born in France, January 15, 1853, to Leon and Harriet (Liberman) Levy, who were also born in that country, and there the mother died in 1883, at the age of sixty years, the father being still a resident of his native land and is nearly sixty-five years old. Leopold, the eldest of their four children, was educated in France and came to the United States in 1869, and for some time lived in New Orleans. In September, 1869, he came to Natchitoches and from that time until 1883 was a clerk in a general mercantile establishment, but in March, 1883, opened an establishment of his own, in the management of which he shows that he is a capable man of business. He was married in July, 1885, to Miss Justine Dreyfus, who was born in Liberty, Tex., in 1865, a daughter of Alphonse and Julia Dreyfus. By her he is the father of two bright little children: Harriet and Moise. Mr. Levy has supported Democratic principles ever since he commenced voting, and expects to continue so to do. He is a member of the A. L. of H. He deserves much credit for the way he has gained his present property, for he is in every sense of the term a self-made man. The first four months of his residence in this State were spent in working for his board and clothes, but now he has an excellent establishment of his own and gives every promise of becoming a wealthy man.

Edwin M. Lindsey, merchant, Robeline, La. In Pointe Coupee Parish, La., on December 28, 1852, there was born to the union of Hugh and Emily (Handy) Lindsey, a son, whom we now take as the subject of this sketch. He was the only child born to this union, and when yet a little child his father died, and his mother married Thomas B. Waters, by whom she had one child, William H. Waters, now a resident of Catahoula Parish, La. Thomas B. Waters died in 1869, but his widow is still living and now makes her home with her son, the subject of this sketch. The mother was a native of Morehouse Parish, La., and the father was born in Wilkinson County, Miss. When Edwin M. Lindsey was but a small child he accompanied his mother and stepfather to Rapides Parish, La., in which he spent his early boyhood on a farm. In 1862 the family removed to Centralia, Ill., and thence in the latter part of 1864, to Cape Girardeau, Mo., from there in 1865, to Rapides Parish again and located in Pineville. Two years later the family removed to Catahoula Parish, and there the stepfather died in 1869 as above stated. The home of Mr. Lindsey continued to be in that parish until 1884, and from 1872 to 1876 he was employed as steamboat pilot on the Ouachita River and its tributaries. From 1876 to 1879 he was engaged in the saloon business in Jonesville, Catahoula Parish, and in the last named year he established a plantation store twelve miles west of Jonesville. This he conducted until the fall of 1884, when he sold out to his half-brother and removed to Robeline. Here he at once established a general store, and his entire attention has since been given to its management. He has been very successful, and is considered one of the leading business men of the place, possessing a first-class store and a large patronage. His present store, which he erected in 1885, is a good frame building 24x66 feet, and besides this he owns another good business property in Robeline, which is 20x50 feet, and which he now rents. On December 15, 1885, his marriage to Miss Rena Rachal, of Sabine Parish, was solemnized, and to them have been born two children: Clarisse and Magdalene who are aged, respectively, four and two years. In politics Mr. Lindsey is a Democrat, and in 1885 he was elected a member of the city council of Robeline, which position he has filled continuously ever since, having been re-elected five times to that position. Ever since a member of the same he has been its secretary and treasurer. He is now serving his sixth consecutive term, which fact is evidence enough of his faithfulness as a public servant, and of his high standing as a citizen. He and wife are very highly respected by all who know them.

Antoine Marinovich, planter, Cloutierville, La. Mr. Marinovich, whose success as a farmer has been very great, was born in Austria on December 8, 1835, and came to America in 1853. Since then he has made two trips to his native country, one in 1867 and the other in 1878. He settled in Natchitoches Parish in April, 1853, and it has been his home ever since. For thirty years he was engaged in merchandising in Cloutierville, and he built up a reputation as an honest, reliable business man which extends far and near. He now resides between four and five miles below Cloutierville, where he owns a fine plantation of 500 acres, 300 acres of which are under cultivation. He is also the owner of several other smaller tracts of land in this parish, and he is now one of the wealthy and substantial planters of the parish. Upon his home plantation he is conducting a plantation store, to accommodate his tenants, and he is a proper representative of the prosperous, enterprising citizens of this community. He has a happy home, where a devoted wife and eleven intelligent children brighten his days. He and wife and family are members of the Roman Catholic Church, are estimable citizens, and are alive to all issues of the day. It is unnecessary to add that Mr. Marinovich is a man of progressive spirit, clear perception, and that his fellow-citizens owe him a debt of gratitude for the advanced state of agriculture in this locality.

James R. Mayben, although still a young man is one of the successful planters of Natchitoches Parish. He is a native of Louisiana, born in Winn Parish on October 25, 1864, his parents, James O. and Nancy (Jones) Mayben, being natives of Alabama and Georgia, respectively. Seven children blessed their union, all, at the present writing, residing in this State. The father pursued farming up to the breaking out of hostilities, in 1861, when he joined the Twenty-second Louisiana Regiment and served his country faithfully throughout the war. He and his wife worship at the Cumberland Presbyterian Church. James R. received his education in the private schools of this county. Deciding, at the age of twenty years, to start out for himself, he rented land, and by energy and perseverance has worked his way up until he now owns 160 acres of good land, forty acres of which are improved. On February 3, 1886, he was united in marriage to Miss Mary E. Brown, one child, Ala M., having blessed their union. He is a member of the Masonic lodge, being a Master Mason, and has held office in the same. He is a very liberal man, and contributes to all public enterprises to assist in the advancement of the good of his parish.

James H. Mumford, M. D., is one of the leading physicians of this section of the country, and as a practitioner of the "healing art" has done not a little to alleviate the sufferings of the sick and afflicted throughout this section. He was born in Onslow County, N. C., February 10, 1827, to Zadoc and Elizabeth D. (Shockford) Mumford, both of whom were born in the Old North State, their union being blessed in the birth of seven children, of whom the subject of this sketch is the eldest. The family emigrated first to Alabama in 1834, and after a residence of about four years in Russell County, they came to Louisiana, the father opening a large farm in De Soto Parish, upon which he resided about six years. At the end of that time he moved to Red River Parish, where he opened another plantation, but a few years later moved back to De Soto Parish, opening a mercantile establishment in Logansport, his capital at that time amounting to about $4,000. This enterprise proved very unfortunate for him, financially, for he was soon after burned out at a loss of about $3,000, but he afterward managed to retrieve his losses in a great measure. He died here in 1876, being a member of the Methodist Episcopal Church and the Masonic fraternity at the time of his death. James H. Mumford was educated in the schools of Louisville, Ky., entering the Kentucky Medical College in 1848, and receiving his diploma in 1850, his preceptor being Dr. S. A. Scruggs. He immediately returned home, and has since devoted his attention to the cause of humanity, and has built up a reputation for ability second to none in this section of the country. In 1851 he was married to Miss Georgia Woodhouse, she being a native of Georgia, and to them eight children have been born: James E. (who is a practicing physician of Sabine Parish), Georgie E., Mary W., Harriet G.

Katie, William B., Edna L. and Lewis. Under the reign of Gov. Moore, Dr. Mumford held the position of sergeant of militia, and was also examining surgeon. His family are members of the Methodist Episcopal Church South.

Samuel Nelken, general merchant, Natchitoches, La. For many years Mr. Nelken has been a prominent resident of Natchitoches Parish, and has enjoyed the reputation of being an intelligent and honorable business man. He was born in Poland in 1847, and is a son of Wolf and Augusta Nelken, who were natives of Poland, and who passed their entire lives in that country. Mr. Nelken remained in his native country until about nine years of age, and then came to the United States, locating in Natchitoches in the fall of 1866. Here he has since made his home, and is a man universally esteemed. He began selling merchandise throughout the country, continued at this for about two years, and then clerked for two more years. In the fall of 1870 he began merchandising for himself, and this he has continued for a period of twenty years, meeting with fair success. Aside from his mercantile interests he is also the owner of about 1,000 acres of valuable land, and also 1,500 acres of timber land. He started out in life for himself with limited means, but by his industry and good business acumen he is now comfortably fixed. He is a stockholder in all the public enterprises of the city, was a member of the city council and school board, and is in every sense a representative citizen. He was married in 1872 to Miss Sarah H. Abram, a native of Poland, born in 1855. They have eight children: Augusta, Wolf, Fannie, Abram, Emanuel, Gettie, Lillian and Bessie. In politics Mr. Nelken is a Democrat. Socially he is a member of the Masonic fraternity (Phœnix Lodge No. 38), Knights of Pythias (Natchitoches Lodge No. 89) and the American Legion of Honor. He is also a member of the I. O. B. B., a Jewish order.

Solomon Nelkin, merchant, Provencal, La. Mr. Nelkin has built up an excellent reputation as a business man, and is a solid and reliable tradesman. He was born in New York City on August 26, 1860, and his early life was spent in his native city, where he received his primary education in the public schools. Throughout his youth, when not in school, he was employed much of the time as a clerk, and when twenty-two years of age, or in 1882, he came to Natchitoches Parish, where for two years he clerked for his brother, Samuel Nelken, in Natchitoches. In 1883 Samuel Nelken established a branch store at Provencal, and of this our subject became manager about a year later. In January, 1888, Mr. Nelkin became the successor of Samuel Nelken, by purchasing from him both the stock of goods and the building in which it was located. He has been its sole proprietor since, and he has done an immense amount of business, being now one of the principal merchants of Provencal. He carries an $8,000-stock, and does an annual business of about $35,000. During the past year he shipped 350 bales of cotton. On November 21, 1888, he had the misfortune to lose his store by fire, the building being entirely destroyed and the stock partially. He at once secured another building, placed in it what goods he had saved, and continued business with but slight interruption. In the early part of 1888 he began upon the site of his former store the erection of his present fine business store, and in the course of a few months it was ready for occupancy. It is a substantially-built structure, 30x90 feet, and is a credit to the town. As soon as it was completed Mr. Nelkin opened up in it a large stock of general merchandise, and he now has a large patronage. He is a young man of good habits, and his courteous and accommodating manners, together with his desire to satisfy the public, has enabled him to acquire both a good trade and a large circle of friends. In politics Mr. Nelkin is a Democrat. He is a pleasant young man, and possesses every qualification for a successful business career.

Jules Honorat Normand is the popular proprietor of Normand's Hotel at Natchitoches, La., an establishment that is admirably conducted, and has a large patronage from the traveling public. Mr. Normand was born in Cloutierville, La., October 22, 1827, to Dr. F. M. Normand and wife, the former of whom was born in France, October 4, 1800, and came to the United States in 1824, settling in Cloutierville, but dying in Natchitoches, September 3, 1873, being a physician, merchant and planter. His wife was Miss Marie Lolette Rachal, who was born in the parish of Natchitoches in 1810, and died here September 20, 1843. Jules Honorat Normand is the eldest of two sons and four daughters born to his parents, three of which family are now living. In 1840 Jules entered the Royal College of Borbon in Paris, France, where he spent seven years, then returned to this country, and for two years taught a public school in the lower part of Natchitoches Parish, the French language taking the place of the English. From 1850 to 1855 he was engaged in farming in this parish, after which he went to Cuba, where, until 1869, his attention was given to planting, the photograph business, and to managing a hospital. In 1866 he returned to his old home, bringing with him seventy-five Chinamen to work on different plantations in this parish, but went back to Cuba and remained there, as above stated, until 1869. He then came back to Louisiana, purchased three plantations in Natchitoches Parish, and was actively engaged in planting and merchandising until 1875, when he discontinued the former occupation and carried on the latter business exclusively in Cloutierville until 1884. He has been a resident of Natchitoches since 1889, and is now conducting one of the best hotels in this section of the State. His marriage, which took place on September 25, 1849, was to Miss Elizabeth Aurelia Anty, who was born in this parish August 30, 1833. To them six children have been born—Maria, Cecilia, Aurelia, Julia, Jules H. and Francois M. Mr. Normand is a Democrat.

William W. Page, merchant, Robeline, La. What is usually termed genius has little to do with the success of men in general. Keen perception, sound judgment and a determined will, supported by persevering and continuous effort, are essential elements to the success of any calling. That Mr. Page has these elements to a marked degree is perceptible to all with whom he comes in contact. He is a native of Natchitoches Parish, La., born nine miles west of the city of Natchitoches, on December 17, 1852, and was one of six children born to

John L. and Elizabeth C. (Holden) Page, who owe their nativity to Amite County, Miss. The parents were married in Natchitoches Parish, La., in 1851, and the children born to this union were named as follows: William W., Emily J., John L., Jr., Elizabeth C. (deceased), and two sons who died in infancy unnamed. The father of these children was a farmer by occupation, and died in 1864, at Fort Darousa, La., whither he had gone to superintend the construction of breastworks. His widow is still living, and resides in Natchitoches Parish, her present home being in Robeline. The home of William W. Page has been in Natchitoches Parish thus far all his life. He received in the schools of the parish a knowledge of the ordinary branches of learning, and throughout his boyhood and youth, when not in school, he labored on the farm. At twenty-one years of age he embarked in farming for himself, and carried this on for about ten years. He was married on January 28, 1874, to Miss Jennie E. Carter, of this parish. In 1883 Mr. Page moved to Robeline, where he has ever since given his attention to merchandising, and where he is classed among the leading business men. His business building, which he erected himself, is 22x65 feet, and is one among the best in the place. It is splendidly stocked with all kinds of general merchandise, and is recognized by the public as an excellent place to trade. Mr. Page is courteous and pleasant to all, and this, together with his desire to satisfy the public, has enabled him to build up a large patronage. His store is one of the largest and best in Robeline, and not one of her merchants are more widely or favorably known. Mr. Page is one of the pioneer merchants of the city, and is the only one who is a native-born citizen of the parish. Mr. Page's marriage resulted in the birth of six children, as follows: John L., William R., Otho O., Luther, Irene, and an infant daughter unnamed. Of these named John L., William R. and Otho O. are deceased. In politics Mr. Page is a Democrat, and in January, 1884, he was elected a member of the city council of Robeline, being re-elected to the same position in January, 1890. Besides his business property Mr. Page owns a first-class residence in Robeline, which he erected in 1885. He also owns considerable land in both the parishes of Natchitoches and Sabine. He is a man in whom the public has implicit confidence, and whose word is considered as good as his bond. Being one of the native sons of Natchitoches, he has an extensive acquaintance throughout the parish, and by all who know him he is very highly thought of.

Harry Percy, civil engineer and surveyor, was born in Ireland, May 4, 1839, and is the second son of Gilbert Percy, LL. D., of County Lutrim, Ireland. The family moved to Canada in 1849, but in 1861 he came to Louisiana, his father and mother returning to Ireland, where they still reside. He joined the Second Louisiana Infantry as private in 1861, and was discharged at Richmond, Va., as a sergeant, and shortly after was appointed lieutenant of engineers, a position he held to the close of the war; since that time he has been engaged in surveying and civil engineering. He was married in 1863, to his cousin Marcella Chaplin, second daughter of Hon. Judge Chaplin, and has two children living: Richard and Maude. He votes the Democratic ticket at all times, and he and family attend the Episcopal Church of which he is a conscientious member.

Edward Phillips, general merchant, Natchitoches, La. Mr. Phillips is a native of Liverpool, England, born on November 12, 1843, and came with his parents, Jacob and Elizabeth (Bailey) Phillips, to the United States in 1848. He located with them in Natchitoches in 1849, and received his education in the schools of that city. In 1861 he joined Company G, Third Louisiana Infantry, Confederate States Army, and served until the close of the war. He was captured at Vicksburg, and was paroled at Shreveport. After the war he began merchandising in this city, and this he has since successfully continued. From 1867 to 1887 the firm was known as Levy & Phillips. Mr. Phillips is a very successful merchant and enjoys an extensive acquaintance and patronage within the town and surrounding neighborhood. His nuptials were celebrated in 1871, with Miss Joanna Lachs, a native of Vicksburg, Miss., born in 1853. They have an interesting family of four children: Robert, Rena May and Violet. Harold, a son, was drowned in Cane River in 1884, and our subject came very near losing his life in the same fatal spot. Mr. Phillips is a stockholder in the Natchitoches Cottonseed Mill, and is one of the leading citizens of the city. He has been a member of the Masonic fraternity, Phœnix Lodge No. 38, since 1866, and is also a member of the L. of H. The father of Mrs. Phillips, Simon Lachs, was born in Prussia about 1826. He came to the United States when in his teens and died in New Orleans in 1872. Her mother was born in Germany in 1836, and died in Memphis, Tenn., in 1873. Edward Phillips was the eldest of six children, three of whom are now living. One brother, Henry, was drowned in Cane River, near where the father lost his life on July 27, 1866. Thus three members of the family lost their lives in this fatal river. His father was born in Prussia, and his mother in Liverpool, England, in 1826. She now resides in Coushatta, La.

Judge David Pierson, of the Eleventh Judicial District, was born in Stewart County, Ga., August 30, 1837, and is a prominent citizen of this parish, respected and esteemed for his sterling integrity, sober, sound judgment, broad intelligence and liberal, progressive ideas. He is a man whose career has been above reproach. His parents, William H. and Mary (Collins) Pierson, were natives of South Carolina, the father born in 1808 and the mother in 1810. The family came to Louisiana in 1847, and settled in Claiborne, now Bienville Parish, where the father followed agricultural pursuits for many years. The mother died in 1848, in Louisiana, and the father received his final summons in Natchitoches, in 1886. Judge David Pierson is one of ten children born to this union, four of whom are now living. He received an academic education at Mount Lebanon Academy, Louisiana, having spent three years there, and then began the study of law, being admitted to the bar of Louisiana in 1859. The same year he located at Winfield, La., and practiced his profession at that place. In 1861 he was elected a delegate to the State Secession Convention, from Winn Parish, was the youngest man in that convention, and was one of

five who refused to sign the ordinance of secession after it was adopted by the convention. In April, 1861, he joined the army and was elected captain of Company C, known as the "Winn Rifles," and was attached to the Third Louisiana Infantry, commanded by Col. Louis Hebert, who afterward was made major-general, participated in the battle of Oak Hills, Mo., Elkhorn, Ark., and other minor engagements. He then followed Gen. Price to Corinth, Miss., and was then in the battle of Iuka, Miss., where he was wounded and captured. In 1863 he was promoted to the rank of major of his regiment, and subsequently to lieutenant-colonel of the same; then later, in the siege of Vicksburg, where he was again wounded, he was part of the time commanding officer of the regiment. After being exchanged he reorganized the regiment and surrendered at Shreveport, in May, 1865. The following year he was elected district attorney of the then Ninth Judicial District, composed of Natchitoches, Rapides, Sabine and Winn Parishes, by the soldier vote, and held that position until the reconstruction, in 1868, or until the adoption of the constitution of 1868. From 1868 to 1876 he was engaged in the practice of law in partnership with W. H. Jack, under the firm name of Jack & Pierson. Judge Pierson removed to Natchitoches in 1866 and in 1876 he was elected judge of the Seventeenth Judicial District, having been nominated without his knowledge and while in Canada for his health. The Seventeenth District was composed of De Soto, Red River, Natchitoches and Sabine Parishes. He held this honorable position until the adoption of the constitution of 1880, when he was elected judge of the Eleventh Judicial District, being re-elected in 1884 and 1888. His term will expire in 1892, after nearly sixteen consecutive years on the bench. The Judge was married in 1866 to Miss Sidney A. Pipes, a native of West Baton Rouge Parish, born in 1847, and they have the following children: Clarence, Alice, Maude and May. Judge Pierson is one of the leading men and one of the prominent characters of North Louisiana. He was a delegate to the National Democratic Convention that nominated Mr. Cleveland at St. Louis, Mo., in 1888, representing the Fourth

Louisiana Congressional District; also president of the Democratic convention for the Fourth Congressional District, in 1884, at Shreveport. He served as the president of the first board of administrators of the Louisiana State Normal School, located under an act of the Legislature, at Natchitoches, and to his efforts and excellent judgment is due, to a large extent, the success of that institution. He has represented the parish of Natchitoches in several Democratic State conventions, and in 1874 was president of the executive committee of the White League of the parish, under the name of "Tax Reform Association," and as such the recognized leader of the revolution that prevented the collection of the 79 mills local taxes, and overthrew the corrupt carpet-bag government. His name has often been mentioned by the press of North Louisiana, in connection with the office of governor of the State. He has never suffered a defeat, either for nomination or election, before the people, for any position to which he has aspired. In all the relations of life, public or private, his character for honesty and integrity has been unquestioned, without blot or stain. Beginning life anew after the close of the war, with no capital save a sound mind and body, and the esteem and confidence of his fellow-soldiers, he has reared and educated a family, attained high rank in his profession, held honorable positions, accumulated enough to make a comfortable home, and is now ready to retire upon a record alike honorable and brilliant.

Charles V. Porter, attorney at law, Natchitoches, La. As a leading citizen of Natchitoches in its professional, business and social life, lending strength to her bar, tone to her finance and grace to her society, Charles V. Porter commands attention from the pen of the historian who would wish to do the town of Natchitoches justice. He was born in De Soto Parish, La.; on January 1, 1857, and is a son of Jacob C. and Sarah A. (Garrett) Porter. The father was born in Georgia, about 1813, came to Louisiana, and settled in Shreveport at an early day, when there were but two or three business houses in the city. He was one of the early merchants of Shreveport, and a citizen of Caddo Parish until about 1856, when he moved to De Soto Parish, and thence to Natchitoches, La., and there his death occurred in 1873. The mother was born in Alabama, and died in Natchitoches Parish, in 1869, when about forty-five years of age. Mr. Porter is the youngest of seven children, only three of whom are now living, and is a self-educated man. He studied law and was admitted to the bar in 1882, after which he immediately began the practice of his profession at Natchitoches. In 1883 he established the Democratic Review in that city, but this he sold in 1887, and for about a year was editor of the Shreveport Daily Democrat. In 1884 his marriage with Miss Violet A. Lachs, a native of New Orleans, was consummated, and to them have been born two children: Charles V. Jr., and Harold. Mr. Porter is a Democrat in his political views and socially is a member of the K. of P. He is a pleasant, courteous gentleman, and has many warm friends. He was elected chairman of the Democratic Executive Committee of Natchitoches Parish in 1887, which position he resigned the following year.

Jacques Alphonse Prudhomme. In no part of Louisiana is agriculture in a more flourishing condition than in Natchitoches Parish, and here Mr. Prudhomme is a leading tiller of the soil, and a prominent and honored citizen. He resides on Oakland plantation, thirteen miles from the city of Natchitoches, which was owned by his father and grandfather before him, the latter having entered it from the Government. It has been his home since 1867, and is a desirably situated and valuable plantation. He, as well as his parents, and grandparents on both sides, was born in Natchitoches Parish, La., his birth occurring on the plantation on which he now resides, April 17, 1838, his father, Pierre Phanor Prudhomme, being also born on this plantation, June 24, 1807, the birth of his wife, Suzanné Lize Metoyer, occurring on the Metoyer plantation, which adjoins the Oakland plantation on the south, November 22, 1818. The paternal grandparents, P. Emmanuel and Catherine (Lambre) Prudhomme, were born in this parish, the former's birth occurring in 1762, he being a son and the third child of Jean Baptiste Prudhomme, who emigrated to the United States from France, and located in Natchitoches Parish, La. The maternal grandparents were Benjamin and Aurore (Lambre) Metoyer. The parents of Jacques Alphonse Prudhomme were married December 21, 1835, and had a family of five children born to them, of whom he was the second, two sons and one daughter now living. The names of the five children are as follows: Catherine Adaline, Jacques Alphonse, Marie Emma, Therese Henriette and Pierre Emanuel. Catherine Adaline died at the age of forty-two, and Marie Emma when fourteen years of age. The mother of these children passed from life May 19, 1852. Their father served as a member of one of the State constitutional conventions, and for two terms was a member of the State Legislature. In 1830 he was captain of a company in the Eighteenth Regiment, of the State Militia. He died October 12, 1865. The subject of this sketch spent his boyhood on the old home plantation, where he was born, and in April, 1853, entered the collegiate Commercial Institute, of New Haven, Conn., which he attended until October, 1856, then returned home. In November of the same year, he entered the University of Virginia, at Charlottsville, which he attended two years, then entered the University of North Carolina, at Chapel Hill, which he attended two years, graduating as a Bachelor of Science in June, 1860. He then returned home, and remained upon the plantation until the following October, when he became employed as a civil engineer upon the central stem of the Mississippi & Pacific Railroad, and was thus engaged until May, 1861. He then entered the Confederate service, in Company H, Third Regiment Louisiana Infantry, and served in that company in the battles of Oak Hill and Elkhorn, until March 7, 1862, upon which day in the latter battle he was wounded by a piece of shell, and shortly after was captured. Eight days later he effected his escape, and returned home. In July and August he assisted Col. W. W. Breazeale in organizing a battalion of five companies of cavalry, of which he was made adjutant. This battalion, with McWater's battalion, formed the Second Louisiana Regiment of Cavalry, and of it he was made adjutant September 21, 1862, continuing in that capacity and participating in

several battles, until April, 1863, when he was severely wounded. He then returned home, but in the month of June, 1863, rejoined his command, and remained with it until July, 1864, participating in a number of engagements, among which was the battle of Mansfield. In July, 1864, he was relieved from duty, on account of his wounds, and was assigned to the position of enrolling officer of the parish of Natchitoches, continuing in this capacity until the end of the war, serving the cause he espoused faithfully until the close of the war. Mr. Prudhomme was married September 6, 1864, to Miss Marie Eliza Lecomte, a native of Natchitoches Parish, a daughter of Ambrose and Julia (Buard) Lecomte, who were also born in this parish. Mr. Prudhomme and his wife have eight children, as follows: P. Phanor, J. Lecomte, Edward C., Marie Cora, Marie Atala, Marie Julia, Marie May and Marie Noelie. Mr. Prudhomme and his wife are consistent members of the Catholic Church, and in politics he is a stanch Democrat. In 1876 he was a candidate of his party for the office of representative, and received the full vote of the whites and a portion of the colored men. He is a member of one of the most prominent families in the State, and is broadminded, liberal and intelligent, one who has the utmost confidence and respect from all classes.

Peter Emanuel Prudhomme, is a well-known and highly-respected citizen of the parish of Natchitoches, his birth occurring on Oakland plantation, thirteen miles southeast of the city of Natchitoches, on January 8, 1844, a son of Peter Phanor and Susan Lize (Metoyer) Prudhomme, a more complete history of whom is given in the sketch of J. A. Prudhomme. Peter E. has resided all his life on the plantation on which he is now living, and the only change in his residence has been from one side of Cane River to the other. At fifteen years of age, or in 1859, he entered Georgetown College, D. C., and continued a student in that institution until the breaking out of the Rebellion, returning home in March, 1861, with the intention of entering the Confederate army, and shortly after returning home he became a member of the Prudhomme Guards of the Twenty-sixth

Louisiana Regiment, as a corporal, and continued with the same command until the end of the war. He was taken prisoner with the surrender of Vicksburg, but was at once paroled, and after rejoining his command was promoted to orderly sergeant, serving as such until the war terminated. He was a brave and loyal soldier to his cause, and after the war returned home. Miss Marie Julie Buard became his wife on January 25, 1866, her birth having occurred on Cane River, six miles below Natchitoches, on April 13, 1845, a daughter of Jean Baptiste and Marie Desiree (Hertzog) Buard, both of whom were born in the parish of Natchitoches. The parents of Mrs. Prudhomme had a family of ten children, of whom she was the sixth, their names in order of birth being as follows: Jean Baptiste, Aspasie, Albert, Emile, Emelie, Marie Julie, Cecile, Felicie, Marie and August Emanuel. Those living are Emelie, Marie Julie, Cecile, Felicie and Auguste Emanuel. The father of these children died on October 14, 1853, and the mother on November 9, 1865. In 1867 Oakland plantation was divided, and that portion east of Cane River fell to the subject of this sketch. In September, 1870, he located upon this portion, and this very desirably situated plantation has since been his home. It is above the point of overflow, and among numerous improvements that have been made is a good residence, 40x40 feet, eight cabins and a good store, in which is kept all kinds of plantation supplies. The plantation is well fenced and in a good state of cultivation. Eight children have been born to Mr. Prudhomme's union, their names being as follows: Jean Baptiste Ovide (born October 24, 1866), Pierre Felix (born March 26, 1867), Susanne Lize (born November 16, 1869), Joseph Edwin (born September 12, 1871, and died October 4, 1882), Emma Laure (born August 23, 1873), Marie Adeline (born July 4, 1875), Raymond Emile (born April 1, 1880), and Felicie Cecile (born September 16, 1882). Mr. and Mrs. Prudhomme and children are consistent members of the Catholic Church, and he is a Democrat in politics, being the present police juror for Ward 9, a position he has held for twelve consecutive years. He is an upright, worthy and honorable man, and he and his family rank among the best citizens of the parish, and are very highly respected. He is at present a member of the parish school board, having been appointed by the governor on May 1, 1889.

Samuel P. Raines, ex-sheriff and farmer of Natchitoches Parish, is one of the substantial, enterprising citizens of the same, and a man who is held in high esteem by all acquainted with him. He was born in Alabama on January 11, 1840, and is a son of James A. and Mary E. (Brian) Raines, the father born in Virginia in 1816 and the mother in South Carolina the same year. The father is still living, and is a resident of Natchitoches, but the mother received her final summons in Alabama in 1841. Samuel P. Raines, the only child born to the above worthy couple, was early trained to the arduous duties of the farm and received the ordinary education of the country boy. He came to Natchitoches in September, 1853, and he has continued the occupation to which he was reared and which has been his life's work. In March, 1862, he joined Company F, Twenty-seventh Louisiana Confederate States Army, and served until the surrender. He was wounded at the battle of Vicksburg. Returning home he continued tilling the soil, and by his progressive ideas and great industry is acknowledged to be far above the average in his chosen calling. He is a Democrat, and in 1879 he was elected sheriff of this parish, which position he held one term. He is now the owner of about 1,400 acres of land. He was married in 1868 to Miss Elizabeth Kieffer, a native of France, and both he and wife are members of the Methodist Episcopal Church South. He is a Mason, a member of Bethany Lodge No. 223 of this parish, and is also a member of the K. of P., Natchitoches Lodge No. 89. He is a stockholder in the Red Hedge Company and the Natchitoches Cotton Seed Oil Mill. He is one of the leading farmers of this parish, and his home is ten miles from the city northeast.

J. J. Rains is a prominent merchant and planter of Ward 5, this parish, and was born in Warren County, Tenn., October 22, 1825, the son of James and Elizabeth (Jackson) Rains, natives of North Carolina. He was the ninth of their ten children and the only one now living. The father was a farmer by pursuit and emigrated from North Carolina to Tennessee in 1811, locating in Warren County, where he resided until his death, October 19, 1848. His widow survived him until 1856. He was a man interested in the welfare of his county, and took an active part in the building of churches, schools and society in general. Himself and wife were worthy members of the Baptist Church. Our subject was educated in the country schools of his native county, and at an early age started out on his own responsibility. At the age of fifteen years and three months (or January 22, 1841), he was united in marriage with Miss Martha Whitlock, also a native Tennesseean, the little town of Marthaville derived its name from her in 1855. Their union was blessed with the following children: James P., Nancy (deceased), George D., Isaac, John F., Salenia, Sarah, Thomas J., Jennie and Perry C. In 1850 he removed with his family to Louisiana and was at that time $20 in debt, but by hard work and perseverance has accumulated quite a fortune, owning 1,380 acres of land, besides having settled on each of his children a plantation of from 320 acres to 640 acres, and also conducts a merchandising business under the firm name of Rains & Small, doing a business of $3,500 annually. Being one of the representative citizens of this parish he has held the position of postmaster for thirty-five years, has been parish assessor for five years (resigning at the end of that time), and was elected a member of the police jury. He and his family worship at the Missionary Baptist Church, of which he is deacon, and is a liberal contributor to all public enterprises for the advancement of the good of his parish. He is sixty-five years of age, in good health and the proud grandfather of sixty-six grandchildren.

H. Raphiel & Bro., merchants, Campti, La. H. Raphiel, the senior member of the above named firm, is an European, born January 11, 1845, and came to this country with his parents when four years of age. He received his education in

the private schools of this parish, and at the age of nineteen years started out on his own responsibility with $900. Through energy and good management he has succeeded in increasing his business, and is now worth $25,000. May, 1874, his marriage to Miss Louisa Betran, a native of Louisiana, took place, and this union was blessed with the following children: Bertha, Esther, Ida, Joseph, Perl, Samuel, Stella, and an infant who died unnamed. Socially, he is a Master Mason, belongs to the Masonic order, Bethie Lodge No. 223, and has represented the same in the Grand Lodge four or five times. Isidore Raphiel was born in this city August 11, 1849, and at the age of twenty-two years entered his brother's business, investing therein $4,000. Miss Johanna Raphiel became his wife August 15, 1879, and they now have one child, Howard. He is a member of the K. of P. and Masonic lodge, and has held the office of secretary in the last named. He is one of the enterprising and progressive men of this part of the country. Besides the merchandising business this firm owns 650 acres of excellent farm land, 300 acres of which are in a good state of cultivation, and worked by sixteen families. The farms are well stocked. Howard and Bertha (Levy) Raphiel, the parents of Howard and Isidore Raphiel, emigrated to this country in 1849 from Europe, and settled in Natchitoches Parish. Of their seven children, four are now living: Howard, Isidore, Lewis and Anna (now Mrs. Sibersky). The father followed merchandising until he was called from his earthly home, June, 1887. His widow still survives him. The entire family are believers in the Jewish faith.

J. P. Readhimer emigrated to this State from Charleston, S. C., where he was born October 20, 1825. His parents, Peter and Harriet (Blewer) Readhimer, were also natives of the above-named city, and of a family of eight children seven are still living, six residing in this State, one having remained in his native home. The father was a cabinet-maker by trade, and he and his wife worshiped at the German Lutheran Church, and were esteemed and respected by all. He was called from his earthly home in 1845, his widow still surviving him, is eighty years of age, and resides with one of her children in this parish. Our subject received his education in Charleston. At the age of nineteen years he accepted a position as clerk, remained there three years, when he received a situation as passenger conductor on the S. C. R. R., which he held until 1865, and in 1868 emigrated to Louisiana, locating in Winn Parish. Here he entered the merchandising business, and later, in connection with this, undertook farming and milling, continuing until 1875, when he decided to come to Natchitoches Parish, and has remained here since following the same pursuits very successfully. He was married in South Carolina in 1855 to Miss Annie Casie, but shortly after their removal to Louisiana she died, leaving five children to mourn their loss. In 1878 he took for his second wife Miss Amanda Gaiennie, a native of this State, and two children have blessed this union — Ephrim and James. They are worthy members of the Catholic Church. Socially he he affiliates with the Masonic order, belonging to Jefferson Lodge No. 5, of Charleston, S. C.; and is a Master Mason.

Dr. Andrew Jackson Roquemore, physician, Provencal, La. Few, if any, industrial or professional pursuits have within the last years made such rapid strides as that of the profession of medicine, and among the leading physicians of Provencal and vicinity, who have availed themselves of all the new ideas and put them in practice, may be mentioned Dr. Roquemore. He was born in Panola County, Tex., on September 6, 1860, and is the son of James and Matilda Roquemore, who were natives of Georgia, but who were married in Texas about 1855. Dr. Andrew J. Roquemore is the third of four children, who are named as follows: Malcom, Jule and James L., all sons. The first two are deceased, but James L. is still living and is a physician of Panola County, Tex., at a place called Jumbo. Dr. Roquemore was but three years of age when his mother died, and but ten when he lost his father. He then went to his grandparents, Moses and Martha Boynton, who resided near Pine Hill, Panola County, Tex., and made his home on the farm with them until he was twenty-four years of

age, receiving in the meantime a good education. In 1883 he began the study of medicine under the direction of Dr. J. E. Wall, of Carthage, Panola County, and remained with him one year, after which, in the fall of 1884, he entered the medical department of the University of Louisville, Ky., from which he graduated on March 1, 1886. He then began practicing his profession in Caddo Parish, La., and six months later he removed to Boyce, La., thence to Provencal, where he has had a paying practice since August, 1887. On January 13 of that year he was wedded to Miss Ida Madora Irvine, daughter of Edward Irvine, the old steamboat captain familiar to the citizens of Tennessee, Louisiana and Texas. Capt. Irvine was a native of New York, but he removed to Texas in 1845, and in 1869 located in Shreveport, La., where he died March 9, 1879. The mother of Mrs. Roquemore, before her marriage, was Miss Harriet Rebecca Watson. She is still living, her home being in Hot Springs, Ark. She has living ten children — five sons and five daughters — all of whom have reached maturity. Mrs. Roquemore was born in Jackson, Tenn., June 3, 1861, and her marriage to Dr. Roquemore has resulted in the birth of two children: Ruthie Lee (born October 16, 1887), and James Edward (born March 6, 1890). Dr. Roquemore and his amiable wife are members of the Baptist Church, and he is Democratic in his political principles. The Doctor devotes his whole attention to the practice of his profession, for which he possesses much ability and has met with good success.

Henry Safford, parish assessor. Like many, and perhaps the most of the representative citizens of this section, Mr. Safford is a native of the parish, his birth having occurred in the city of Natchitoches, November 25, 1860. Henry and Harriet (Airey) Safford, his parents, were born in Beach Island, S. C., and Natchitoches, La., the former being a son of Henry and Eliza (Burr) Safford, and was reared to manhood in Georgia, graduating from Oglethorpe University of that State. In early manhood he removed to Louisiana and located in Natchitoches, where he was married about 1858, and where he pursued the practice of law throughout the remainder of his life, dying in March, 1883. His wife was a daughter of Thomas L and Annette (Whitcomb) Airey, the former a native of Baltimore, Md., and the latter of Montpelier, Vt., and in 1873 Mrs. Safford passed from life. Henry Safford is the second of four children born to his parents, their names being: Annette Eliza, Henry, Harriet Rebecca, and Whitcomb Burr. Henry spent his boyhood and youth in this town, which place has been his home all his life, with the exception of a few years after the death of his mother, which were spent in the northern part of the parish and at Mount Lebanon, La. When about nineteen years of age, he returned to Natchitoches, and for several years he attended to the management of his father's estate, and later on, for two years he was engaged at farming. In 1878 he was elected to the office of assessor of the parish, and his present term will not expire until 1892. He makes a good officer, and is discharging his duties in an acceptable manner. In politics he is a Democrat, and is strongly opposed to the rechartering of the State lottery. He is a substantial citizen, and has a large circle of warm friends.

A. E. Sompayrac, representative of Natchitoches Parish, is a native Louisianian, born in this parish November 7, 1843, his parents, Ambros B. and Roseline (Deblieux), also natives of this State. They were united in wedlock in 1842, and their union was blessed by six children: Alex, Aline and Fronie, now living. Our subject's father was a farmer by occupation, and cultivated 600 acres of good land, always took an active part in the improvement of his parish, and assisted in the building up of churches, schools and the societies, in the early days of Louisiana, and died in April, 1890. A. E. Sompayrac was educated at Alexandria University of Louisiana, but soon after the breaking out of the late war in 1861 he dropped his studies and took up the Confederate cause, joining Company K, Twenty-seventh Louisiana, and was in the siege of Vicksburg, where he was captured, paroled and transferred to the west side of the Mississippi River, and at the time of surrender, was at Mansfield, La. On returning home,

he worked for his father on the farm, and, July 14, 1866, he was united in the holy bonds of matrimony, with Miss Annette Airey. One child was born to them, Alex H., who passed away August 11, 1887, at the age of twenty years. Our subject now owns 2,500 acres of land, 300 acres of which are under cultivation, the farms being well stocked and containing cotton-gins and grist-mills. He was chosen, and is the present representative of his parish, which goes to show how much he is respected. He has always taken an active part in the building up of churches and all educational matters. He is a member of the Catholic, and his wife of the Episcopal Church.

McDaniel Scarborough is a tiller of the soil of Ward 6, Natchitoches Parish, La., and his plantation comprising 400 acres is well improved and the seventy-five acres which Mr. Scarborough has succeeded in putting in a tillable condition is very fertile. He was born in Darlington District, S. C., October 13, 1823, being sixth in a family of seven children, two now living, born to the marriage of Noah Scarborough and Margaret Josey, both of whom were born in the Palmetto State, the former in 1777, and the latter in 1797, their deaths occurring in Georgia, in 1849 and 1839 respectively. The immediate subject of this biography came to Louisiana in 1849, and first settled in Jackson Parish, but after some time becoming dissatisfied with his location he moved to Natchitoches Parish, and for twenty-five years resided on Spanish Lake, after which he came to his present place of residence, which is situated about three miles south of Robeline. Mr. Scarborough gave four years of the best part of his life to service in the Confederate army, but gave them willingly, for he was a stanch Southerner, his only regret being the defeat of the cause. Like so many of the progressive and successful men of this parish he has made his own way in the world, and the plantation on which he resides has been earned by hard labor since the Rebellion. He is a Democrat, politically, and is now a demitted Mason. In 1850 Mrs. Eleanor (Culpepper) Hargrove, who was born in Georgia, in 1828, became his wife and in time the mother of his four children: Daniel C., Anna, Aelo and Georgia.

Daniel C. Scarborough, district attorney for the Eleventh Judicial District, was born in Jackson Parish, La., October 5, 1852. and is the eldest of a family of seven children born to the union of McD. and E. M. (Culpepper) Scarborough (see biography), the father a native of South Carolina, born in 1823, and the mother of Georgia, born about 1828. The former now resides in Natchitoches Parish, and there the mother died in 1887. The paternal grandfather, McJosie Scarborough, died in South Carolina. Daniel C. Scarborough was reared upon the plantation and worked on the same for his father until twenty-one years of age, when he began educating himself. In 1873 he entered Shreveport University and remained there until July, 1875, when he returned to Natchitoches Parish and taught school for nine months. Then in connection with teaching he read law and continued his former pursuit until April 4, 1876, when he came to Natchitoches. Here he entered the law office of Jack & Pierson; worked for them during the day and read law at night, being admitted to the bar July 4, 1878, at Monroe, La. He then came home and formed a law partnership with Hon. William M. Levy, with whom he continued until April, 1880, when Mr. Levy was appointed to a position on the supreme bench, in which position he died in 1884. Mr. Scarborough then formed a partnership with Judge L. B. Watkins, who in 1886 was appointed to a similar position, and who is now one of the State supreme judges. In November, 1879, Mr. Scarborough was elected to his present position, re-elected in April, 1884, and so great was his popularity that he was elected to that position for the third time in 1888. His present term will expire in 1892. His strong, good sense, his knowledge of human nature, his calm conservatism and his genuine legal ability were soon perceived, and he has gained the general confidence of the people. Since 1886 the firm of Scarborough & Carver has existed, and is well and favorably known in this part of the State. Mr. Scarborough was married January 4, 1880, to Miss Lucy Paxton, a native of Louisiana, and to them have been born an interesting family of four children: Zama, William P., Daniel C. and Immogene.

Mr. Scarborough is a Democrat through and through in his political views, and socially he is a member of Phœnix Lodge No. 38, A. F. & A. M., and a charter member of Natchitoches Lodge No. 89, K. of P., of which he was the first chancellor. Although a thoroughly self-made man, he has gained an honorable place among his brother practitioners, and is one of the leading lawyers of this part of Louisiana.

N. F. Scopini, a leading planter of Ward 3, Natchitoches Parish, was born in this parish April 19, 1835, being the second child of eight born to Francis and Nolete (Pero) Scopini, who died in 1840. The father emigrated from Italy to Louisiana in 1816, locating at Campti, and busied himself with farming, which he followed for ten years, and then went into the merchandise business, remaining in this until his death in 1854. While in the old country he served as a soldier in the war between France and England, being taken prisoner by the English, and on his release he came to Louisiana. After coming to America he joined the Masons, being an honored member of a lodge of that order. Our subject was educated in the private schools of the country, and when arriving at the age of twenty-five started out in life for himself, entering into the mercantile business, with a capital of $1,000. Continuing in this business for fourteen years, and controlling a stock of $18,000, he sold out to settle on his present 7,000-acre plantation, 800 being well cultivated and stocked; he is also the owner of four gins, one being situated on the plantation. On January 29, 1852, our subject wedded Miss Ellen Lattier, a Louisianian by birth, being born in Rapides Parish, and to them have been born two children: John F. and Mattie (now Mrs. Atria Rubor, and the mother of one child, Norbert F.) In religion he and family worship with the Catholic Church.

Cyrus S. Searing, real estate agent and surveyor, Natchitoches, La. The principal necessity to the success of the real estate business, and the safest and surest forms of investment, is to have reliable agents who are thoroughly posted on their city and locality. Such a one has Natchitoches possessed in Mr. Searing, who has resided in this parish since 1886. He was born in Mobile, Ala., on December 25, 1854, and is the son of Robert B. and Artemesia A. (Sibley) Searing. The father was born in Newark, N. J., in 1821, and died in New Orleans in March, 1890. The mother was born in Alabama in 1839, and now resides in New Orleans. The parents settled in Alabama about 1848, and in 1861 came to Louisiana, settling in New Orleans, where the father resided until his death. He was a cotton merchant by occupation, and purchased extensively for the mills of Europe. Cyrus S. Searing, the eldest of five children, three of whom are living, first attended the New Orleans High School, and in 1870 entered Ronoake College at Salem, from which he graduated in 1873. He then returned to New Orleans and engaged in business with his father, with whom he continued until 1879. He then began civil engineering and surveying, in which he has since been engaged, and his work has been principally by contract for the United States Government. He removed to Natchitoches in 1886, and in connection with his former occupation, he is deep in the real estate business. He was married in 1887 to Miss Fanny S. Gillispie, who was born in Natchitoches in 1869, and who is the daughter of Dr. George E. and Fanny Gillispie. They have one child, Cyrus S., Jr. In politics Mr. Searing is a Democrat, and he is a member of the Episcopal Church. Mrs. Searing is a member of the Catholic Church.

Joseph Henry Stephens, a prominent and influential business man of Provencal, La., and the present mayor of that city, was born in the parish of Natchitoches, about fifteen miles southeast of the city of Natchitoches, September 12, 1847. He was the son of Joseph G. and Mary E. (Vascocu) Stephens, the former a native of Darlington District, S. C., born August 22, 1818, and the latter a native of Red River Parish, La., born in 1823. The father left his native district, with an uncle, at fifteen years of age, and accompanied him to Mississippi, locating near Vicksburg, where he made his home with his uncle for six years. When about twenty-one years of age he came to Louisiana, and located in Natchitoches Parish, where he was married at the age of twenty-five to Miss Mary E. Vas-

cocu, and where he resided for a period of thirty-one years, engaged in farming and saw-milling. He served in the Crescent Regiment during the last two years of the Civil War, and was a faithful and efficient soldier. In the fall of 1871 he removed to Harrison County, Tex., where he pursued the vocation of a farmer and stock-raiser, and continued this until his death in 1876. He was a Democrat in politics, and was a man who had the confidence and respect of all who knew him. His widow survived but two years, her death occurring in 1878. Joseph Henry Stephens was the second in a family of eleven children, seven of whom grew to maturity, and three sons and three daughters now living. The names of the eleven children in the order of their ages are as follows: James J., Joseph H., William B., Lawrence W., George W., Irene, Alice, Laura C., Eliza A., Louisa J. and Walter G. Those living, besides our subject, are: Lawrence W., Laura C., Eliza A., Louisa J. and Walter G. Joseph H. Stephens attained his growth on his father's farm, in this parish, and his first educational training was obtained in a private school. Later he attended a French school three years, and when in the sixteenth year of his age, or in the spring of 1864, he entered the service of the Confederate army, in Company B, Bird's battalion, and served in the courier service until the end of the war. He then returned home, and for two years afterward was engaged in the saw-mill business in connection with his father. In 1868 he purchased a saw-mill of his own, and gave his attention to saw-milling until 1878. In the fall of that year he removed to Natchitoches, engaged in merchandising, and carried on a successful business there until 1881. In that year he was engaged in the same business at Provencal, which town had just been founded, and, as the partner of Thomas Gregory, he continued merchandising until December 31, 1889, under the firm title of Stephens & Gregory. They had an immense business, and ranked among the leading merchants of the parish. In the winter of 1885-86 they erected a fine business building, which is 32x110 feet, and which they still own. It is a substantially built structure, and is the best building in the town. Mr. Stephens was married May 7, 1871, to Miss Isabella C. Whitfield, a native of Arkansas, and daughter of George W. and Mary (Johnson) Whitfield. Mr. and Mrs. Stephens are the parents of six children, as follows: Edwin Lewis, Ida L., George W., Joseph Henry, Isabella and Sudie Belle. Mr. Stephens is a member of the Masonic Lodge, and also of the A. L. of H. In politics he is a Democrat. He was elected mayor of Provencal in 1888, and is the present competent incumbent. In the same year he was appointed by the governor justice of the peace, and he has also held that office ever since. In the fall of 1888 he was also appointed a member of the school board of the parish of Natchitoches, and he has likewise held this position ever since. He has, therefore, for the past two years, held three official commissions from the governor of the State. Mr. Stephens is a broad-minded, liberal-hearted man, and one who possesses much executive ability. Being a native of Natchitoches, he is widely known throughout the parish, and by all citizens he is recognized as thoroughly reliable in every respect, and one whose opinions are worthy the attention of all. He is entirely self-made, and the position he has won does him credit. The eldest son of Mr. Stephens, Edwin Lewis, completed a commercial course from Keatchie College at fourteen years of age, and is now a member of the junior class in the Louisiana State Agricultural and Mechanical College or University, in which institution he has already been the recipient of merited honors. Besides his literary training, he is a skillful operator. Miss Ida L. Stephens the eldest daughter of Mr. Stephens, is now a student in Keatchie College.

William B. Stille, merchant, Robeline, La. Mr. Stille deserves honorable mention as one of the prominent young merchants of Robeline. He first saw the light of day in Sabine Parish, La., his birth occurring on August 4, 1860, and is the son of Joseph D. and Hattie B. (Smith) Stille, the former a native of New Jersey, and the latter a native of Virginia. To the parents were born six children—five sons and one daughter—all living and named as follows: Anna E., William B., Joseph D., Walter D., Elliott O. and Norrie A. The

mother of these children died in 1878, after which the father married Miss Emma J. Pierson, and they now reside at Many, La. He has two children by this union, Lillian P. and Mary A., both living. Joseph D. Stille, the father of our subject, is an old and honored citizen of Many, La., and for a great many years he has been a merchant of that place. When William B. Stille was five years of age his parents removed to Sabine Town, Sabine Parish, Tex., where the father was engaged in merchandising, and where our subject spent his youth. He secured a good common-school education, and at the age of fifteen years he entered the employ of R. B. Stille & Co., one of the leading mercantile firms of Many. About one year after he entered its employ, his uncle, R. B. Stille, died, and our subject's father, James D. Stille, succeeded the firm of R. B. Stille & Co., continuing the business ever since. After his uncle's death William B. Stille entered the employ of his father, and continued with him in the same store as clerk and book-keeper until March, 1889. At that time, with the means he had thus earned, he removed to Robeline, where he engaged in business for himself. Immediately after locating in this place, he purchased a lot and upon it he erected a business building, which is 23x70 feet, and which is not only one of the neatest, but one of the most substantially built buildings in the city. In this he placed a first-class stock of general merchandise, and on July 15, 1889, he opened it up to the public. Though it has been but little more than a year since it was opened, Mr. Stille has already built up a good patronage, and now ranks among the foremost business men. Mr. Stille was married on October 9, 1889, to Miss Ione M. Yarbrough, the only daughter of Maj. J. J. Yarbrough, of Mansfield, La. They have one child, a son, born September 4, 1890. Mr. Stille is strongly Democratic in his political principles, and when a resident of Sabine Parish he held the office of constable for four years, filling that position ably and in a satisfactory manner. He is a young man of good habits, and possesses every qualification necessary for a successful business career. He is careful and painstaking with his patrons, and is one whose word and judgment are thoroughly reliable.

A. N. Timon, one of the successful farmers of Ward 3, this township, is a native Mississippian, born in Wilkerson County April 13, 1847, the son of John and Mary (Jackson) Timon, the father a native German, and the mother from Tennessee. The father emigrated to Mississippi from Germany when quite young, and was here married in 1830. This union was blessed with seven children, five still living. He followed the merchandising business the greater portion of his life, and died in 1851, his widow dying in 1853. She was a member of the Baptist Church. A. N. Timon received his education in the private schools of Mississippi, and at the age of fourteen years started to work on a farm, remaining there three years, when he took up the Confederate cause, and enlisted as a private with the sixty-day troops, which disbanded after a short time. Later he entered Company D, Twenty-first Mississippi, under Capt. Brandon, and was in the engagement at Berryville, where he was wounded very severely, carried to Mount Jackson, was there furloughed and returned home, where he was at the time of surrender. He then accepted a position as manager of a farm, and January 29, 1879, was united in wedlock to Miss Alberta Chapman, a native Louisianian, and their union was blessed with two children: Benjamin F. and Sarah L. Our subject now owns 1,500 acres of land, 1,000 under cultivation and 500 acres rented, which he superintends himself. His farm is well stocked, and contains five gins and one grist-mill. He is a very liberal man, and contributes largely to all public enterprises.

Gervais L. Trichel, sheriff of Natchitoches Parish, La., is a native-born resident of this parish, and the confidence which the people have in him is therefore intelligently placed, for they have known him from infancy, and have had every opportunity to judge of his character and qualifications. He was born on December 21, 1842, and is a son of Leonard and Zelia (Perot) Trichel, natives also of Natchitoches Parish, La. The former was born in 1819, and was a farmer by occupation, he died here in 1887. The mother was born about 1824, and now resides here. Gervais L. Trichel, the eldest of eleven children, four of whom are now living, was educated in the schools of Natchitoches. In 1861 he enlisted in Company D, Third Louisiana Infantry, Confederate States Army, and upon the re-organization of the company in 1862, he was elected first lieutenant of Company D, which position he held until cessation of hostilities. He was wounded at the battle of Iuka, Miss., and was made a prisoner of war at the siege of Vicksburg. Returning to Louisiana after the war he engaged principally in farming, and this he continued until 1880, when he became deputy sheriff of Natchitoches Parish. This position he held for four years, and in April, 1884, he was elected to the position of sheriff. Four years later he was re-elected to the same office, his present term expiring in 1892. Mr. Trichel is a capable and efficient officer, and a popular man and citizen. He was united in marriage to Miss Emma E. Owen, a native of Mississippi, in Jackson Parish in 1865, and the result of this union has been four children: Annie Celeste, Martha Estelle, Lelia Ethel and Vivian Oleida. Mr. Trichel is a member of the Masonic fraternity, Lake Village Lodge No. 196, and a charter member of Natchitoches Lodge No. 89, K. of P. He is a Democrat in politics, and is one of the most popular and accommodating men in the parish.

Charles E. Trichel, deputy sheriff of Natchitoches Parish, and a representative of one of the old families of this portion of Louisiana, was born in Natchitoches Parish, on December 25, 1850, and is a son of Leonard and Zelia (Perot) Trichel. He was the fourth of nine children, and his early impressions were at once directed toward the channels of agricultural pursuits. He received a fair education in the common school, and continued to till the soil until 1882, since which time he has held his present position. He is eminently suited to the position and fills it to the satisfaction of all. His marriage occurred in 1878, to Miss Josephine E. Bullard, who was born in Mississippi in 1859, and the fruits of this union have been three children: Charles M., Clarence E. and Annie C. Mr. Trichel is a Free Mason, a member of Phœnix

Lodge No. 38, and is also a charter member of Natchitoches Lodge No. 89, K. of P. In politics he affiliates with the Democratic party.

J. C. Trichel. The mercantile interests of this section have been ably represented since the close of the war by Mr. Trichel, who is also devoting some of his time and attention to agriculture. In addition to this he has been honored with the position of president of the police jury of Natchitoches Parish, a position he is filling with marked ability. He was born here on October 22, 1832, to J. B. and Cephalide (Perot) Trichel, who were also born here, the death of the father occurring in the year 1839. The paternal grandfather of Mr. Trichel was also born in this parish, and died here about the year 1790, being a member of one of the oldest families of the State. Mr. Trichel passed from life in 1851. J. C. Trichel is the eldest son in a family of seven children, of whom two survive. He received the advantages of the common schools, and in 1850 entered the mercantile establishment of Walmsley Bros., as clerk, and continued in that position for seven years, after which he became a member of the firm, and continued as such until the business was broken up by the opening of the Rebellion. In April, 1861, he joined Company G, Third Louisiana Infantry, Confederate States army, and served until the war closed, being a true and faithful soldier to the cause he espoused. After the cessation of hostilities he resumed general merchandising, of which establishment he is still the proprietor, and farming also received his attention. He is an uncompromising Democrat, and in 1884 he was elected by the party he has so long represented, to the position of police juror for Ward 1. He is now president of the police jury of this parish. He is a stockholder in the Cotton Seed Oil Mill, and the Red River Hedge Company. He was married in 1865 to Miss Kate Johnson, who was born in this parish, and by her is the father of four children: J. C., Gilbert P., Kate Lee and Evelina. Mr. Trichel is a member of Natchitoches Lodge No. 89, of the K. of P., and A. L. of H.

John M. Tucker is an attorney at law of Natchitoches, La., and needs no introduction to the people of this region, for, in addition to being one of the eminent lawyers of the State, he was born here on December 24, 1856, to J. M. B. and Caledonia (Marrs) Tucker, who were born in Tennessee in 1828 and 1838, respectively. The father was also a talented lawyer, and in early manhood came to this section, and at the time of his death, which occurred in Natchitoches, January 20, 1890, he was the oldest member of the Natchitoches bar. Although he possessed brilliant attainments, he was very retiring in his disposition, and his ability only showed itself in its full force when he was studying or discussing some knotty point of law, or when he was pleading his cases. His widow survives him, being a resident of this town. Of a family of eight children born to them, the subject of this sketch is the second, and only seven are now living. Like the majority of the youths of his day he was given the advantages of the common schools, and later determined to follow in his father's footsteps and make the profession of law his calling. He first began his studies in 1877, and in October, 1882, he graduated before the Supreme Court of Louisiana, at Shreveport, and immediately began practicing in his native city, forming in 1885 a co-partnership with W. G. McDonald, which existed until 1887. Mr. Tucker was then alone one year and in the month of October, 1888, formed his present partnership with Ex-Attorney-Gen. M. J. Cunningham, they constituting one of the strongest and most talented law firms in this part of Louisiana at this time. They have been employed in many important cases, but on all occasions have shown marked ability in their management. Mr. Tucker has always been devoted to his calling and as he has shown that he is a man of unswerving integrity, and as he possesses many admirable traits of character, he is well liked and popular both at home and abroad. He is a Democrat of the uncompromising stripe, and is ready at all times and under all circumstances to defend his views and to champion what he thinks to be right. He has been the promoter of his own success, and as he started in life with limited means his success commands respect from all. Socially he is a member of Natchitoches Lodge No. 89 of the K. of P.

Richard B. Williams belongs to that independent and intelligent class, the planters of Natchitoches Parish, La., and is possessed of much genuine merit and strength of character. He was born in Perry County, Ala., September 18, 1829, and is a son of John and Elva (Edmonds) Williams, both of whom were born in Georgia, the former in 1807. He was a son of John Williams, his wife being a daughter of Signor Edmonds, her birth occurring in 1812. Her union with Mr. Williams took place about 1828, and to them eight children were born, their names in the order of their birth being as follows: Richard B., Sarah A., John D., Frances, James E., Martha, Nancy and George. Sarah A., Frances and Martha are deceased. The parents of these children died in Vernon Parish, La., where they settled in 1859, having reached a ripe old age. The subject of this sketch was reared to manhood in his native parish, and throughout this time he worked on his father's farm in summer time and attended school during the winter. In 1843 the family moved to Bibb County, Ala., and in 1848 to Union Parish, La., starting on November 28, and after a long and toilsome journey reached their destination in February, 1849. Mr. Williams remained in Union Parish for about ten years, during the first eight of which he farmed and the last two clerked in a store. His marriage took place in Union Parish on February 26, 1854, to Miss Helen M. Wade, who was born in the State of Tennessee on October 14, 1835, being a daughter of Dr. Absalom Wade. In 1859 Mr. Williams removed from Union Parish to Winnfield, Winn Parish, and there, after clerking two years, he was elected to the position of parish recorder and parish treasurer, which offices he filled acceptably for ten years. For a number of years during his residence in Winnfield he was engaged in mercantile pursuits, but in 1872 he resigned his official positions and removed to Montgomery, Grant Parish, La., where he kept a mercantile establishment for two years, at the end of which time he turned his store over to his son, J. H. Williams, who has conducted a successful establishment ever since, and is now one of the principle merchants and most prominent business men of the place.

Meanwhile, before leaving Winnfield, Mr. Williams purchased two large tracts of land, each of which contained more than 300 acres, one lying on Red River, in Grant Parish, just above Montgomery, and the other on the opposite bank of the river, in Natchitoches Parish. After transferring his mercantile interests to his son, he turned his attention to farming, and has followed that pursuit ever since. He continued to reside in Montgomery until 1881, when he came to this parish, locating on Highdie plantation, which he had purchased in 1880, which contains over 1,000 acres. Here he resided until 1888, when he removed to a point nearly two miles farther down the river, and directly opposite the town of Montgomery. Since 1880 he has made several purchases of land, until his plantation reached the enormous size of 4,000 acres, in 3,300 acres of which his son, J. H., has a half interest. No better land can be found on Red River, for the soil is very productive, and above the point of overflow. He has made extensive improvements since locating on his present farm, one of which is a handsome residence. His barn is also a fine structure. His marriage has resulted in the birth of four children: James Henry, William Thomas, Malinda Annette and John Alexander. Mr. and Mrs. Williams are members of the Baptist Church, and he is a Democrat. He is a gentleman of much intelligence, and being strictly honest, and possessing kindly and agreeable manners, no planter on the Red River is more widely or more favorably known.

Received too late for alphabetical insertion:

George Easterbrook came to Louisiana in the spring of 1883, and settled near Colfax. He was born at Widecombe-in-the-Moor, Devonshire, England, on June 9, 1842, and is consequently in his forty-ninth year. He is a descendant of a long line of old yeomen, for whom the old country was for hundreds of years famous. His father, the late Mr. Daniel Easterbrook, quitted farming life when the subject of this sketch was a child, and after becoming possessed of the necessary qualifications, was appointed to the onerous position of manager of the oldest brewing concern in the famous brewing center in England, Burton-on-Trent, from which issues the world-renowned Bass and Allsopp Ales. There his sons George and John (the latter now residing in Texas), were first initiated into the mysteries of brewing. A severe and long continued attack of acute rheumatism, obliged George to look to another profession for a livelihood. He chose that of shorthand reporting, and as a stenographer, he, almost constantly in a delicate state of health, performed very severe and arduous labor on the London Press. In 1875, at the request of his brother-in-law, Mr. William Palmer, he purchased for that gentleman an extensive saw-mill outfit, and accompanied it to St. Petersburg, Russia, where in the face of great obstacles, chiefly caused by the frightful severity of a winter season in those polar latitudes, he succeeded in erecting and running it. Residing there during several years, he of necessity made himself familiar, not only with the habits and customs, but also with the peculiarly interesting and intensely poetic language of the northern barbarians, a sad feature of whose life has recently been eloquently portrayed to America, and the whole civilized world, through the pages of The Century, by the caustic but truthful pen of Mr. George Kennan. Returning to London, Mr. Easterbrook turned his attention to the working of the bankruptcy laws in the United Kingdom, and managed an important department in a large bankruptcy house and mercantile agency, based on somewhat similar lines to those of the well-known American institution of Bradstreet. There his mercantile education may be said to have been completed. In 1883 he was obliged to leave England, and he came to Louisiana in search of a warmer climate, and one better suited to the health of his son, whose constitution suffered in the too-bracing atmosphere of England. He is fully satisfied that by taking this course he has succeeded in his object. Mr. Easterbrook takes a lively interest in all matters agricultural, and notwithstanding that his abilities with his pen fit him for very different duties in life, he asserts that he never feels so contented or at home as when on the plantation. After several attempts had been made to induce him to accept the position of stenographer to the district court of Natchitoches (a recent law rendering it obligatory on all clerks of court to attach such an official to their several courts), he has finally accepted the position. Formerly he was engaged in assisting his brother to manage the business of the Farmers' Union store at Colfax. Mr. Easterbrook married, in 1865, his cousin, Miss Amelia A. Palmer, of Hennock, Devonshire, and Melrose Hall, London, by whom he has had several children, the only one of whom now living is the son referred to above, George Augustus Easterbrook, born at Ashburton, Devon, July 12, 1873. Mr. Easterbrook has an unbounded belief in the future of Louisiana, as the garden spot of the world, and in that of our country generally, and is in particular proud of it as a great representative of the dominant Anglo-Saxon race. He hopes and believes that the common interests of humanity are certain to be helped by a long-continued union of interests, on both sides of the Atlantic. He loses no opportunity of familiarizing himself with all matters, political, social and religious, affecting the welfare of the citizens of the commonwealth, into which he has thrown his lot. He is, to use the words of Burns, "a chiel among us taking notes, and faith he'll prent 'em." His letters to the old home of his fathers have induced several other Englishmen to come to Louisiana with their families, to settle. They are all imbued with the law-abiding principles, ingrained in the best of the emigrants from Europe, i. e., the very class whom the American people are discovering to be the best suited for transplantation on our soil.

Yours very truly
William H. Jack

SEE PAGE 350.

SEE PAGE 350.

INDEX

NOTE: *Since the text of the present publication is taken from a larger work*
still used and cited by some researchers, the original pagination has
been retained. *Index entries correspond to the old page number that*
appears at the top left or right of each leaf. *The "a" and "b" desig-*
nations after each number indicate the specific column on that page.

A. F. & A. M. [Masonic Lodge]:
312b, 313a
Aaron, Hannah: 314a
Abbot, A. L.: 299a
Abram, Sarah H.: 361b
Adams, Adam C.: 320b
  Benjamin: 320b
  Briant: 320b
  Christena: 320b
  Clarlia Forteneau Ginger: 320b
  John Q.: 320b
  Johnson: 320b
  Josiah: 320b
  Lora: 320b
  Lucy: 320b
  Pollie Holding: 320b
  Richard: 320b
  Roselia: 320b
  Whart: 334b
Adams House (Hotel): 315a
Adeyches Indians, 295a
Addison, J.: 302b
  J.D., Dr.: 302a, 318b
  John D., Dr.: 318b
  Sarah Ann: 332b
African Baptist Church: 313b
African Methodist Church: 313b
Agues, John A.: 297a
Airey, Annette: 370b
  Annette Whitcomb: 370a
  F.W.: 305b
  Harriet: 369b
  T.H.: 301b, 303b
  Thomas L.: 370a
  Thomas H.: 312b
Airhart, Peter: 302a
  William: 304b, 305b
Alabau, T. Rev.: 311b

Alexandria, LA: 312a, 312b
Alexander Cemetery: 318b
Allen, James: 305b
Allen, LA: 348b
Ame, Rev.: 309a
Anastase (var. Anassthase), Rev.
  Pere: 294b, 309a
Anderson, Randolph H., Dr.: 308a
Andrien (Andrieu), A. Rev.: 311b
Anduze, Rev.: 311a
Anthony, C. C.: 297b
Anti-Lottery League: 329b
Antoine, Widow: 297a
Anty, Mr. _____: 297a
  Aurelia: 313b
  Elizabeth Aurelia: 362b
  Louis: 296b
  Valery: 297a
Archange, Rev.: 309a
Areaux, T. H.: 301b
Arail (var. Anail), M. R.: 310a
Armand, E. Rev.: 311b
Armstrong, Alexander B.: 321a
  Barney: 321a
  Barnie L.: 321a
  David H.: 334a
  Jennie: 321a
  John N: 321a
  Lizzie Butler: 321a
  Lizzie Nye: 321a
  Lula: 321a
  Mary: 321a
  Mary Rogers: 321a
  T. C.: 300b, 338b
Arroyo del Durasno: 297b
Asher, _____ Mr.: 314b
  P. L.: 315a
Assinais Indians: 295a

Atkins, Abigail: 321a
    Alice Boal: 321b
    John: 321a
    Lizzie: 321b
    Maggie May: 321b
    Mason F.: 321a
    Medora: 321b
    Edmond: 310b
Attahoo River: 297a
Aubree, Rev.: 317a
Augustin, (free negro): 296b
Avoyelles Indians: 295b

Babers, A.J.: 321b
    Elizabeth Stokes: 321b
    John W.: 321b
    Lee A.: 321b
    Lula: 321b
    Mary M.: 321b
    M. E. Watson: 321b
    Nettie: 321b
    Pearl: 321b
    William A: 321b
Backen, P. M.: 302a
Bacon, Thomas S., Reverend:
    312b
Badgers, Mary: 313b
Badin (see Bodin)
Bahn, Bertha: 314a
Bailey, Elizabeth: 363b
Baird, A. M.: 302a
    A. W.: 297b
    B. H.: 297b, 302a
    C.B.: 297b
Baker, H. H.: 315b
Baldwin, Issac: 299a, 300a
Balliss, Francois, Rev.: 309a
Bank of Natchitoches: 314a
Banks, Nathaniel P., Gen: 318b
Baptist Church of Natchitoches:
    313b
Baptist Church of Robeline
    (Spanish Lake): 316b
Barbee, Agarine Dulliam: 321b
    A. V.: 322a
    J. L.: 321b
    Joseph L.: 322a
    Leslie: 321b
    M. A. Carter: 322a
Barbes, W. H.: 310b

Barbier, Francois Gaspard: 308b
Barbin, Arestides: 319b
Barker, Celia
Barlow, John A: 300b, 302b
Barnabie, Rev.: 309a
Barnes, G. W.: 314a
Barnes, Robbie: 314a
Barron, L. G.: 303a
    L. R.: 304b
    V. A.: 302b
    Virgil A.: 301a
Bartlett, F. G.: 297b
Baruch, Charlotta: 333a
Bason, Juliania: 320b
Bath, H.: 311a
Baton Rouge: 312b
Battle Ground Plantation: 295b
Baum, _____Dr.: 309b
Bayou Amulet: 310a
Bayou Blue: 296b
Bayou Boine: 297a
Bayou Bourbeaux: 311b
Bayou Castor: 297a
Bayou Cie: 311b
Bayou, Derbanne (Dearbonne): 297a
Bayou Deyet: 297a
Bayou Dieu Domini [Dugdemona?]:
    297a
Bayou Dole: 311b
Bayou Jeat: 297a
Bayou Kisatchie: 293b
Bayou Moreauville: 311b
Bayou Nantachi: 297a
Bayou Pierre: 297a, 297b, 311b,
    312a
Bayou Rapides: 336b
Bayou Tete du Cheval: 297a
Bayou Tortoise: 297a
Beasley, James: 297a
Beattie, Taylor: 305a
Beaudry, Frank: 318a
Beaulieu, Jean M. Rev: 311a,
    322a
Beckham, Asa: 297a
Behan, W. J.: 315b
Bellevue, _____: 311b
Bellewood, LA: 330b
Bennett, Joseph: 313b
Benoist, Antoine Gabriel Francis:
    322b
    Alphonse, 322b

92

Benoist, Amanda: 322b
    Catherine Sanguinet 322b,
        323a
    Celine Cloutier: 323a
    Charles Francis: 322b
    Clemence: 322b, 323a
    Felix: 323a
    Jacques Louis: 322b
    Jules: 322b
    Julia: 322b
    Julie (Mrs. Chopin):
        334b
    Ludwick: 323a
    Neuville: 323a
    S. H.: 301b
    Suzette: 322b, 323a
    Suzette (Rachal): 322b
    Victor Sanguinet: 322b
    Victor Sanguinet, Jr.: 323a
    William R.: 323a
Bermudas [LA]: 297a
Bernstein, Adolph: 323b
    Albert M.: 324a
    Arnold: 324a
    Augusta: 323b, 324a
    Bertha: 323b, 324a
    Charlotte Yachetsky: 323b
    Gustave: 323b
    H.: 300b
    Henry: 324a
    Issac: 323b
    Joseph: 323b
    Julian: 324a
    Julius: 323b
    Mary: 323b
    Maurice: 323b
    Nettie: 324a
    Philip: 323b, 324a
    Rebecca: 323b
    Robert: 323b
    Rosalie Marks: 324a
    Rudolph: 324a
    Samuel: 323a, b, 324a
Berry, Giles: 297b
Berry and Ingram brick kilns: 318a
Berry and Thompson, firm of: 299a
Bertrand, Anna: 324b
    Charles, Jr.: 324a,b
    Charles, Sr.: 324a
    Charles III: 324b
    Clemence: 324b

    Eloise: 324b
    Florentine: 324b
    Francois: 324a, b
    Francois of Charles, Jr.: 324b
    Harriet: 324b
    Harriet, of Charles, Jr: 324b
    Leopold: 324b
    Lise Woods: 324b
    Mary F. Rachal: 324a, b
    Woods: 324b
Bertrand: see also Betran
Besson, Julien: 296a
    Pierre: 296a
Betran, Louisa: 368b
Beulah Plantation: 335a
Big Bend: 311b
Big Island: 311b
Biloxi (Boluxa): 294a
Biloxi Fort: 295a
Binet, Mr.: 312b
Bishop, J.M.: 302a
Bisteneau (var. Bastriano) Lake:
    296b
Black, Samuel: 302b
Black Lake: 296b
Blackburn, W. Jasper: 320a
Blackman, W. F.: 320a
Blacksher, D. A.: 299a, 314b
    F. C.: 316b, 317a
Blackstone. E. S.: 297b, 302a
    M.: 304b
    M. P.: 302b
Blair, J. D.: 297b, 305b
    J. J.: 297b
Blake, John: 316b, 329a
Blanc, J. B., Rev.: 311a
Blanchard, C. P.: 303a
    Edward O.: 301a, 312a
    Newton C.: 320b
    O. P.: 297b
Blower, Harriet: 368b
Blondel, [Philippe], Comm.: 295a, 308b
Bludworth, A.: 299a
    Alfred: 312b
    James: 297a, 305a
    P., coroner: 299b
Blunt, A. Rayford: 304a, b
Boal, Alice: 321b
Boatner, Congressman: 320b
Bodin, Gaspard: 296b
Boisnette, J. B.: 296b

Bonvellon, P.:   297a
Bordelon, Hilaire: 298a
   Hypolite: 296b, 318b
   L. F.:   298a
   Louis: 319b
Bordinave, V.:   306a
Borman, Alex: 319b
Bosley, J. R.:   297b, 298a, 302a
Bossier,_____: 320a
   Gen.:   297b
   Francois: 296b
   J. J.:   302b
   J. Jules: 300b, 310a
   L. A.:   300b
   P.:   306a
   P. E.:   301a
   Pierre, Gen.:   304a
   Pierre, E., Gen: 303b
   Placide: 297a, 306a, 319b
   S. Mrs.:   297b
   S. S.:   301b, 302a
   Sylvester: 303b
   T.:   301a
   Theophile: 301a
Bouis, Benjamin Joseph: 301a
   Edward: 325a
   Emelie Chamard: 324b
   Leo: 325a
   Louis V.:   325a
   Mary M. Hartman: 325a
   Oscar: 325a
   P. F.:   324b, 325a
   P. V.:   324b
   Stella: 325a
Boulard, Madame: 318a
Boult, D. H.:   301a, 302a, 303b,
   D. H., Jr.:   300b
   W. H.:   301b, 302b
Bowie, James: 309b
   Rezin P.:   309b
Bowman, Alex: 320a
Boyce, Charles W.:   319b
   Henry: 300a, 320a
   M.:   303b
   Michael: 297b, 301b
   Victor (emancipated slave):
      301b
Boyd, Thomas D.:   314a
Boynton, Martha: 369a
   Moses: 369a
Brady, W.:   310a

Braimer, G. M.:   299a
Brandon, Capt.:   374a
Breazeale, Adeline Prudhomme:
      325a
   B. B.:   306a
   Cammilla: 325b
   Cammilla Leacht: 325b
   Elisha: 314a
   H. P.:   302a, 303a, 307b, 308a,
      314b, 325a
   Hopkins P.:   325b
   Maude: 314a
   N. M., Mrs.:   297b
   Phanor: 300b, 307a, 313a, 314b
   W. O.:   297b, 302a, 303a
   W. W.:   302b, 306a, 325a, 366a
   Winona: 325b
Breazeale Battalion,   Natchitoches
      Rangers: 326a
Breazeale, Payne & Harrison: 297b
Breazeale Union, 346b
Breda, A. P.:   302b, 303b
   Alexander P., Dr.:   308a, 325b
   Edmee, 326a
   Elice Hertzog: 326a
   Elmira: 326a
   Emma: 326a
   J. E.:   300b, 311a, 313a,b
   J. Emile: 325b, 326b, 327a
   J. Ernest: 300b, 325b
   J. P.:   297b
   John P., Dr.:   325b, 326a,b
   John P., of J. Ernest: 326a
   Joseph E.:   326a
   Marie Emee Tauzin: 327a
   Marie Helmina D.:   325b, 313a
   Philip :   301a, 308a
Brent, W. L.:   320a
Brevel, Batazar: 297a
Brian, Mary E.:   367b
Britton, Mary: 309b
Bronaugh, M.:   300a
Brooks, J. C.:   297b
Brosset Island [Isle Brevel]:
      297a
Brosset,
   M. C.:   303b, 305b
   Oliver: 301b
Brown, D.:   298a
   Inil: 297b
   J. W.:   298a

94

Brown (con't)
  M.: 316a, 317a
  Martin: 316b
  Mary: 297b
  Mary E.: 361a
  T. D.: 297b
  Tally D.: 301b, 351b
  T. M.: 301b
  W. W.: 298a
Brown's Hotel: 318b
Bryan, Mary E.: 307a
Bryant, Hardy: 297b
Buard, Albert: 367a
  Aspasie: 367a
  August Emanuel: 367a
  Cecile: 367a
  Emelie: 367a
  Felicie: 367a
  J.: 304b
  J. B. O.: 309b
  Jean Baptiste: 367a
  Jean Baptiste, Jr.: 367a
  Julia: 366b
  L. A., Miss: 297b
  Louis: 309a
  Marie: 367a
  Marie Desiree Hertzog: 367a
  Marie Julie: 367a
Bubst, L. Rev.: 309a
Buckner, E. E.: 300b, 314b
Buckstone, M. C.: 297b
Buie, Ann: 336a
Building and Loan Association:
  314b
Bullard, C. A. 300b
  Charles A.: 300a
  Henry A.: 299b, 319b, 320a
  J.L.: 297b
  Josephine E.: 374b
Bullard & Campbell, firm of: 311a
Bullitt, B.W.: 302a
  Benjamin: 300b
  Benjamin, Sheriff: 300b
Bunch of Cannes: 296b
Bundanis, M.: 298a
Burdick, L. H.: 301a, 307a, 310a,b
  317a
  M.F., Mrs.: 316b
Burke, Col.: 303a
  Mary Ann: 336a
  Mr.: 312b

Peter: 336a
R. E.: 301a, 302a, 303b, 306a,
  310b. 311a
Burkett, Amy Dora: 327b
  Ann Cannon: 327a,b
  Ana Elizabeth: 327b
  Armecy Hendrick: 327b
  Claudie Idell: 327b
  Daniel Winfred: 327b
  George Washington, 327a
  George Washington, Jr., 327b
  Isabella Mahala Carroll: 327b
  Isadora Jane: 327b
  J. N.: 303a
  James Clifford: 327b
  James Madison: 327a,b
  James Madison, Jr.: 327b
  Jesse Allen: 327b
  John Norvel: 327b
  Josiah Newton: 327b
  Mable: 327b
  Margaret Elizabeth: 327b
  Mary Francis: 327b
  Thomas Benton: 327b
  William Jasper: 327b
  Zuella: 327b
Burnett, David S.: 300b
  David: 303b
Burns, Henry: 310a
  W. M.: 299a
Burnside, Emmet: 328a
  Jane Graham: 328a
  John: 327b
  L. R.: 327b, 328a
  Martha Jones: 327b
  Robert H.: 328a
Butt, Emeline: 358a
Butler, Annie L.: 328b
  Bessie L.: 328b
  Bettie Williams: 328b
  Carrie Campbell: 328b
  J.W.: 297b, 304b
  John W.: 328a,b
  Julia A. Hailey: 328a
  L. W., Dr.: 308a
  Lizzie: 321a
  Maggie L.:
  Thomas: 320a
  W.B.: 303a,b, 306a
  William B.: 328b
  Woodson B.: 328a,b

Busy (Bussi), M: 304a
Buvens, Annie Kathleen: 329a
    Cecilia: 354b
    Ella F. Hogue: 329a
    J. E.: 316b
    James Monroe: 329a
    John G.: 328b, 329a
    M. F.: 316b, 317a, 329a
    Monroe F.: 328b, 329a
    Peter: 328b
    Robert Elmer: 329a
    Sarah A. Dendy: 328b, 329a

Cade, S.M.: 298a
Cadillac, Antoine Lamotte: 295a,b
Caddo Indians: 296b
Cajahdet (Caddo Indian): 296b
Caldes (Caldar), Francois de,
    Rev.: 309a
Calves, R.S., Dr.: 310b, 313a, 313b
Caldwell, J, II.: 317a
Caldwell Family: 316b
Calhoun, Meredith: 318a
    N. P.: 298a
Cameron, Charles A., Rev.: 312b
    Emily F.: 344a
Camp Salubrity: 305a
Camp Villero: 305a
Campbell, ___ Judge: 300a
    Carrie: 328b
    J. G.: 300a, 304a, 341b
    James G.: 319b
    Joseph G.: 312a
    William S.: 301a
Campbell & Co., W. S.: 298a
Campe, Rev: 309a
Campte: 302a, 311b, 318b
Canary Islanders: 295a
Cane River: 297a, 309b, 324a
Cannon, Ann: 327a,b
    James D.: 301a
Capers, H.: 316b
    Hickson: 307b
Capitaine (Captain) Pierre:
    297a
Caporal, E. L.: 307a
Carey, Nancy: 355b
Carnahan, A.: 298a, 301b
    John: 299a
Carr, John C.: 299b, 300a,b, 301a

Carr (Cont'd):
    Mortimer: 319b
Carroll, Frank L.: 330a
    Isabella Mahala: 327b
    Lula Pearl: 329b
    Lula Prothro: 329b
    M.: 298a
    Monroe W.: 329b, 330a
    J. F.: 318b
    John F., Dr.: 308a
    M. W.: 318b
    Sarah J.: 330a
Carter, A. V.: 303a, 307b
    A. Everly: 331a
    Americus V.: 330a,b, 331a,b
    Bessie: 330b
    Bessie Lee: 332b
    Elizabeth A.: 330a
    Eva T.: 331a
    Floy Belle: 332b
    Harmon: 332b
    I. F.: 307b
    Issac F.: 330a,b, 331b, 332a
    J. F.: 300b, 317a
    Jemima Cole: 330a
    Jennie E.: 363a
    John J.: 332a
    Josie L.: 332a
    Laura L.: 331a,b
    Lillian Lee: 331a
    Lizzie: 314a
    Lucile: 332a
    M. A., Miss.: 322a
    Margaret U. Holden: 330a, 331b
    Martha Ann Estes: 332a
    Martha Ponder: 330b
    Mason T.: 331a
    Mattie J. Ponder: 331b
    Nettie J. Wagley: 332b
    Norwood W.: 331a
    Ponder S.: 330b, 331a
    S. L. Miss.: 316b
    Sallie: 332b
    Sarah Ann Addison: 332b
    Sarah L. Smith: 331a
    Silas E.: 331a
    Thadeus A.: 330a, 331a,b
    Thomas: 330a
    W. A.: 300b, 307b
    Willian: 330a
    William E.: 331a

96

Carter (cont'd):
  William Harmon: 332b
  William O.: 330a
Carter & Son, firm of: 330b
Carver, Ada Whitfield Jack: 351b
  M. H.: 300b, 303a, 310a,b, 314b,
    317a, 351b
Cashmere Plantation: 355b
Casie, Annie: 369a
Caspari, Charles: 333a
  Charlotta (Baruch): 333a
  David: 333a
  Dora: 333a
  Emanuel: 333a
  Gustave: 333a
  Joseph: 333a
  Julia: 333a
  Leopold: 303a,b, 305a, 306a,
    313a, 314b, 315a,b 333a
  Richard L.: 300b, 306b, 314b
    333a
  Samuel: 333a
Cassady, A. E.: 305a, 312b
  Albert E.: 308a
Castenado, Appoline: 342a
Catholic Church, Robeline: 316b,
  317a, b, 318a
Cauley, Marion: 318b
Cayacaille, Natchitoches Indians:
  296a
Census, 1785: 294a
  1890: 294a
  and assessment, 1858: 294a
  and assessment, 1870: 294a
Centina, Elodiscia: 354a
Chagneau (Chaigneau), Widow: 297b
Chaler, A.: 298a
  F. F.: 306a
  P. O.: 298a
  Terence: 298a
Centenary College: 328b
Chamard, Emelie: 324b
  Marie B.: 296b
Chaplin, Brazeale & Chaplin,
  firm of: 314b
Chaplin, Chichester, Judge
  300a,b, 302a, 304b, 311a,
  313a, 314b, 316a, 363b
  C., Jr.: 306b, 310b, 313a
  F. P.: 303a
  Marcella: 363b

Chaplin (Cont'd)
  T.P.: 306a
  Thomas P.: 300b, 313a
Chapman, Alberta: 374a
  B. F.: 313a
  Benjamin F.: 300b
  Monroe: 351b
Charbonneau (var. Chabineau),
  Widow: 296a
  Charleville, Aurora Rachal:
    333b
  John Baptist: 333b
  Joseph: 333b
  Landry: 333b, 334a,b
  Pauline DuPrey: 334a
  Victoire Verdon: 333b
Charrio, Pierre: 296b
Chelletre, Etienne: 298a
  Pierre: 297a
Chesteraur Indians: 296b
Chevalier, Emile [f.m.c.]: 298a
Chickasaw Indians: 294b
Chief of the Flour (Indian): 295b
Chinn, T. W.: 320a
Chopin, Cora Henry: 335a
  Eugenie: 335a, 346b
  J. B.: 334b
  Julie Benoist: 334b
  Lamy: 303a, 334a
Chopin & Benoist, Plantation: 298a
Chopin, LA: 334b, 335a
Chorin, A. Rev.: 311b
Christy, Charles F.: 301a
Churches; Religious Organization
  see: Adayes Mission
      African Baptist
      African Methodist
      Baptist
      Free Sons of Israel
      Lutheran Benevolent Soc.
      Methodist
      Methodist Episcopal
      St. Francis, Catholic
      South African Colored
      Trinity English Protestant
        Episcopal
Clamons, J. A.: 302b
Clanton, G. L.: 298a
  M. F.: 298a
Clark, J, A.: 306b
  Joseph: 298a 316a

Clark (cont'd)
   Joseph, Mrs. 316a
   Patrick: 300a
Clear Lake: 297a, 311b
Clifton, Catherine: 353b
   J. B.: 317a
Closseau, Gilbert: 297a
Cloutier, Alexis Jr.: 296b
   Celine: 323a
   Clara Prudhomme: 323a
   Edouard: 315a
   Emile: 306a
   J. B.: 298a, 309b
   Neuville: 323a
Cloutierville: 311b, 324a
Cobb, T.: 306a
Cockerham, J. W.: 314b
Cockfield, A. R.: 315a
   Anglo Puritan: 335a,b
   Belton Theodosia: 335a
   E.J.: 305b
   Hannah: 335a
   Justin Compere: 335a
   Ladson Hartley: 335a
   LeRoy Akron: 335b
   Letitia Everett: 335a
   Lilly Connie: 335a
   Marcia: 335b
   Moma Eble: 335b
   Stanley Forno: 335b
   Taney Autun: 335b
   Tustin Level: 335a
   W.: 304b
   William Ebeneezer Joseph: 335a
   William H.: 335a
Cockfield and Benoit Plantation:
   298a
Cockrell, Simon: 301a
Coffee, Fannie: 314a
   Florence: 314a
Coe & Loupart, firm of: 299b
Cole, Jemima: 330a
   Josiah L.: 319b
Colfax, La.: 294a, 313b, 318a
Collier, L., Mrs.: 316b
   Mary: 339b
Collins, Mary: 364a
Colored Methodist Church of
   Robeline: 316b
Colton, John: 302a
Commercial Hotel: 318b

Compere, J. M.: 298a
Conant, Florentin: 296b
   Jean [f.m.c.]: 298b
Conde, Dr.: 322b, 323a
   Mary Ann: 323a
   Mary Ann (La Ferne): 323a
Condet, Justine: 302b
   Noel [f.m.c.]: 298a
Convent of Divine Providence: 314a
Cook, G. J.: 317a
   G. J. & Co.: 316b
   W. M.: 316a
Coons, J. M.: 313a
Cooper, Harriet: 354a
   John W., Rev.: 354a
Corbett, Ida: 314a
Cortes, Benjamin V.: 300b
   Jean F.: 302a, 304a
Cortez, John E. [F.]: 304a
Cosgrove, Annie: 336a
   Burdette: 336a
   Burke Eddie: 336a
   Hugh: 335b
   J. H.: 301a, 303a, 307a,b,
     310b, 311a, 313a, 314a, 315a
     335b, 336a,b
   Julia A. Johnson: 336a
   Mary Ann Burke: 336a
Cote Breda: 326b
Cotes D'Afrique: 311b
Cotton Seed Oil Mill: 375a
Cottonport, La.: 311b
Coughlin Buildings: 318b
Coulon de Villier: 308b
Court, District: 299a,b, 300a
Court, Parish: 300a,b
Coushatta Point: 302a
Courtesse, Louis: 297a
Couty, Andre V., Dr.: 308a
Couty (var. Coutant), Paul: 296b
Cowser, W.R.: 298a
Cox, J. H.: 316a
   W. C.: 316b, 317a
Cox & Thomas: 316b
Crain, Alfred P.: 336b
   Annie, Mrs.: 318a
   Elizabeth Wood: 336b
   George A.: 336b
   Penn, Dr.: 308a, 336b, 337a
   Robert A., Col.: 336b
   Virginia S. Terrett: 336b

Crawford, James: 299b
Crenshaw, H. R.: 307a
Creole culture: 319a
Crette, Marie J.: 296b
Criswell (var. Chriswell),
  Martha: 346a
Crocheron, Sherman B., Dr.:
  308a
Crockett, Annie Mary: 336a
  Charles Frederick: 337a
  Charles William: 336a
  David: 309b
  Jennie B. Hunter: 336a
  Mary Deniston: 337a
  Walter Henry: 336a
  William: 337a
Cromie, James: 300b, 307a
Cross, T. J.: 314b
Crow, Issac: 296a
  Michael: 296a
Crozat, Antoine: 295a
Cruz (var. Craz), Miguel Rosalie
  de la: 296b
Culpepper, Eleanor: 370b
Cuney, Frederick, Rev.: 311b
Cunningham, A. B.: 306b
  Ann Buie: 336a
  Anna Peyton: 338a
  C., Dr.: 331a
  Cecile Hertzog: 338a
  Charlotte: 338a
  Ida G.: 338a
  Ivy: 338a
  J. H.: 300b, 304b, 307b,
    330b, 336a
  John H.: 338a
  Laura: 338a
  M. E., Mrs.: 307b
  M. J.: 300b, 315a, 375b
  Milton C.: 338a
  Milton J.: 304b, 319b, 336a,
    337b, 338a
  Milton J., Jr.: 338a
  Sidney: 338a
  Thalia Tharp: 338a
  V. G., Rev.: 313b
  William T.: 338a
Curry, Augustus J.: 338a
  M. F., Mrs.: 338a
Cushing, Col.: 305a

Dagobert (var. Ragobert), Rev.:
  309a
Daily, Amanda M.: 338b, 339b
Dallas, Henry: 302b
Dalrymple, Lizzie: 341a
Danglais (var. Dinglis), Dr.:
  304a
Daniel, Amanda Daily: 339b
  Anson W.: 338b
  Caroline Gay: 339a
  E. B., Widow: 298a
  Emma A.: 338b
  John P.: 338b
  Joseph L.: 338b, 339b
  Josephine I.: 338b
  L.: 316a,b, 317a
  Lambert: 338b, 339a
  Lambert Jr.: 338b
  Larkin O.: 338b, 339a,b, 340a
  Laura A.: 338b
  Lee: 338b
  Mary Collier: 339b
Darby, Louisiana historian: 308b
Darden, Lucitta: 330b
David, Elizabeth: 297a
Davidson, E. C.: 304b
  T. G.: 320a
Davion, E.: 298a
Davis, Dorphey: 348b
  H. J.: 351b
  L. F., Mrs.: 298a
  Maria: 351b
  R. A.: 316b
Dawson, John B.: 320a
de Alvarado, Muscoso: 294b
de Bienville, Jean Baptiste Le
  Moyne: 294b, 295a,b
Deblieux, A.: 298a, 304b, 305a
  Alexander L.: 340a
  Alexander Louis: 340b
  Aurore Metoyer: 340a
  Camille: 340a
  Cecile: 314a
  E. V.: 298a, 340a,b
  E. Valery: 305b
  Euphrosine Tauzin: 340a
  J. N.: 298a
  Jefferson: 340a
  Julie: 340b
  Julie Prudhomme: 340a
  (cont'd)

99

Deblieux (con't)
  Leon: 340a
  Leston: 340b
  Louis A.: 301a
  Marie: 340a
  Matilda Valery: 340a
  Roseline: 370a
  Stella: 340a
Decker, John: 316a
Dehuste, Indian Chief: 296b
De la Motte, M.: 308b
de Lattin,
  see Lattier
Deslouche, Augustinia: 313b
De Louche, F.: 298a
Deloche, J. E.: 315a
Delouches, Landry: 301b
  Sylvan: 301b
Delvaux (var. Dalvaux), Rev.:
  309a
de Mezieres, Athanase: 296a
Dendy, Sarah A.: 328b, 329a
Deniston, Mary: 337a
De Peyster, Gen.: 312b
Derbanne (var. Derbonne), L. G.:
  298a
  J. A.: 306a
  Louis: 296b
Derouen, E.: 297a
De Russy: 306a
  John A.: 300b
  L. G.: 303b, 304a, 312a
De Russy Cemetery: 318b
de Soto, Antoine Bermudez: 296a
  Hernan, explorer: 294b
  Manuel: 296b
  Marcel: 296a
Despallie, Matthew: 309b
de Vargas, J. F.: 310b, 311a
De Veles, Rev.: 309a
d'Iberville, Pierre LeMoyne:
  294b, 295a
Dicharry, P. F., Rev.: 311b
Dickerson, F. M.: 298a
Dietrich, Albert: 314a
Dismukes, A. L.: 303a
  Ada Ruth: 340b
  Charles H.: 340b
  Katie C. Jack: 340b
  M. L.: 300b, 314b
  Marcus L.: 340b, 341a

Marcus L., Jr.: 340b
Mary: 340b
Mary Jane Hager: 340b
Thomas H.: 340b
Dixon, J. M.: 298a, 341a
  Jared S.: 341a
  Lizzie Dalrymple: 341a
  Mary, Widow: 298a
Doak, D. P.: 314b
  Doak, Thomas: 314b
  W. C.: 314b
Dobbin, J. C.: 358b
Dobbs, Annie M.: 354a
Dodd, T. E.: 316b
Donaldsonville, La.: 312b
Douglas, W. T., Rev.: 312b
Dover, A.: 316a
Dowden, S. G.: 303a
Dranguet, B.F.: 306b
  Benjamin F.: 341a,b
  C. F.: 300b, 310b
  Charles F.: 341a,b, 342a
  Charles F., Jr.: 341b
  Eliza [Elizee]: 341b
  Eliza Greneaux: 341b
  Laura: 341b
  Lelia: 341b
  Louis A.: 341b
  Marie Helmina: 325b, 326a
  Victoria Celeste Tauzin: 341a,
    341b
Drunkard's Bayou: 296b
Dreyfus, Alphonse: 359b
  Julia: 359b
  Justine: 359b
Drury, George: 327a
Dubois, Antoine: 297a
  J. B.: 297a
Ducasse, Jules: 315b
Ducose, J.: 311a
Ducournau, A.: 315b
  Appoline Castenado: 342a
  Estelle: 342a
  J. A.: 298a, 310b, 342a
  J. A., Jr.: 315a,b, 342a
  J. A., Sr.: 325a
  John B.: 342a
  Lelia Sompayrac: 342a
  Louis: 342a
  Lucile: 342a
  Mary Rival: 342a

100

Ducournau & Breda, firm of:
    311a
Ducournau & Son, firm of: 314b
Duels: 303b
Duerson, James, Dr.: 308a
Dugas, Clemence: 342b
Duke. Peter: 308a
Dulanois, Indian: 295a
Dulliam, Agarine: 321b
Dumas, John: 302b
    R.: 311b
Duncan, G. W.: 313b
    R. L.: 298a
Dunlap, James, Judge: 299b
Dupleix, Clemence Dugas: 342b
    L.: 298a, 305b, 306b, 310a
    Louis: 342b
    Y.: 342a
Dupre, Adolphe, Widow: 298a
    Marie A.: 296b
    Pauline: 334a
Durier, Anthony, Rt. Rev.:
    312a
Du Roy, Michel: 296b
Dussausoy, L., Rev.: 311a
Du Tisne (var. Du Pisne):
    295a

Easterbrook, Amelia A. Palmer:
    377b
    Daniel: 376b, 377a,b
    George Augustus: 376b, 377a,b
    John: 377a,b
Ecore Rouge: 296a
Eddelman, Viola: 356a
Edmonds, Elva: 376a
    Signor: 376a
Edmondson, H. V. C.: 306a
Edwards, William: 316a
Egan, James C.: 319b
    William B.: 319b
Egypt Post Offie, La: 341a
Elam, J. B.: 304b, 320b
Elie, Pierre: 296b
Ellis, George H.: 355a
Ellzey, J. A.: 318a
    J. H.: 298a
    William: 298a
Ely, H. A.: 310a

Espy, K.: 306a
Estage
    see: Lestage
Estes, Martha Ann: 332b
Eustache, Rev.: 309a
Ezernack, ____: 303a
    Della: 314a 303a
    Edward: 300b
    Joe: 298a, 310a
    Joseph: 302b, 303b
    Mary Odalie: 314a

Fairfield, LA: 311b
Fairmont, LA: 311b
Farmer's Alliance: 321a, 322a,b,
    331a, 346b, 348b
Farris, W. W.: 318b
Farson, Azenor, Sr: 298a
Faulkner, R. L.: 302b
Faure, Olandine: 356a
Favrot, Col.: 358a
Fearing, Martin: 312b
Featherston, John: 309b
Ferguson, R.W.: 307b
Fires: 299b
    in Natchitoches: 296a, 342a
    in Provencal: 318b
Figari, H., Rev.: 311b, 322b
Fisher, J., Senator: 339b
    M. C.: 316b, 317a
Fitzgerald, E. F.: 310b
Flanner, Daisy Sers: 343b
    Eugene: 343b
    Joseph: 343a
    Josephine: 343b
    Leo: 343b
    Ricardo: 343b
    T. J., Dr.: 343a
    Thomas Boyce: 343a
    Thomas J.: 307b
    Thomas J., III: 343b
    Thomas Jefferson, Jr.: 342b,
    343a,b
Flannigan, Elizabeth: 330a
Fleming, ___ (police juror): 303a
    Bartholmie: 300b
    E. B.: 298a
    J. B.: 302a, 303a
Flournoy, James S.: 304b

Fonteneau, Clarlia: 320b
  G.: 302a
  L. T.: 306b
Fonteneau Hotel: 311a
Ford, W. L.: 314a
Fort Claiborne: 299a
Fort Jesup: 304a, 312b, 316a
Fort Rosalie (Natchez): 295b
Fortson, Lizzie: 314a
Foster, A. T.: 318a
  J. W.: 299a
  Lucretia Maude: 352a
  T. J.: 298a, 306b
Fox, Lula: 344b
  Rosanna T.: 328a
Franciar, Father: 311b
Francois, Jean, Rev.: 309a
Franklin, LA: 312b
Frazier, John: 299a
Frederic, Ben: 298a
  Edward: 298a
  Honore: 298a
Frederique, Marie R.: 296b
Free Sons of Isreal: 313b
Freedman's Bureau: 304a
Freeman, _____(explorer):
    305a
  John: 302a
  R. W.: 303a, 316b, 317a
Freeman Family: 316b
Furlong, N.: 301b

Gaiennie, Amanda: 344a, 369a
  Aurora: 344a
  Aurore: 349a
  Denis: 344a
  Emeline: 344a, 346b
  F.: 306a
  Francois: 343b
  Francois, Gen.: 297b,
   304a
  Heloise: 344a
  [H]Eloise Metoyer: 350a
  Heloise Metoyer: 343b, 344a
  Louise: 344a
  Mathilda: 344a
  Mathilda A.: 350a
  Valery: 343b, 344a
  Valery, Jr.: 344a

Gaines, Maj.: 350a
Galhen Derzelin (Dezzelin):
  298a
Gallien, E. J., Mrs.: 298a
  Neuville: 297a
Gallion, H. P.: 302a
  James H.: 316a
  Joseph: 306b
  Zachery T., Dr.: 308a, 313a
   314b, 315a
Gallo, Marquis de: 295a
Galop, J. L., Rev.: 311b
Galvez: 294a
Gamble, Charles R.: 344a
  E. J.: 315a, 344a,b
  E. Lillian: 344b
  Emily F. Cameron: 344a
  Emma J.: 344b
  Harry P.: 344b
  Sarah S.: 344b
Gandy, W. W.: 306a
Garland, Rice: 320a
Garrett, Sarah A.: 365a
Garza Hotel: 315a
Gay, Caroline: 339a
  Elizabeth Nash: 344b
  F. C.: 316b, 344b
  Howard: 344b
  L. B.: 316b, 317a
  Lafayette: 344b
  Louis B.: 344b
  Nena: 344b
Gay Brothers, firm of: 316b
Gay family: 316a
Gayarre, Charles: 315a
Geanty, Josephine: 313b
Gegg, N. & Son, firm of: 348a
Gelot, Father: 311b
Genoe, John: 310a,b
Gentille, Joseph, Rev.: 311b,
  312a
Gentry, Louis, Widow: 298a
George, A. B.: 319b
Gergaud, L., Rev.: 311b
Gibbs, W. R.: 318a
Gilbreath, W. A.: 307b
Gillen, Daniel L., Dr.: 308a
Gillespie, Fanny: 372a
  Fanny S.: 372a
  George E., Dr.: 372a
  J. L.: 301a

102

Gillespie (Cont'd)
   James L.: 313a
Ginger, Clarlia Fonteneau: 320a,b
Ginstiniani, E., Rev.: 311b
Givanovitch, Marco: 298a
Giustiniani, Rev.: 311b
Gizirnac, Gregoire: 297a
Gloster, Rev.: 311b
Goings, John: 313b
Gondaux, Theophile, Dr.: 308a
Gooch, W. D.: 298a, 299a
Graham, Jane: 328a
Grand Batture Island: 297a
Grand Marsh: 297a
Grande Ecore: 294b, 296b, 297b
   318b, 335b
Grant, Capt.: 315b
   Richard: 298a
   U. S., Gen.: 305a
Grant's Point, Al: 318a
Grappe, Alexis: 296b
   Francois: 296b, 318b
   J. P.: 298a
   T. L:.: 303a
Green, _____ (gambler): 309b
Green & Brogan, firm of: 318a
Greenwood, La: 312b
Gregory, Agnes: 345a
   Charles: 345a
   Mary: 345a
   Martha Hamlin: 345a
   Mattie: 345a
   Plummer: 345a
   Octavia: 345a
   R. W.: 318b
   Richard C.: 345a
   Richard W.: 345a
   Thomas, 345a,b, 372b
   William S.: 345a
Greneaux, Alma: 346a
   Amelia Lemee: 345b
   C. E.: 298a, 306b, 315a
   Charles E., Judge: 345b
   Charles E. (merchant): 345b,
     346a
   Charles E: 299b, 300a,b,
     301a, b, 310b, 314b,
     319b
   Eliza: 341b
   Irma: 346a
   L. A.: 298a, 301a, 345b

Greneaux (continued)
   Lem: 310b
   W. S.: 303b, 310b
Griffin, Josephus F., Dr.: 308a
Grillet, J. B. T.: 297a
Grosse, F., Rev.: 312a
Guillory, Felicite: 297a
Guion, Elijah, Rev.: 312b
Gurney, George: 298a
Gurley, H. H.: 320a
   Capt: 309a
Guy, G., Rev.: 322b

Hailey, J. Fuller: 316b
   Julia A.: 328a
   L., Mrs.: 298a
Haithorn, H. H.: 302a, 303a
Hale, T. B.: 299a
Hall, D. W.: 318a
   D. W. & Co.: 318b
   Ida Lillian Jack: 351b
   W. P., Judge: 351b
Haller, Pauline: 314a
   T.: 305b
Halloway, G. W.: 306a
Hamilton, A. W.: 300b, 301a, 306a
   P. H.: 302b
Hamlin, Charles, Dr.: 301a, 306a,
     308a, 310b, 345a
   John: 345a
   Martha: 345a
Hammett, R. C.: 306a
   R. E.: 298a, 301b, 302a,b
     303a
Handy, Emily: 359b
Hanson, L.: 310a
Hanson & Brazier Sawmill: 318a
Hargrove, Eleanor Culpepper: 370b
Harkins, W. D.: 310a, 311a
Harmansan, John H.: 320a
Harper, J. D.: 299a
   S. D.: 298a
Harrison, Anna K.: 344b
Hart, S. M.: 298a
   T. M.: 301a
Hartman, Mary M.: 325a
Harville, H.: 298a
Haurd, E. D., Rev.: 311a

Haurut (var. Hanrut), M.L.:
  298a
Hawthorne, T. W.: 318a
Hazelton, L. S.: 299b, 300b
Heard, D. M., Dr.: 308a, 312b
Hebert, Louis, Gen.: 349b, 364b
  Pauline, 358a
Henderson, M.: 298a
Hendricks, Armecy: 327b
  J. F.: 298a
Henry, Bessie: 346b
  Cora: 346a,b, 335a
  Emeline Gaiennie: 346b
  Eugenie Chopin: 346b
  John: 346a
  John H. : 346a,b, 347a
  Joseph: 293b, 303a,b, 305a,
    311a, 314b, 315b, 335a,
    346a,b
  Joseph, Jr.: 346a
  Joseph, Sr.: 346b
  Joseph C., Jr.: 346b
  Joseph H.: 346b
  Mable: 346b
  Martha C.: 346b
  Martha Chriswell: 346a
  S. J.: 300b
Henry & Co.: 298a
Herron, A. S.: 319b, 320b
Hertzog, Cecile: 338a
  Elcey: 326a
  Emile, Heirs of: 298a
  Henry: 298a, 326a
  Hypolite: 298a, 302a
  J. F., Widow: 298a
  Jean Francois: 297a
  John: 304b
  Laure LeComte: 326a
  Marie Desiree: 367a
  Matthew: 298a, 314b, 315b,
    319a
  Richard: 315b
  Richard, Widow: 298a
  Theodore: 305b
Hertzog family: 306b
Hewitt, John E.: 307a
Hiestand, W. H.: 300b
Highdie Plantation: 376b
Higtower, Lelia: 314a
Hill, Adeline S.: 348a

Hill (cont'd)
  Bertha L.: 348a
  "Black Jack": 347a
  Cora L.: 348a
  Emily Lake: 347a
  Eswell: 348a
  Flowers: 348a
  J. H.: 315a
  James H.: 347a,b, 348a,
    349a
  James H., Mrs.: 317a
  Joseph: 297a
  John G.: 347a
  Matilda: 348a
  Mary M. Hyams: 348a
  Rosa: 348a
  Samuel H.: 348a
Hill & Caldwell, firm of: 316b
Hill & Jones, firm of: 314a,
  347a
Himel (var. Hemell),Maria F.:
  297a
Himes, R. L.: 314a
Hines, B. M.: 298a
Hogue, Mr.: 316b
  A. H.: 329a, 344b
  Ella F.: 329a
Hogue & Gay Bros., Firm of: 344b
Holden, Elizabeth C.: 363a
  Elizabeth Flannigan: 330a
  Margaret: 330a
  Margaret U.: 331b
  Pollie: 320b
Hollingsworth, Anna A.: 348b
  Clarence W.: 348b
  Sarah McCracken: 348a
  W. W.: 348a
  William R.: 348a,b
Hollis, E.: 312b
  T. T.: 298a
Hollon, W. A.: 306a
Holmes: 303a
  Isaac: 301a
  J.: 313a
  John: 302b
  Willis: 302b, 303b, 310a,b
Home Co-operative Cotton Seed Oil
  Co.: 314b, 357a
Homer, LA.: 311b
Hongo, Eli, Dr.: 308a

Honmett, Albert T.: 349a
    Callie I.: 349a
    Celia Barker: 348b
    Clara L.: 349a
    Dorphey Davis: 348b
    Eugene R.: 349a
    L. E.: 348b, 349a
    Leola M.: 349a
    Lucy E.: 348b
    Parlee Jones: 348b
    Roger H.: 348b
    Robert E.: 348b
Hopkins, Walter D.: 316a
Hopkins & Barber: 316a
Hornsby, J. R.: 302b, 304a
Hotham, J. G.: 299b
Hough, T. J., Rev.: 313b
Howe, Mrs.: 316a
    J. E.: 307b
Howell, W. F.: 298a
Hubley, D. W.: 307a,b
Huerta, J., Rev.: 309a
Hughes, James C.: 301a
    Millie: 314a
    Nellie: 314a
Hughes & Carter, firm of: 316a
Hunt, T. C.: 298a
    Thomas C.: 306b, 309b
Hunter, Jennie B.: 337a
    Robert A.: 319b
    T.: 313a
    Thomas: 298a
    William: 312a
Huppe, J. B. T., Widow: 298a
Hyams, Mr.: 299b, 314b
    Aurore Gaiennie: 349a
    Thomas, Lieut.: 307a
    Denis J.: 350a
    E. L.: 298a, 306b
    Eleazar L.: 349a
    Eleazar L. (son of H. M. &
      Mathilde Gaiennie): 350a
    Eliza Levy: 349a
    Emily E.: 349a
    Emily E. Prudhomme: 349a
    Emily Eloise: 350a
    Emily Prudhomme: 348a
    H. M.: 313b, 314a, 315a
    Henry M.: 300a, 319a, 348a,
      349a,b, 350a
    Jackson D.: 349a

Hyams (cont'd)
    John P.: 349a,b
    Kosciusko: 349a
    Mary Lucile: 350a
    Mary P.: 348a
    Mary R.: 349a
    Mattie A.: 350a
    S. M.: 289a, 298a, 301b,
      309b, 310a
    Samuel M.: 300b, 301a, 305b,
      348a
    Samuel M,. Jr.: 349a,b
    Samuel M., III: 349b
    Valery G.: 350a
Hyatesses Indians: see Yatasse
Hyman, William P.: 319b
Hypolite [emancipated slave]: 301b

Infant, Rev.: 309a
Inwood, Capt.: 326a
Irion, Alfred B.: 319b, 329b
Irvine, Edward: 369b
    Harriet Rebecca Watson: 369b
    Ida Madora: 369b
Isbell, R. S., Rev.: 316b
Isle Brevelle, La.: 294b, 312a
Israel, Jacob: 310a
    Mrs.: 318b

Jack, Ada Whitfield: 351b
    Catherine Clara Wellbone: 350b
    Ella: 321b
    Ella G. McIntyre: 351b
    Ida Lillian: 351b
    John W.: 351,b
    Mary C. Whitfield: 351b
    Mary Kate: 351b
    Patrick: 350b
    W. H.: 304b, 310b, 315b, 319
      320a, 364b
    Whitfield: 351b
    William C., Prof.: 350b
    William H.: 300b, 314b, 351b
    William Huston: 350a,b, 351a,b
Jack & Pierson, firm of: 364b,
    371a
Jackson,_____: 299b
    Albert Sidney: 353a
    Aurelia Townsend: 353a

Jackson (cont'd)
    Edmond W.: 351b, 352a
    Edward F.: 352a
    Eliza Ann: 352a
    Elizabeth: 368a
    Elmo Murray: 353a
    Eugene M.: 352a
    G. L.: 317a
    Hardy: 352a
    Howard H.: 352a
    Isaac: 352a
    James Hardy: 352a
    Jennie: 353a
    John: 352a
    John Milton: 352a,b
    Lelia Pierson: 353a
    Lucretia Maude Foster: 352a
    Maria Davis: 351b
    Mary: 374a
    Mildred: 353a
    Nancy Little Rutland: 352a
    R. E.: 303a
    R. L.: 304a
    Richard Ervin: 352a,b, 353a
    Richard Ervin, Jr,: 352a
    Robert Lockridge: 352a
    Sallie B.: 352a
    Sarah Little: 352a
    Warren: 351b
    William Leftwich: 352a
    William W.: 352a
Janin, Joseph: 298a
    Jules V., Dr.: 304b, 308a
Jenkins, Ben., Jr., Rev.: 316b
    W. A.: 306b
Jennings, F.: 302a,b, 303a,b
Joe, negro: 299b
Joffrion, Oscar: 320a
Johnson,_____: 303a
    _____, Gov.: 305a
    C. R.: 299a
    F., Dr.: 298a, 303b, 304a
    "Happy": 309b
    Henry: 320a
    J.: 306b, 311a
    J. C.: 304b
    J. P.: 303b
    Joseph P.: 302b
    Josiah S.: 299a, 300a, 320a
    Julia A.: 336a

Johnson (cont'd)
    L. D.: 306a
    Mary: 373a
    R. M., Col.: 345b
    Wm. R.: 300b
Joliet (explorer): 294b
Jones, _____, Judge: 300a
    Annie M. Dobbs: 354a
    B. F.: 298a
    C. K.: 314b, 315a
    Carroll: 302b, 303a, 353a,b
    Carroll, Jr.: 353b
    Catherine: 353b
    Catherine Clifton: 353b
    Cora: 353b
    Crokette K.: 313a
    Ernest W.: 354a
    Floresten: 353b
    H. T.: 301b
    Harriet Cooper: 354a
    Hattie: 354a
    Henry: 300b
    James: 354a
    James R.: 354a
    James W.: 353b, 354a
    Jerry M.: 353b
    John R.: 299a
    Laura: 353b
    Lillie: 354a
    Louis T.: 353b
    Maria L.: 353b
    Martha: 327b
    Martha (dau. of Carroll):
       353b
    Mary: 353b
    Matthew: 353b
    Nancy: 360b
    Parlee: 348b
    R. B.: 319b
    R. C.: 305b
    Roland; 320a
    Rachal: 353b
    Thomas P.: 301a, 312b
    William C.: 353b
    William P.: 313a
Jonquiere, Marquis de la: 295a
Jordan, A. G.: 298a
    John: 299a
Josey, Margaret: 370b

K. of P.: [?Knights of Pythias]:
313a
Kaffe, A.: 315a
   Adolph: 313a, 315a
   H. & Bros.: 314b
Kearney, G. W.: 306a
   George W.: 300b, 301a
   J. S.: 306a
   Nena: 314a
   Sam D.: 314a
Keatchie College: 332a, 373a
Keatchie, LA: 311b
Keegan, J. E.: 317a
   James E.: 303a, 316a,b
Keer, David: 312b
KeKouen, LA: 312a
Kellogg, Gov.: 303a
Kelly, Henry B.: 319b
   J. F.: 305b
Kennan, George: 377a
Kerry (var. Kairey), Pierre: 296b
Ketcheart, W. S.: 298a
Keyser, Ellen: 354b
   Elodiscia Centina: 354a
   Hamlin: 354b
   J. C.: 314b, 354a
   John: 354b
   Joseph C.: 354a,b
   Josephine Raggio: 354b
   Paul: 354b
Keyser & McKenna, firm of: 310a
Kieffer, Elizabeth: 367b
Kile, Alice E.: 354a
   Alma: 354b
   Camille L.: 354b
   D. W.: 315b
   Daisey C.: 354b
   Eliza B. Power: 354b
   George: 311a
   George W.: 354b, 355a
   Jacob: 298a, 302a, 304b
   James: 306a
   Joseph F.: 354b
   Joseph H.: 354b
   Lucile: 354b
   May Pearl: 354b
   S. W.: 313a, 315b, 354b
Kilgore, Eliza A. Taylor: 355a
   George A., Judge: 355a,b,
   356a
   George Morton: 355b

Kilgore (cont'd)
   John: 355a
   Julia: 355a
   Kathleen: 355b
   Mary A.: 355a
   Mattie: 355a
   Mittie Morton: 355b
   Nettie: 355a
   Robert: 355a
   Robert Oliver: 355b
Killen, J. M.: 318a
King, George R.: 300a, 319b
   I. H.: 317a
   J. F.: 320b
   R. R.: 298a
King & Blacksher, firm of: 299a
Kingston,___: 311b
Kirkland, Pauline Hebert: 358b
   Theresa: 358a
Knight, D. R.: 355b, 356a
   Daniel: 356a
   Ellen: 356a
   J. : 302a,b
   Maude P.: 356a
   Nancy Carey: 355b
   Spear: 355b
   Thomas: 356a
   Viola Eddleman: 356a

Labombarde, Pierre: 296b
LaCaze, Etienne: 297a
Lac de Mure: 318a
Lachoniere Island: 297a
Lachs, Joanna: 636b
   Simon: 364a
   Violet A.: 365b
Lacoste, Adolph L.: 356a
   Olandine Faure: 356a
La Coste, Timothy: 356a
Lacour, Gasparte: 298a
La Cour, Gaspard: 296b
La Poule d'Eau: 297a
Lac Toure Noire: 297b
La Ferne, Bardet, Dr.: 323a
   Constance: 323a
   Mary Ann: 323a
LaFontaine, L. D. C.: 301a
   P.D. Cailleau: 300b
Lake, Emily: 347a
Lake aux Meures: 296b

Lake Burnside: 328a
Lake Clark: 316a
Lake Ocassee: 294a, 315b
Lamalathie (var. Lamalthie),
   Therese: 297a
Lamarlaire, Eugenie: 356b
   John, Gen.: 356b
Lambert, Lamarque A, Dr.: 308a
Lambre (var. Lambie):
   ____: 302a
   Aurore: 366a
   Catherine: 365b
   Remy (Reiny): 297a, 310b
   Ursin: 298a
   Valsin, Mrs.: 298a
Lancaster, ____: 310a
Land, Thomas T.: 319b
Landreaux, ____: 299b
Landry, Bazilide: 357b
   Doralise: 357b
Langlois, A.: 297a
   Augustus: 299a
La Place, John: 298a, 302b, 309b,
   310a,b
   John J.: 305a
Laplante, Marcel: 298b
La Plante, O.: 306a
La Renaudiere (var. Larnodier),
   Nanet: 296b
La Salle, Rene Robert Cavalier,
   Sieur de: 294
Lasso, Leandre: 297a
Lattier (var. de Lattin),
   Ellen: 371b
   Firmin: 298b
   Theodore: 298a
   Theodul[e]: 306b
Latham, Louis: 296a
Laurents, Benoit: 309b
Laurent, F.: 296b
   W. A.: 307b
Lauve, Armand: 296b
   Nicholas: 309a
Lavespere (var. Lavispierre),
   Benoist: 298a
   Melanie: 322b, 334a
Lavois, Gov. of Los Adayes: 296a
Lawalle, Marguerite: 342b
Lay, Madison: 314a
Leacht, Cammilla: 325b
Leando, J. M.: 297a

Le Blanc, A.: 297a
Lebour, Ch., Rev.: 311b
Lecomte, A.: 318b
   Ambrose (Le Compti): 297a,
      298a, 315a, 366b
   Ambrose H.: 301b
   F. : 298a
   Julia Buard: 366b
   Laure: 326a
   Nelken: 311a
   Marie Eliza: 399b
   Marie Perine [free mulatto]:
      296b
Lecompte, LA: 312a
Le Compte's Race Track: 304a
LeConnait, Y. M., Rev.: 311b
Le Court, Marie Pelagie [free
   woman of color]: 296b
LeCourt (La Cour) de la Prelle
   Islands: 297a
Lee, Anna: 338a
   C. R.: 307b, 317a
   F. B.: 298b
   James N., Dr.: 308a
   Patrick: 323a
   Patrick O.: 309b
Lee Family: 316a
Lee & Gilbreath, firm of: 307b
Leech, Ebenezer: 296b
Le Gendre, Ernest: 306b
Legur, Jean: 297a
LeMaitre, F., Madame: 296b
Lemee, A.E.: 300b, 302a,b,
     303a,b, 310a,b, 314b, 315a,b
   Adolph: 303b, 357a
   Alexis, Sr.: 356b
   Alexis E.: 356b, 357a,b
   Alexis M.: 357b
   Amelia: 345b
   Amelie: 357a
   Cecile: 357a
   Daisy: 357b
   Desiree Morse: 357b
   Eloise: 357b
   Emma: 357a
   Eugenie: 357a
   Eugenie, Mrs.: 298a
   Eugenie Lamarlaire: 356b
   Ida: 357a
   Peter E.: 357a
   St. Ange: 357a

Lennon,____: 299b
Le Noir, Antoine: 297a
Leolia, LA [Robeline]: 317a
Leonard, A. H.: 320a
Leopold, J. C.: 298a
Leray, F. X., Rev.: 312a
Le Roy,Charles: 302b,303b,
304b, 311a
Lestage, B. (B. L. Estage):
296b
Lester, J.: 302a
James: 301b
W. W.: 309b
Levasseur (var. Lavasseur):
E.: 305b
J.F.: 296b
M.: 297a
Leveque, Aloysia: 357b
Bazilide Landry: 357b
Benjamin: 357b
Celeste: 357b
Doralise Landry: 357b
Evelina: 357b,
Joseph A., Dr.: 308a, 357b
Joseph M.: 358a
Justinian: 357b
Lize: 357b
Louis: 357b
Lucy: 358a
May: 357b
Samuel: 357b
Theresa Kirkland: 358a
Vincent: 358a
Levissee, A. B.: 320a
Levouzet, F., Rev.: 311b
Levy, Annie: 314a, 359a
Bertha: 314a, 359a, 368b
Bessie: 359a
C. H.: 313b
Charles H.: 314b, 358a,b, 359a
Clyde P.: 359a
Edgar: 359a
Edna: 359a
Eliza: 349a
Emily A. Pierson: 358b
Emeline Butt: 358a
H. M.: 313b, 315a
Harriet: 359b
Harriet Liberman: 359b
Henry M.: 314b, 359a
J. S.: 298a

Levy (cont'd)
John B.: 310b, 358a
John S.: 313a
Joseph: 318a,b
Justine Dreyfus: 359b
L. : 314a
Lelia: 359a
Leola: 359a
Leon: 359b
Leopold: 359a,b
M. H.: 315b
Mahlon H.: 359a
Mary: 359a
Moise: 359b
Myrtle E.: 305b
Paul: 359a
Samuel: 314a, 359a
William M.: 304b, 306a, 359a,
371a
Levy & Kaffie, firm of: 327a
Levy & Phillips, firm of: 311a,
Lewis, E. T.: 320b
George W.: 312a
J. B.: 304b
J. L.: 299a
S.: 299b
Seth W.: 319b
William B.: 300a
L'herisson, P. F.: 314a,b, 315a
Liberman, Harriet: 359b
Lindsey, Clarissa: 360a
E. M.: 317a
Edwin M.: 359b, 360a
Emily Handy: 359b
Magdalene: 360a
Rena Rachal: 360a
Lindsey Family: 316b
Ling, C. H.: 314a
Lisso, Morris: 303b
Litchenstein, B. H.: 300b
H.: 311a
Little, J. W.: 310a,b
John: 352a
Nancy Rutland: 352a
Sarah: 352a
Little Nas: see Nassau
Little River: 296b, 297a, 309b
Litton, John: 297a
Livingstone, Edward: 320a
Llorens (var. Florens), M. B.:
303a

Loccard, James: 300b
Logan, Darius, Rev.: 313b
Loggy Bayou: 309b
Long, S. G.: 318b
    Sarah J.: 330a
    William: 313a
Loper, B. D.: 316b
Lord, J. G.: 343a
Los Adayes: 294a, 295a, 296a,
    297a, 308b
Los Tres Llanos: 296a
Loupart & Coe, firm of: 299b
Love, Edward: 299b
    [see also Lauve]
Lovett, E. C., Mrs.: 316b
    John A, Dr.: 308a
Lutheran Benevolent Society:
    313b
Lynch, F., Mrs.: 298a
    L. L.: 306b

Machen, M. F.: 300b
Magnolia Plantation: 319a
Magnes (var. Maynes or Magney),
    J. Francois, Rev.: 299b, 309a
Mahle, John H.: 301a
Mailleux, Pierre: 297a
Malle, _____: 307a
Manhiem, H.: 317a, 318b
Manning, Thomas C.: 319b, 320a
Mansfield, LA: 305b, 311b
Mansfield Female College: 336a
Many, La: 300b, 305b, 312a
Marcy, L.: 298b, 302a
Margil, Antonio (Anthony), Rev.:
    308b
Marinovich, Antoine: 303a, 360a,b
Marks, Rena: 324a
    Rosalie: 324a
Marksville: 311b
Marmoulet, Rev.: 309a
Marontini, J. B.: 298b
Marquette, _____Pere: 294b
Marrs, Caledonia: 375b
Marsden, B. W.: 304b
Marsello, Father: 308b
Marshall, Henry: 320a
Marthaville, Martha's Bulletin
    307b

Marthaville, People's Republic:
    307b
Martin, _____: 302b
    Rev.: 311a
    Amazi, Dr.: 352b
    Augustus, Bishop: 311a,b, 312a
    322a
    F., Rev.: 311b
    J. H.: 298b
    J. J. A.: 305b
    Joseph: 297b, 298b, 302b
    Louis F.: 301a
    Marcellet: 296b
    Margaret C.: 359a
Martin Family: 297a
Mascaroni, A., Rev.: 311a
Masson, Ernest: 304b
Matthews, William: 298b
Maximin, Brother: 309a
May, Capt.: 302a
Mayben, Ala M.: 361a
    James O.: 360b
    James R.: 360b, 361a
    Mary E. Brown: 361a
    Nancy Jones: 360b
Maynard, J. M.: 311b
Melvin, W. C.: 304b
Merchants & Planters Protective
    Union: 315b
Mercier, F.: 296b
Messi(var. Messie):
    Jerome: 298b
    Jules E.: 303a
Methodist Church
    Natchitoches: 312a, 313b
    Robeline: 316b
    Episcopal : 313b
    Episcopal of Provencal: 318a
Metoyer, A. P. [f.m.c.]: 298b
    August, Widow [f.w.c.]: 298b
    Aurore Lambre: 343b, 366a
    Benjamin: 298a, 343b, 366a
    Ben, widow: 298a
    Dominique: 296b
    F.: 313a
    F. B.: 302a
    Felix: 310a
    Heloise: 343b
    [H]eloise: 350a
    J. B., widow [f.w.c.]: 298b
    J. C.: 302b

Metoyer (cont'd)
  Joseph: 296b
  N. P.: 298b, 302b
  Octave V., Capt.: 357a
  P. G.: 298b
  P. T.: 296b
  Suzanne Lize: 365b, 366b
  T. F.: 298b
  Tranquillin [f.m.c.]: 298b
Mezieres, H. P.: 300b
Mezierre, F. A.: 303a
Michele, Vincente: 296a
Mickelbury, King: 313b
Miles, E. J.: 306a
Military Units: 305a, 306
Minard, L. Rev.: 311b
Minden, LA: 311b
Miro, Estevan, Gov.: 296b
Mitchell, Ed.: 302b
Moncure, John C.: 319b
Monette, Theo.: 302b
Monette Ferry: 335b
Monroe, George: 310b
Moon, J. M.: 319b
Moore, John: 320a
  Thomas O.: 319a,b
Moorman, George: 315A
  J. M.: 317a
Moreau, Alex, Widow: 298b
  J. B.: 298b
  L.: 298b
Morentine & Calhoun, firm of: 318a
Morentine & Rachal, firm of: 318a
Morey, Frank: 320b
Morin, J. B.: 286b
Morin, Louis, widow [f.w.c]: 298b
Morris, Aaron: 306b
  John: 314a
Morrison, Charles H.: 319b
Morrow, W. P.: 298b, 303b, 305b,
    310b, 313a
  William P.: 301a
Morse: B. P.: 305b
  Desiree: 357b
  George W.: 301a,b
  Isaac E.: 319b, 320a
  James C.: 300b
  P. A.: 301b, 304a, 313a
  Peabody Atkinson: 357b
Morse & Butler, firm of: 249a
Morse rifle: 301b

Morton, Mittie: 355b
Morvant, Francois: 297b
Moses, S.: 318a
Mosley, M. C.: 300b
Moss, James W.: 306a
Mount Lebanon: 329b
Mount Lebanon Academy: 364a
Mount Lebanon College: 330b, 370a
Mumford, Edna L.: 361b
  Elizabeth D. Shockford: 361a
  George E.: 361a
  George Woodhouse: 361a
  Harriet G.: 361a
  James E., Dr.: 361a
  James H., Dr.: 361a
  Katie: 361b
  Lewis: 361b
  Mary W.: 361a
  William B.: 361b
  Zadock: 361a
Murdock, Andrew: 313b
Murphy, Denis V.: 301a
  John E.: 303b
  M.: 299a
  Patrick: 297b, 300b
Murray, William: 296a, 299a,b,
  300a
Myers, ____: 310a
  H. C.: 300a,b, 310a
  M. C.: 302b
  Philip: 310a, 313a
Myrick, J. T.: 318a

McAlpine Plantation: 334b
McCabe, Ross: 299a
McCain, H.V.: 305b
  J. M.: 305b
McClendon, H.R.: 302b, 303a
McCook, J.B.: 316b
  J.J.: 315b
  J. M. H.: 317a
  James, 316a
McCoquedale, D.: 318a
McCleary, James: 320a
McCracken, Sarah: 348a
McCollough, Ben., Gen.: 328b
McDaniel, F.: 310b, 311a
  Mrs.: 318b
McDonald, J. W.: 301b
McDonald, W. G.: 300b, 375b

111

McEnery, Samuel D.: 305a
McFier:
  see McTier
McIntosh, R. M.: 307b
McIntyre, Ella G.: 351b
McKenna, Hugh: 310a
McKnight, H.: 315b
  H. M. N.: 298b
  James: 301b
McLaughlin, Richard K.: 296a
  Robert K.: 299a
McLaurin, J. L.: 298b
McMillen, W. L.: 303b
McNeely, W. W.: 305b
McNutt, Isaac: 299a
McPeak, Roger: 297a
McTier, George: 300a
  Reine: 298b
McVoy, A. D., Jr., Rev.: 316b
McWilliams, Jacob: 314b

Nacogdoches, TX: 297b, 305a
Nalley, J. C.: 318a
  S. E.: 318a
Narces, Jean: 297a
Nash, C. C.: 305b
  Christopher C., Dr.: 308a
  Elizabeth: 344b
  J. V.: 317a
  Valentine: 344b
Nash & Sons, firm of: 316b
Nassau, _____ Mr.: 309b
Natchez Indians: 295b
Natchitoches Chronicle: 301b
  306a,b
Natchitoches Cottonseed Mill:
  364a
Natchitoches Daily Union: 307a
Natchitoches Daily Vindicator: 307a
Natchitoches Democratic Review:
  336a
Natchitoches Enterprise: 307a, 325a
Natchitoches Fort: 295b
Natchitoches Indians: 294b, 295a,b,
  315a
Natchitoches Land & Railway Co.: 315b
Natchitoches Opera House Company: 315a
Natchitoches People's Vindicator: 307a,
  311a, 336a
Natchitoches Railroad Company: 333a

Natchitoches Record: 307a
Natchitoches Red River News:
  310b
Natchitoches Register: 307a
Natchitoches Spectator: 307a
Natchitoches Times: 307a
Natchitoches Union: 306b, 307a
Nelken, Abram: 361b
  Augusta: 361b
  Bessie: 361b
  Emanuel: 361b
  Fannie: 361b
  Gettie: 361b
  Lillian: 361b
  S.: 314b, 315b
  Samuel: 318a,b, 361b, 362a
  Sarah H. Abram: 361b
  Solomon: 361b, 362a
  Wolf: 361b 315a
Nelson, S.: 315a
Nemitts, J. C. H.: 306b
New Orleans: 295b
Newsham, J. P.: 320a
Newspapers: 306b, 307
  [See also name of individual
  papers.]
Nicholas, free Negro: 296b
Nicholls, Francis T.: 305a
Noel, Smith: 306a
Normand, Aurelia: 362b
  Cecilia: 362b
  Elizabeth Aurelia Anty: 362b
  Francois M., Dr.: 297b, 298b,
    300a, 304a, 308a, 362a,b
  Francois M.: 362b
  Jules: 313b
  Jules H., Jr.: 303a, 362b
  Jules Honorat: 362a,b
  Julia: 362b
  Maria: 362b
Normand Hotel: 315a
Norris, J. W.: 313a
  Joseph W.: 301a

Officials,
  Land office: 309b
  Legislative: 304b, 305a
  Natchitoches Parish: 300b,
    301-303
  State, from NW LA: 319-320

112

Officials (cont'd)
  Town of Natchitoches: 310
O'Flaherty, Eliza: 333b
Ogden, Henry W.: 319b
Olcutt, Judge: 300a
Old River: 296b, 297a, 312a
  315b
Oliver, Lucy, Widow: 298a
Ortise, U.: 297a
Osborn, John: 300a
Oswalt, Emma: 314a
Overton, W. H.: 319b, 320a
Owen, Emma E.: 374a
Owings, Amelia: 298b
  W. P.: 302a

Packard, S. B.: 305a
Packer, Prof.: 338b
  J. P.: 298b
Page, Elizabeth C.: 363a
  Elizabeth C. Holden: 363a
  Emily J.: 363a
  Irene: 363a
  Jennie E. Carter: 363a
  John L.: 363a
  John L., Jr.: 363a
  John L., son of: 363a
  Luther: 363a
  Otho O.: 363a
  W. W.: 316b, 317a
  William R.: 363a
  William W.: 362b, 363a,b
Paillette (var. Poillet), Jean J.:
  296b
Paire [see Pavie]
Palmer, Amelia A.: 377b
  William: 377a
Pantaleon (var. Pantaloon),
  Bernard: 297b
Papillon: 296b
Parker, _____: 315b
Parmer, William: 309b
Parson, Samuel: 301a, 305b, 310a
Parvie [see Pavie]
Pascual, Father: 311b
Patterson, D. A. W.: 298b
  E. L.: 299a
Pavie (var. Parvie, Paire),
  Charles: 309a
  Rev.: 309a

Payne,_____: 311a
  J. F.: 301a
  John F.: 309b, 313a
  William: 301a, 302a,b, 303a,b,
    313a,b
Pearre, A. W.: 298b
Pegues, C. M.: 319b
Penn, A. G.: 320a
Perchi, Archbishop: 312a
Percy, Gilbert: 363b
  H. : 301b
  Harold: 363b
  Harry: 301a
  Marcella Chaplin: 363b
  Maude: 363b
  Richard: 314a, 363b
Perier, Governor: 295b
Perini, A.: 310a
Perkins; John, Jr.: 320a
Perot, Brevil[l]e: 304a
  Cephalide: 375a
  Charles: 298b
  Cyriac: 298b
  John L.: 298b
  L.: 318b
  Mortimer: 304b
  Nolete: 371b
  Owen: 298b
  Zelia: 374a,b
Perot's Plantation: 294b
Perrault, Rene: 297a
Persinger, Elias L., Dr.: 308a
Peters, J. H.: 305b
Petite Ecore: 297a
Peyson, B., Col.: 305b
Peyton, Col.: 349a
  Anna: 338a
Phillip, Capt.: 334a
Phillips, E.: 310a
  Ed: 313a
  Edward: 359a, 363b, 364a
  Elizabeth Bailey: 363b
  Esther: 359a
  Harold: 364a
  Henry: 304b, 364a
  Jacob: 363b
  Joanna Lacks: 363b
  Rena May: 364a
  Robert: 364a
  Violet: 364a

Physicians: 308a
  [See also individual names.]
Pickett, Hosea: 302a
Piedferme (var. Piedfirme), J.B.:
  297a
Piegay, A., Rev.: 311b
Pierro, John M.: 296b
Pierson, A.H.: 298b, 301b,
  302a, 304b
  Aaron H.: 359a
  Alice: 364b
  C.: 306b
  Clarence: 313b, 314b, 364b
  D.: 314b, 332a, 339b
  David: 300a, 305b, 314b,
    315b, 364a,b, 350b, 365a
  Edward L.: 310b
  Emily A.: 358b
  Emma J.: 373a
  J. F.: 305b
  Lelia: 353a
  Margaret C. Martin: 359a
  Mary Collina: 364a
  Maude: 364b
  May: 364b
  Sidney A. Pipes: 364b
  William H.: 364a
Piper, D. M., Miss.: 346a
Pipes, Sidney A., Miss.: 364b
  W. H.: 314b
Pitts, William W., Dr.: 308a
Plaisance, Baptiste: 297a
  F.: 298b
  Issac: 298b
Plauche, A. J.: 342a
  J. B.: 299a
Pleasant Hill, LA: 351b
Poche, Luc: 298b
Poiret, ____: 309a
  Chevalier de: 296a
Poissot, (var. Poisseau):
  Athanase: 296a
  Paul: 297a
Polk, Leonidas, Bishop: 312a
Ponder, Amos: 300b
  Lucitta Darden: 330b
  Martha: 330b
  Mattie J.: 331b
  S. D.: 303a
  Silas: 330b
  Silas D.: 300b

Ponder (cont'd)
  W.A.: 298b, 302b, 305a, 307b,
    316a, 317a, 331b
  William: 302a
  William A.: 330b
Pope, Lt.: 302a
Porter, ____ Mr.: 314b
  C.V.: 307b, 310b, 315a
  Charles V.: 300b, 314b, 365a,b
  Charles V., Jr.: 365b
  Harold: 365b
  J. M.: 307b
  Jacob C.: 365a
  James B.: 298b
  James F. 297a
  Sarah A. Garrett: 365a
  Violet A. Lachs: 365b
Postlewait's Salt Works: 309b
Potts, S. M. & Son, firm of: 307b
Poullain, Father: 311b
Powell, H. W.: 301b
  William B., Dr.: 308a
Power, Eliza B.: 354b
Prairie Nabutscahe: 296a
Prairie River: 311b
Prairie Yanecoocoo: 297a
Presely, S. C.: 307b, 330b
Pressnell, Mrs.: 316b
Prevots, Ben: 305b
Price, Congressman: 320b
  Gen.: 364b
Prickett, Col.: 304a
Procelle, Joseph: 297a
Prothro, James E.: 298b
  Joseph E.: 298b
  Joshua: 298b
  Lula: 329b
  S.C.: 298b
  W. M.: 317a
Prothro Hotel: 315a
Prosser, R. H., Rev.: 312b
Provencal, LA.: 318a
Provencal Land & Improvement Co.:
  318a
Provots, Charles: 299b
Prudhomme, A.: 311a
  Adeline: 325a
  Adolphe: 298b
  Catherine Adaline: 366a
  Catherine Lambre: 365b
  (cont'd)

Prudhomme (cont'd)
  Charles N.: 349a
  Clara: 323a
  E.: 298b
  Edward C.: 366b
  Emanuel: 297b
  Emily: 348a
  Emily E. Hyams: 349a
  Emma Laure: 367a
  Felicie Cecile: 367a
  G.: 298b
  J. A.: 315a,b
  J. Alphonse: 314b
  J. B.: 298b
  J. LeComte: 366b
  Jacques Alphonse: 365b,
    366a,b
  Jean Baptiste: 349a, 365b
  Jean Baptiste Ovide: 367a
  John: 298b
  Joseph Edwin: 367a
  L.: 301b, 302a
  Lestan (Lectan): 298b, 301b
  Marie Adeline: 367a
  Marie Atala: 366b
  Marie Cora: 366b
  Marie Eliza LeComte: 366b
  Marie Emma: 366a
  Marie Julia: 366b
  Marie Julie Buard: 367a
  Marie May: 366b
  Marie Noelie: 366b
  Narcisse: 298b
  Neuville: 298b
  P. E.: 303a
  P. L.: 306a
  P. S.: 314b
  P. Emmanuel: 365b
  P. Phanor: 366b
  Paul: 297a
  Peter Emanuel: 366b, 367a,b
  Phanor: 298b, 304a
  Pierre Emanuel: 366a
  Pierre Felix: 367a
  Pierre Phanor: 365b, 366b
  Raymond Emile: 367a
  St. Ann: 298b
  Suzanne Lize: 367a
  Suzanne Lize metoyer: 365b
    366b
  Theophile: 298b

Prudhomme (cont'd0
  Therese Henriette: 366a
Prudhomme Station: 294b, 315b
Pucketts, C. J. C.: 298b, 303b
  L. Q. C.: 298b
Pugh, W. W.: 319b

Quinnity, John: 297a
Quintanillo, Luis de, Brother
  [Father]: 309a
Quiqualtanqui, Indian Chief: 294b
Quirk, Edmond: 297a
  William B.: 297a

Rabalais, Joseph: 296b
Rabelais, P.: 306b
Raby, Henry: 304b
Rachal, Antoine: 296b
  Aurura: 333b
  Clementine: 324b
  J. B.: 304b
  Julien, Jr.: 334a
    [See also erroneous listing
    as Louis Julien]
  L. B.: 298b
  L. J., estate: 298b
  Louis Julian: 322b
  Louis Julien [Julien Jr.]:
    334a
  Marie Lolette: 362b
  Melanie Lavespere: 334a
  [Marie Melanie] Lavaspere, Mad-
    ame: 366b
  Mary F[lorentine]: 324a,b
  Rena: 360a
  Suzette: 322b
  Sylvester: 304a
  Victor: 298b
Rachal Family: 306b
Ragan, John A.: 301b
Raggio, John A.: 304b
  F. P.: 310b
  Josephine: 354b
Ragobert: see Dagobert
Raines, Elizabeth Kieffer: 367b
  James A.: 367b
  Mary E. Brian: 367b
  Samuel P.: 301a
Rains, C. F.: 310a

Rains (cont'd)
  Elizabeth Jackson: 268a
  G. P.: 303b, 306a
  George D.: 368a
  Isaac: 368a
  J. J.: 302a, 303b, 318a, 367b,
    368a
  James: 368a
  James P.: 368a
  Jennie: 368a
  John F.: 368a
  Martha Whitlock: 368a
  Nancy: 368a
  Perry C.: 368a
  Salenia: 368a
  Samuel P.: 367b
  Sarah: 36
  Thomas J.: 368a
Rains & Small, firm of: 368a
Rambin, Andre: 309a
  Andrew: 296a
Rami, Geago: 296b
Raphiel, Anna: 368b
  Bertha: 368b
  Bertha Levy: 368b
  Esther: 368b
  Howard, Jr.: 368a,b
  Howard, Sr.: 368b
  Howard (son of Isidore):
    368b
  Ida: 368b
  Isidore: 368b
  Johanna: 368b
  Joseph: 368b
  Lewis: 368b
  Louisa Betran: 368b
  Perl: 368b
  R.: 318b
  Samuel: 368b
  Stella: 368b
Raphael & Brother, firm of:
  318b
Ratbois, B.: 297a
Rauscheck, Mr.: 316a
Read, Watson: 298b
Readheimer, Amanda Gaiennie:
  369a
  Annie Casie: 369a
  Ephrim: 369a
  Harriet: 368b
  Harriet Blewer: 368b

Reidheimer (cont'd)
  J. G.: 318b
  James: 369a
  Peter: 368b
Rechatin, J., Rev.: 311b
Redmond, H.: 303a
  W.H.: 303b, 310b
Red River Hedge Company: 315a,
  375a
Red Rever News Republican: 307a
Reese, G. W.: 301a
  W. M., Rev.: 316b
Reid, J. H.: 306b
Review Bldg.: 313b
Reynolds, J. W.: 298b
Richardson, R. C., Dr.: 305b
Rigolet de Bon Dieu:294b,
  296b, 297a, 309a
Ringrose, W. B.: 315b
Rio Pedro: 297a
Ripley, E. W.: 320a
Rippardo, Governor of Los Adayes:
  296a
Ritter, Charles, Rev.: 312b
Rivers, Emile: 310b
Riviere aux Cannes: 296b, 297a
Rival, Mary: 342a
Robeline, LA: 296a, 316, 317a
Robeline News: 307b
Robeline Public and Private
  Academy: 329b
Robeline Publishing Co.: 307b
Robeline Reporter: 307b, 330b,
  332a
Robertson, E. W.: 320b
  S. B.: 306a
  Thomas B.: 320a
Robinson, G. W.: 351b
  N. A.: 326a
  W. B.: 298b
Robins, W.J.: 303b
Robson, D.: 304b
Rockwood, John: 305b
Rogers, Mary: 321a
  P. C.: 301a
Root, James A., Dr.: 308a
Roper, E. B.: 306b
  J. W.: 298b
Roquemore, Andrew Jackson, Dr.:
  318b, 369a,b
  James: 369a

Roquemore (cont'd)
  James Edward: 369b
  James L.: 369a
  Jule: 369a
  Malcom: 369a
  Matilda: 369a
  Ruthie Lee: 369b
Roques, C.N. [f.w.c.]: 298b
Rosenthal, Benny: 314a
Ross, Anna Lee: 338a
  John F.: 338a
  W. C.: 302a,b, 303a, 304b
Rost, Emile: 298b
  P. A.: 296a
Roubieu, Ausita: 346a
  F. [Jr]; 304b
  Francois: 298b
  Francois, Widow: 298b
  Pauline: 343a
  [See also Rubor]
Rougot (var. Roujot), John B.:
  296b
Rouquiere, Francois: 297a
  J. B. O.: 298b
  Madam: 296b
Rouquiere Family: 297a
Roujot, Commandant: 308b
Roulleaux, N. J., Rev.: 311b
Roy, LA, post office: 335b
Rubor, Atria: 371b
  Mattie Scopini: 371b
  Norbert F.: 371b
Russ & Hollingsworth, firm of: 348b
Russ, G. W.: 310a
  S. E., Jr.: 348b
Russell, Bessie: 314a
  S. D.: 305b
  Samuel: 318b
  Samuel D.: 350a
  Sammel P.: 313a
  W. E.: 305b, 310a,b
Rutland, Nancy, Mrs.: 352a
Ryan, Michel, Judge: 300a

Safford, _____ (Tax assessor):
  294a
  Annette Eliza: 370a
  H.: 314a
  Harriet Airey: 369b
  Harriet Rebecca: 370a

Safford (cont'd)
  Henry: 303b
  Henry, Sr.: 320a, 369b
  Henry, Jr.: 369a, 370a
  Whitcomb Burr: 370a
St. Amans, B.: 301b, 310a
  B. V.: 313a
  C. E.: 298b, 299a
  J. F.: 298b
St. Denis, Louis Juchereau de:
  295a,b, 308b
  Jr.,_____Juchereau Chevalier
  de: 296a
  [Louis, Jr.] Widow: 297b
  Marie des Neiges de (Mme.
  Antoine Manuel Bermudez de
  Soto): 296a
St. Francis, Catholic Church of
  Natchitoches: 299b, 308b
  309a, 311b, 312a
St. Germain, Damas: 298b
St. John the Baptist Catholic
  Church, Cloutierville: 322
St. Joseph College: 313b
St. Louis de la Mobile: 295ba,b
Saline Bayou: 297a, 309b
Salter, J. D.: 318b
Salverte, _____French officer:
Sampite, A.: 298b
Sanchez, ___ grant of: 296a 295b
Sandels, John, Rev.: 312b
Sandiford, J.W.: 305b
  W.D.: 304b
Sandige, John M.: 319b, 320a
Sanguinet, Catherine: 322b, 323a
  Charles: 323a
  Mary Ann Conde: 323a
  Simon: 323a
Sans Quartier, Pierre: 297a
Santes, Joseph: 297a
Sarpy, C. A.[f.m.c.]: 298b
  Jerome [f.m.c.]: 299a
Savoy, B.: 297a

Scarborough, Aelo: 370b
  Anna: 370b
  D. C.: 300a, 314b, 315a,b
  Daniel C.: 370b, 371a,b
  Daniel C., Jr.: 371a
  Eleanor M. Culpepper Hargrove:
  370b, 371a

Scarborough (cont'd)
  Georgia: 370b
  Immogene: 371a
  J. F.: 298b, 306a
  Josiah S.: 305b
  Margaret Josey: 370b
  McDaniel: 370b, 371a
  McJosie: 371a
  Noah: 370b
  William P.: 371a
  Zama: 371a
Scarborough & Carver: 371a
Schools: 307b, 308a, 313b, 314a,
  319a
Schroeder. F. H.: 306a
Schuman, H.: 315a
  Theodore: 310a
Scisson, A. P.: 301b, 302a
Scopini, Ellen Lattier: 371b
  Francis: 371b
  John F.: 371b
  Mattie: 371b
  N. F.: 371b
  Nolite Perot: 371b
Scruggs, S. A., Dr.: 361a
  S. O., Dr.: 299a, 304b
  Samuel H., Dr.: 308a
Scott, Thomas W.: 319b
Searing, Artemesia A.: 372a
  C. S.: 314b
  Cyrus S.: 371b, 372a
  Cyrus S., Jr.: 372a
  Fannie S. Gillespie: 372a
  Robert B.: 372a
Seay, W.A.: 320a
Sedella, A. D., Rev.: 309a
Seigler, D., Col.: 310a
Seiger, A.: 313a
Self, D. W.: 305b
Sellers, Thomas B., Dr.: 308a
Serr [Sers], L. C. & Co.: 318a
Sers, Daisy: 343b
  Felix: 306b
Severin, Edward: 299a
Shackleford, S.B.: 306b
Shaffrach, ___?: 311a
Sharp, Hubbard: 313b
Shaumburg (var. Shamnerg),
  Barthelemy: 296b
Sheib, Edward, Dr.: 314a
Sherburne, F. B.: 304a

Sherman, W. T.: 350a
Shockford, Elizabeth D.: 361a
Shreveport, LA: 312b
Shreveport Railroad Convention:
  310b
Sibersky, Anna Raphiel: 368b
Sibley, Artemesia A.: 372a
  Horatio: 313a
  John, Dr.: 293a, 297b
  R. H.: 305a
  S. H.: 301a
Sibley Lake: 304a
Sicily Islands: 295b
Silvie, Emile: 302b
Simon, H.: 314b
Simmons, P. A.: 300b, 302b
  S. S.: 299a
Simms, John: 299a
Simon, H.: 315a
  P. E., Rev.: 311b
  Simeon: 313b
Sims, Samuel: 299b
Sisters of Mercy: 312a
Sisters of the Sacred Heart:
  313b, 314a
Skinner, Dr.: 326a, 327a
Slaves, emancipation of: 301b
Slay, B. D.: 317a
Slocum, Charles: 297b, 301a
Smith, A. L.: 314a
  C. J.: 303b
  Edmund: 302a
  G. L.: 320b
  George: 299a
  Hattie B.: 373a
  J. B.: 302a, 313a
  J. F.: 300b, 305b
  J. Fisher: 305a
  J. T.: 303a
  Jerry: 298b
  John: 297a
  John N.: 299a
  John B.: 298b
  Mollie: 355b
  N.: 313b
  N. T.: 314b
  Robert E.: 331a
  Sarah L.: 331a
  T. M.: 298b,
  Thomas: 303a
  W.: 301b

Smith (cont'd)
  Wm.: 298b
Sohano, John: 296b
Soldini, Joseph: 299a.
Sompayrac, A. B.: 298b
  A. E.: 315a
  Adolphe: 303b, 312a
  Alex E.: 370a,b
  Alex II: 370b
  Aline: 370a
  Ambrose: 299a, 301b, 312a
  Ambrose B.: 370a
  Annette Airey: 370b
  C. E.: 298b
  Emile: 304a
  Fronie: 370a
  Hypolite (Emancipated slave):
    301b
  Jules: 299a, 301b, 304b
  Lelia: 342a
  Roseline Deblieux: 370a
  Victor: 303b, 312a
  Virginia: 336b
Sons of the Revolution, Louisiana
  Society of: 314b
Sora, J. M., Rev.: 309a
Sorrentini, C., Rev.: 311b
Soumande Family: 322b
South African Colored Church:
  313b
Southern H & B Association: 314b
Spafford [see Safford]
Spanish Lake: 296b, 297b, 312a,
  314a, 327b, 330b
Spanish Town: 312a
Sparta: 302a
Speight, W. R.: 313a
Spring Creek: 312a
Springville, La.: 302a
Sprowl, Jonathan: 298b
  William: 298b
Spurgeon, T. M.: 302a
Squires, M. L.: 301b
Spencer, W. B.: 320b
Stamper, N.: 316a
  N. A.: 316a, 317a
Stamper's Steam Mill: 316b
Stanislaus, Rev.: 309a
Stathart, A. H.: 298b
Stehle, R. W., Rev.: 311b
Stelle, J. D.: 315b

Stephens, Mr.: 314b
  Alice: 372b
  Edwin Lewis: 373a
  Eliza L.: 372b
  George W.: 372b, 373a
  Ida L.: 373a
  Irene: 372b
  Isabella: 373a
  Isabella C. Whitfield: 373a
  J. H.: 308a, 313a, 315b,
    345b
  J. S.: 298b, 301b, 314b
  J. S., Jr.: 313b, 315a
  James J.: 372b
  Joseph G.: 372a
  Joseph H.: 318a
  Joseph H., II: 372b,
  Joseph Henry: 372a,b, 373a
  Joseph S., Dr.: 308a
  Laura C.: 372b
  Lawrence W.: 372b
  Louisa J.: 372b
  Mary E. Vascocu: 372a
  Sudie Belle: 373a
  Walter G.: 372b
  William B.: 372b
Stephens & Gregory, firm of:
  318a,b, 372b
Stevenson, John A.: 305a
Stewart, W. B.: 298b
Stille, Anna E.: 373a
  Elliot O.: 373a
  Emma J. Pierson: 373a
  Hattie B. Smith: 373a
  J. D.: 338b
  Joseph D.: 373a,b
  Lillian P.: 373a
  Mary A.: 373a
  Norie A.: 373a
  R. B.: 373b
  R. B. & Co.: 373b
  Walter D.: 373a
  William B.: 373a,b
Stokers family: 316a,
Stokes, Elizabeth: 321b
Stone, G. W.: 299a
Stowe, Harriet Beecher: 334b
Strickland, George: 299a
Strong, W. A.: 301b, 305b, 319b
Strong & Morse, firm of: 298b
Strong, Walcott & Morse: 299a

Sudduth, Mrs.: 311a
   E., Mrs.: 327a
Sullivan, _____Mrs.: 305b
   Mary C.: 314a
Surlls, A.C.: 310a
Sydic, Louis: 297a

Tabor, D.F.: 301a, 313a
   Rufus: 311a
   W. F.: 313a
Tahon River: 297a
Taliaferro, R. W.: 311a
Tapalcote, village of: 297b
Tauzin, _____: 299b, 304a
   _____, Miss.: 313b
   Briant: 300b
   J. E.: 299a
   John M.: 306a
   Marcellin: 299a
   Marie Emee: 327a
   T. E.: 299a, 304a
   T. E., Mrs.: 299a
   Theophile E.: 300b
Tax Assessments: 294a
Tax Reform Association: 303b, 304a
Taylor, Eliza A.: 355a
   Gen.: 346a
   James: 300a, 301b
   Jane: 355a
   John, Judge: 355a
   Zachary, Gen.: 349a
Teal, Capt.: 315b
   James: 297a
Terrett, Burdett A.: 336b
   George A.: 336a
   James P.: 336b
   Virginia Sompayrac: 336b
Tessier, H. V.: 299a
   Emma: 314a
Texas & Pacific Railroad: 315b
Texas Masonic College: 336a
Tharp, Edgar: 314a
   Thalia: 338a
   W. A.: 299a
Thirteen Club: 313b
Thomas, Gary: 299b
Thomas, James E., Dr.: 308a
   John W.: 308a
   Philemon: 320a
   Shadrack: 299b

Thomasson, J. C.: 318b
Thompson, G. W.: 299a
   John: 297a
   Sarah: 297a
   T.: 301b
Thorn, J. T.: 299a
Three Cabins: 296a
Tibbetts, S. M.: 312a
Tierra Blanca: 297b
Tiger Island: 312a
Timmon, A. N.: 374
   Alberta Chapman: 374a
   Benjamin F.: 374a
   John: 374a
   Mary Jackson: 374a
   Sarah L.: 374a
Tomac, Natchitoches Indian
   Chief: 296b, 318b
Tompkins, L. L.: 304b
Tonti, Henri de: 295b
Torres (var. Taurus), Joseph:
   296b
Townsend, Aurelia: 353a
   William: 301b
Trezevant, Peter J.: 319b
Trezzini (var. Trezziur), J. B.:
   299a
Trichel, Annie C.: 374b
   Annie Celeste: 374b
   Baptiste: 296b
   Cephalide Perot: 375a
   Charles E.: 301a, 374b, 375a
   Charles M.: 274b
   Clarence F.: 374b
   Emma E. Owen: 374b
   Evalina: 375a
   G. L.: 301a, 305b, 314b
   Gervais L.: 374a,b
   Gilbert P.: 375a
   H. F.: 303b
   J. B.: 375a
   J.C.: 303a, 306a, 310b, 314a,b
      315a, 375a
   J.C., Jr.: 313b, 375a
   J.T.: 315a
   John: 318a
   Kate L.: 314a
   Kate Lee: 375a
   L.: 302a
   Lelia Ethel: 374b
   Leo: 299a

Trichel (cont'd)
    Leonard: 301b, 302a, 374a,b
    Lucien: 299a
    Martha Estelle: 374b
    Severin: 299a
    Syl.: 302a
    Vivian Oledia: 374b
    William: 302b
    Zelia Perot: 374a,b
Trinity English Protestant
    Episcopal Church: 312a
Trudeau, Felix: 297b
True, S. B.: 313a
Truly, F. : 316b
Tucker, Caledonia Marrs: 375b
    J. M. B.: 299a, 300b, 309b
      310a, 375b
    James B.: 300b
    John: 309b
    John M.: 300b, 375a,b
Tully, Ephraim: 309b
Tunica Indians: 295b
Tunnard, ____: 303a
    W. H.: 300b, 302b
Tuomey, W. L.: 310a
Turner, _____ Capt.: 305a
    Edward D.: 300a
    M. T., Rev.: 312b
    Richard H.: 299a
    T. B.: 299a

Ugarte, Commandant of Nacogdoches:
    297b
Umphrey, John S.: 305a
Union-Greenback-Labor Party: 304b
Union Brick Manufactoring Co.:
    314b
Union Publishing Co.: 306b
Upton, Mr.: 316b

Vail, Daniel H.: 312b
Valentin, Rev.: 309a
Varnird, Rev.: 309a
Varnum, Engineer: 315b
Vascocu (var. Vascoco, Vascoeu):
    Chme.: 302a
    Francois: 297b
    Louis: 296b
    Mary E.: 372a

Vaugine, Commandant: 296a, 297b,
    308b
Vega, Jose de la: 297a
Vercher (var. Vircher, Vercheve),
    C.: 306b
    Jacques: 296b
Verdon, Victoria: 333b
Verrina, L. C. M. A., Rev.:
    311b
Vickers, M.: 306b
Victor (emancipated slave): 301b
Vienne, Adolphe: 299a
    Emile: 305b
    Emile, Widow: 299a
    F.: 303b
    Francois: 301a
    Gabriel: 299a
    J. B.: 302b
Villedaigle, P.: 296b
Villefranche, (var. Villfranche)
    Maria Louise: 296b
Vincent (var. Vinson), W. G.,
Vitry, Pierre, Rev.: 309a
Voce, Col.: 305a,b
Voorhies, Albert: 319b

Waddell, H. Y.: 301b
    Hugh Y.: 309b
Wade, Absalom: 376a
    Helen M.: 376a
Wagley, Nettie J.: 332b
    Philip: 299a
Walker, John: 297a
    J. W.: 301a
Wall, J. E., Dr.: 369b
Wallace: J. T.: 315a
    James: 299a
Walmsley, C.C.: 302a, 303b,
    313a
    G. S.: 299a
    H.: 311a
    H. A.: 315b
    H. B.: 303a, 305b, 315b
    Hugh: 311a
    L. R.: 303b
    Mrs.: 312a
    P. S.: 306b
    W. T.: 301b, 309b
Walmsley Bldg.: 311a
Walmsley Bros.: 375a

Walmsley, Carver & Co.: 336a
Walsh, H.P.: 299a
Walters, Rev.: 313b
Wamack, Jesse: 301b
Warmoth, Henry C.: 305a
Warner, B.F.: 306a
Washington, Mary E.: 314a
Waters, Thomas B.: 359b
    William H.: 359b
Watkins, J. D.: 320a
    L. B.: 300b, 371a
    Lynn Boyd: 319b
    Tilman: 310a
Watson, Harriet Rebecca: 369b
    M. E., Miss: 321b
Waugh & Gentry: 318a
Weaver, H. J.: 303a
Wells, J. M.: 304a, 309a, 318a,
    319a
    T. Monk: 318a
Westerfield, W. E.: 315b
Wheeler, Charles: 303a
Whitcomb, Annette: 370a
Whitfield, George W.: 299a, 373a
    Isabella C.: 373a
    Mary Johnson: 373a
White, Charles: 314a
    Ed. D.: 320a
    Henry: 310a
    O.: 304b
    Thomas C.: 302a
Whitlock, Martha: 368a
Whitted, E.: 299a
    William: 298a
Wiggins, J. C.: 318a
Wiley, S. B.: 296a
Wellbone, Catherine Clara: 350b
Williams, Bettie: 328b
    Boling: 304b
    Elva Edmonds: 376a
    F.: 301a,b, 302a, 312a
    F. E., Widow: 299a
    Frances: 376a
    Frederick: 313a
    George: 303b, 376a
    Helen M. Wade: 376a
    J. H.: 376a,
    J. R.: 299a, 304b, 310a
    J. O.: 303a
    James E.: 376a
    James Henry: 376b

Williams (cont'd)
    John, Sr.: 376a
    John, Jr.: 376a
    John Alexander: 376b
    John D.: 376a
    John F., Dr.: 308a
    John R.: 313a
    Malinda Annette: 376b
    Martha: 376a
    Nancy: 376a
    Rawle: 299a
    Richard B.: 375b, 376a,b
    Sarah A.: 376a
    Warren: 299a
    William: 299a, 301b
    William Thomas: 376b
Williamson, J.: 306a
Wilson, E. K.: 300a
    K. B.: 316a
Wiltz, L. A., Gov.: 336a
    Louis A.: 305a
Winnsborough Sun: 307a
Winship, J.: 299a
Winter, William: 325a
Witherspoon, Ad.: 313b
Wolfson, J. A.: 301a
Wood, Capt.: 315b
    Elizabeth: 336a
    John D.: 306b
Woodhouse, Georgia: 361a
Woods, Amanda: 333a
    Clementine Rachal: 324b
    Lise: 324b
    Richard: 324b
Wray, J. W.: 301b
Wright, Amos: 303a
    Isaac: 309a
Wright & Beasley: 336a
Wyche, William: 299a

Yamey, V., Father: 311b
Yaneau, Y., Rev: 311b
Yarborough, Ione M.: 373b
    J. J.: 373b
    William: 313b
Yattassee Indians: 295a,b,
    296a,b
Yazoo Settlement: 295b
Young, John: 297a
Young's Bayou: 297a

www.ingramcontent.com/pod-product-compliance
Lightning Source LLC
Chambersburg PA
CBHW071830090426
42737CB00012B/2223